FRETBOARD BIOLOGY
COMPREHENSIVE GUITAR PROGRAM

"The Knowledge without the College"™

LEVEL 2

This textbook accompanies the Level 2 course at Fretboardbiology.com

©2021 Joe Elliott. Please do not distribute or reproduce this material. This program represents a lifetime of work teaching guitar players like you how to be better musicians. If you think this program is great, please encourage your friends to sign up for the course and go through it with you. They will get more out of the program, and you will feel better knowing that you aren't hurting fellow artists by just giving away their work. Thank you.

Music Biology Publishing

Copyright © 2021 Joe Elliott

All rights reserved. Except as permitted under the U.S. Copyright Act of 1976, no part of this book may be reproduced in any manner whatsoever without written permission from the publisher, except in the case of brief quotations in critical articles or reviews.

The paper used in this publication meets the minimum requirements of the American National Standards for Information Services - Permanence of Paper for Printed Library Materials,
ANSI Z39.48-1984.

ISBN 13: 978-1-7362942-2-2

DEDICATION

I would like to dedicate this to all the great teachers out there who are passing along their knowledge and experience.

ACKNOWLEDGMENTS

In any project like this, it is hard to thank all of the people who have been instrumental in its development and success. I've been fortunate to have the support and friendship of many people along the way. I've somehow been wise enough to listen to those who know more than me, too. I encourage everyone to live that way.

I would like to start by thanking my wife, Eileen, for all the support, encouragement, and freedom to take on this monstrous project—and the faith that it would be a success—as well as all the years of putting up with the stresses of being married to a professional musician. My interest in music was fostered and supported by my parents, Jack and Marian Elliott, who always had a house full of big band and classical music, and my older siblings, Dave, Mary, and Dan, who exposed me to a lot of great music growing up ike the Trashmen, The Beatles, The Stones, Sergio Mendes, Chicago, Sly, and Crosby, Stills, and Nash.

There were several people who were very influential in my development as a musician and educator that I would like to acknowledge: Fred Brush for showing so many great musicians to me in my formative years. Glen Johnston for exposing all of us "Montana Boys" to the real musicians in person at Montana State. Kent Erickson for drilling me on theory on our long road trips. Carl Schroeder for your unique way of getting your points across back in the day when I was in your classes in LA. You certainly shaped my way of teaching and managing a classroom. Keith Wyatt for the steady example of professionalism in guitar education. Combining great guitar talent with an organized mind is a great combination for any student. Scott Henderson for your relentless intolerance of mediocrity. You still scare me into working harder. Don Mock for being such an egoless sharer of your knowledge and gifts. You'll probably never know how many lives you affected with your pragmatic approach. Howard Roberts for all the lives you changed teaching guitar players real-world skills and shaping the most innovative guitar program that's ever existed. Bruce Buckingham for feeding me the right information at the right time. Eric Paschal for always finding the best in all your students. And Dan Gilbert for the energy you pumped into every class and the motivation to practice more than I've ever practiced.

For this project I was very fortunate to be surrounded by a team of amazing and intelligent musicians and specialty experts such as Ricky Peterson, Sean Nilson, Eliot Briggs, Bill Lafleur, Luke Elliott, Carter Elliott, John Krogh, Harry Chalmiers, Kevin Sullivan, Tony Axtell and the McNally Smith College of Music "guitar department in exile"—Tim Lyles, Paul Krueger, Chris Olson, Mike Salow, Dave Singley, and Eva Beneke—for test-driving this Fretboard Biology method for seven years.

None of this would have happened without the dedicated work of my business partner in the Fretboard Biology program, Todd Berntson, and his wife, Monique. There's a lot of skill and talent in that duo and it was only through Todd's insistence that this project was launched.

Lastly, I would like to thank all the great musicians and students I have had the pleasure to work with over the past 40 years.

TABLE OF CONTENTS

ACKNOWLEDGMENTS	v
LEVEL 2 INTRODUCTION	1
UNIT 1	3

- Theory - Intervals
- Fretboard Logic - Pattern II Major Pentatonic and Major Scales, Mixing Open and Barre Chords in Progressions, Intervals: 2nds and 3rds on One String, Octave Shape Family Tree
- Technique - Alternate Picking with 8th-Note Subdivision
- Rhythm Notation - Meter, Measures, Barlines, Notes, and Rests
- Rhythm Guitar - Folk Rhythm Guitar
- Improvisation - Soloing with a Straight 8th-Note Subdivision
- Practice - Continue Practice Routine Development

UNIT 2	29

- Theory - Measuring and Constructing Intervals
- Fretboard Logic - Pattern IV Major Pentatonic and Major Scales, Mixing Open and Barre-Chord Voicings, Intervals: 2nds and 3rds on Adjacent Strings
- Technique - Alternate Picking with a Syncopated 8th-Note Subdivision
- Rhythm Notation - Note Heads and Stems, Flags
- Rhythm Guitar - Folk Rhythm Guitar
- Improvisation - Soloing with Syncopation- Straight 8th-Note
- Practice - Continue Practice Routine Development

UNIT 3	47

- Theory - Major, Minor, Augmented, and Diminished Triad Formulas, Suspended 4th Formula
- Fretboard Logic - Pattern V Major Pentatonic and Major Scales, Introduction to Triad Super Shapes, Intervals: 4ths and 5ths on Adjacent Strings
- Technique - Alternate Picking with 16th-Note Subdivision
- Rhythm Notation - Meter and Time Signatures
- Rhythm Guitar - Folk Rhythm Guitar, Introduction to Fingerpicking
- Improvisation - Soloing with Straight 16th-Note Subdivision
- Practice - Continue Practice Routine Development

UNIT 4 — 71

- Theory - Analyzing Triads, Chord Symbols
- Fretboard Logic - Pattern I Minor Pentatonic and Natural Minor Scales, Triads and Triad Super Shapes, Intervals: 6ths on Adjacent Strings
- Technique - Alternate Picking with Syncopated 16th-Note Subdivision
- Rhythm Notation - Note and Rest Values
- Rhythm Guitar - Folk Rhythm Guitar, Alternating Bass Fingerpicking
- Improvisation - Soloing with Syncopated 16th-Note Subdivision
- Practice - Continue Practice Routine Development

UNIT 5 — 103

- Theory - Triad Construction
- Fretboard Logic - Pattern III Minor Pentatonic and Natural Minor Scales, Three-String Major Triad Shapes, Intervals: 6ths and 7ths on Non-Adjacent Strings
- Technique - Alternate Picking with 8th-Note Triplets
- Rhythm Notation - Dots and Ties
- Rhythm Guitar - Folk Rhythm Guitar Progressions
- Improvisation - Soloing with 8th-Note Triplets
- Practice - Continue Practice Routine Development

UNIT 6 — 127

- Theory - Harmonizing the Major Scale with Triads
- Fretboard Logic - Pattern V Minor Pentatonic and Natural Minor Scales, Patterns I and III Major Triad Arpeggios, Three-String Minor Triad Shapes, Intervals: 2nds and 3rds on Top Three Strings
- Technique - Alternate Picking with Syncopated 8th-Note Triplets
- Rhythm Notation - Spacing and Grouping of Notes
- Rhythm Guitar - Classic Rock, Common Power Chords
- Improvisation - Soloing with Syncopated 8th-Note Triplets
- Practice - Continue Practice Routine Development

UNIT 7 — 159

- Theory - Chord Families and Analyzing Chord Progressions in Major Keys
- Fretboard Logic - How Pentatonic Shells Fit Together on the Fretboard, Patterns II and IV Minor Triad Arpeggios, Voice Leading, Intervals: 4ths and 5ths on Adjacent Top Three Strings
- Technique - Alternate Picking with 16th-Note Triplets
- Rhythm Notation - Note Grouping with 8th Notes
- Rhythm Guitar - Classic Rock, Open-A Power Chord Vocabulary
- Improvisation - Soloing with 16th-Note Triplets
- Practice - Continue Practice Routine Development

UNIT 8 — 183

- Theory - Harmonizing the Minor Scale, Analyzing Chord Progressions in Minor Keys
- Fretboard Logic - How the Major and Minor Natural Scales Fit Together on the Fretboard, Patterns II, IV, and V Major Triad Arpeggios, Voice Leading, Intervals: 6ths on Non-Adjacent Top Four Strings
- Technique - Alternate Picking with Syncopated 16th-Note Triplets
- Rhythm Notation - Note Grouping with 16th-Note Measures
- Rhythm Guitar - Classic Rock, 1st Inversion Power Chords
- Improvisation - Soloing with 8th-Note Shuffle Groove
- Practice - Continue Practice Routine Development

UNIT 9 — 221

- Theory - Constructing the Blues Scale
- Fretboard Logic - Patterns II and IV Blues Scale, Patterns I, III, and V Minor Triad Arpeggios, Practical Major Triad Shapes in each Octave Shape, Intervals: 7ths on Non-Adjacent Top Four Strings
- Technique - Alternate Picking with Various Articulation Devices
- Rhythm Notation - Common Meters Other Than 4/4 Time
- Rhythm Guitar - Classic Rock Using Pattern III Triad Shapes
- Improvisation - Soloing with Chord Tones
- Practice - Continue Practice Routine Development

UNIT 10 — 247

- Theory - Level 2 Summary
- Fretboard Logic - Patterns I, III, and V Blues Scale, Suspended 4th Arpeggios, Practical Minor Triad Shapes in Each Octave Shape, Intervals: Octaves on Non-Adjacent Strings
- Technique - Notating Pick Direction
- Rhythm Notation - Clarity in Notation
- Rhythm Guitar - Classic Rock, Triad Shapes on String Set 2-3-4
- Improvisation - Soloing with Chord Tones
- Practice - Continue Practice Routine Development

APPENDIX 1 - GLOSSARY OF TERMS — 275
APPENDIX 2 - FAMILY TREES — 281

LEVEL 2 INTRODUCTION

Fretboard Biology Level 1 established a strong foundation in the major areas of the program: Theory, Fretboard Logic, Technique, Rhythm Guitar, Improvisation and Practice techniques. Regardless of your prior musical background, I recommend that you start at Level 1 because this is where I introduce Fretboard Biology's unique approach to organizing Music Theory and the fretboard. If you're experienced, you can complete these Units quickly while still benefiting in a big way from learning the system and terminology. If you are also a teacher yourself, you will learn a proven method that you can apply when you teach your own students. If all of this is new to you, take as much time as you need to understand and master the material.

Level 2 Content

In the Theory Modules you will learn about recognizing and building intervals and recognizing and building triads. Building on your knowledge of intervals and triads, you will learn to harmonize the major and natural minor scales. This provides the foundation for harmonic analysis. You also learn the Blues scales.

In the Fretboard Logic Modules you will continue learning the organization system for the fretboard – the expanded CAGED system. As part of this, you will learn how all scales, arpeggios, and chords fit into what we'll call the "Family Tree" of the fretboard. The Family Tree helps keep all the fretboard information organized in an easily-understood system. You will learn the rest of the major and minor pentatonic shells and the major and natural minor scales found within as well as all five patterns of the Blues scale. You will learn how all scales fit within the Family Tree. You will also begin your study of arpeggios, starting with major and minor triad arpeggios as well as sus4 arpeggios. You will learn how all arpeggios fit within the Family Tree, too. Chord studies include mixing barre and open-string chord voicings in progressions. You will learn about the "super shape" system, which helps you understand three-string major and minor triad chord shapes all over the fretboard. You will learn the practical triad chord shapes within each Octave Shape as well. You will also learn all interval shapes found on the fretboard—from minor 2nds to the octave.

The Technique Modules explain alternate picking for the following subdivisions: 8th notes, 16th notes, 8th-note triplets, and 16th-note triplets and how to handle syncopation.

In the Rhythm Notation Modules you will learn to notate rhythms clearly. The guiding principle will be: "Music should look the way it sounds".

The Rhythm Guitar Modules study Folk and Classic Rock.

In the Improvisation Modules you will learn to solo in grooves that use the subdivisions explained in the Technique Modules. The concept of chord tone soloing is introduced. This is all presented in the context of good storytelling through motif development and the use of the elements of contrast.

As discussed in the last Level, this is a progressive course. Each Module in each Level builds on the information from the previous one. You'll get the most out of the program by staying with the sequence.

About Practicing

If you have worked through Level 1, you have started to develop a practice routine. You may have also noticed that as the number of things to practice increases, it becomes more and more of a challenge to get in all into one session. In Level 2, you will learn how to split up your task list into multiple routines so the work doesn't become overwhelming.

UNIT 1

Learning Modules

> **Theory** - Intervals

> **Fretboard Logic** - Pattern II Major Pentatonic and Major Scales, Mixing Open and Barre Chords in Progressions, Intervals: 2nds and 3rds on One String, Octave Shape Family Tree

> **Technique** - Alternate Picking with 8th-Note Subdivision

> **Rhythm Notation** - Meter, Measures, Barlines, Notes, and Rests

> **Rhythm Guitar** - Folk Rhythm Guitar

> **Improvisation** - Soloing with a Straight 8th-Note Subdivision

> **Practice** - Continue Practice Routine Development

THEORY

Intervals

The term interval refers to the distance between two notes. So far, we have discussed intervals in terms of half steps and whole steps. Using terms like half steps and whole steps as the only way to describe the distance between two notes becomes very impractical when measuring greater distances, such as "3 1/2 steps".

Terms like minor 3rd or perfect 4th provide an easier way to describe greater distances than saying "3 1/2 steps", which is a minor 3rd, or "5 1/2 steps", which is a perfect 4th. Similarly, we wouldn't say two walls are 144 inches apart. We'd say they are 12 feet apart, right? Having a thorough understanding of intervals, along with key signatures, is essential to understanding the rest of Theory. Don't slight this Unit in any way; in fact, take your time and review this material until you have a strong understanding before you move on. You'll be glad you did.

Let's take a look at a few definitions:

Melodic Interval

A melodic interval is two notes played one after another (ascending or descending).

Harmonic Interval

A harmonic interval is two notes played at the same time.

Simple Interval

A simple interval is an interval an octave or smaller in size.

Compound Interval

A compound interval is an interval larger than an octave.

Let's dig deeper into the world of intervals. We will use two terms to describe intervals: quantity and quality.

Interval Quantity

Quantity is a term used to describe the general distance between two notes based on the number of letters used in the musical alphabet. Quantity is determined by counting lines and spaces on the staff.

Quantity refers to the number of letters of the musical alphabet involved in a particular interval. For example, the distance from C to the D has a quantity of two, so it is called a "2nd". The term "2nd" is used because there are two letter names involved when measuring the distance: C and D. The interval from C to E is called a "3rd" because there are three letter names involved: C, D, and E. Take a look at the quantities of the intervals in the table below.

Table of Interval Quantities

INTERVAL QUANTITY	LETTERS USED
2nd	C - D (two letters: C, D)
3rd	C - E (three letters: C, D, E)
4th	C - F (four letters: C, D, E, F)
5th	C - G (five letters: C, D, E, F, G)
6th	C - A (six letters: C, D, E, F, G, A)
7th	C - B (seven letters: C, D, E, F, G, A, B)
8th	C - C (eight letters: C, D, E, F, G, A, B, C)

Now that we have discussed quantity, we need a way to describe the more specific and exact measurement between two pitches. The term "quality" is used to describe an interval with more precision.

Interval Quality

Quality indicates the exact measurement of an interval based on the number of half steps between two notes. Terms like major, minor, perfect, diminished, and augmented refer to the quality of an interval.

The quantity of the interval between C and D♭ is a 2nd, and the quantity of the interval between C and D is also a 2nd. But while these two intervals are both 2nds, they sound very different because the distances between them differ by a half step. In other words, the general distances (quantities) are the same, but the exact distances (qualities) are obviously different. The chart below shows that C to D♭ is a half step and the distance from C to D is a whole step. Both are 2nds because there are two letter names involved, but while they both have the same quantity, they have different qualities.

Look the table below. The left column lists the terms used to name an interval by combining quantity with quality. This table shows the precise number of whole and half steps of all simple intervals.

Table of Interval Qualities

INTERVAL	NUMBER OF HALF STEPS
Minor 2nd	1 half step
Major 2nd	2 half steps (1 whole step)
Minor 3rd	3 half steps (1-1/2 whole steps)
Major 3rd	4 half steps (2 whole steps)
Perfect 4th	5 half steps (2-1/2 whole steps)
Augmented 4th	6 half steps (3 whole steps)
Diminished 5th	6 half steps (3 whole steps)
Perfect 5th	7 half steps (3-1/2 whole steps)
Augmented 5th	8 half steps (4 whole steps)
Minor 6th	8 half steps (4 whole steps)
Major 6th	9 half steps (4-1/2 whole steps)
Minor 7th	10 half steps (5 whole steps)
Major 7th	11 half steps (5-1/2 whole steps)
Perfect 8th	12 half steps (6 whole steps)

Study this table and memorize it. It may seem daunting, but the investment of your time and energy now will pay huge dividends later as you go through this program.

Intervals and the Major Scale

In the major scale, the distance from the tonic to each of the other scale degrees is always the same regardless of the key. The interval formula never changes. As a result, the major scale can be used to measure intervals much like a tape measure is used to measure physical distances. If you bought two different tape measures at two different hardware stores and put them side by side to measure the same board, you would get the same measurement from both tape measures. This is because the distances between the inch markers—the intervals—are fixed, standardized, and never change. They are always the same.

Similar to a tape measure, the major scale has a fixed interval formula that never changes. The distance between scale degrees remains the same regardless of the key. We will use the major scale as a consistent and reliable measuring tool for intervals. Examine the interval distances from the tonic to each of the scale degrees of the C major scale:

Major Scale Intervals

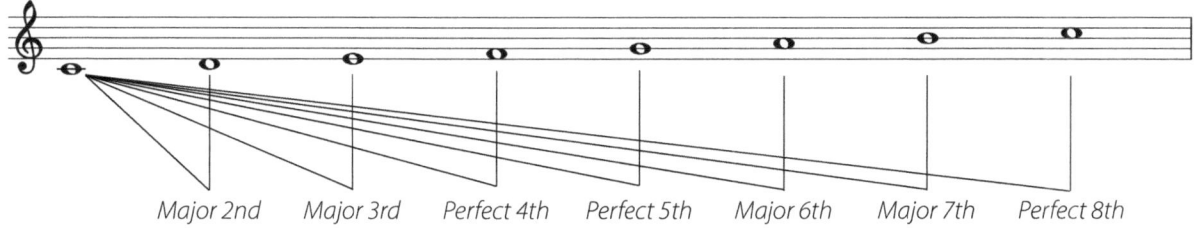

Remember, these distances are the same in all major scales and never change regardless of the key:

- From the tonic to the 2nd scale degree is always a major 2nd
- From the tonic to the 3rd scale degree is always a major 3rd
- From the tonic to the 4th scale degree is always a perfect 4th
- From the tonic to the 5th scale degree is always a perfect 5th
- From the tonic to the 6th scale degree is always a major 6th
- From the tonic to the 7th scale degree is always a major 7th
- From the tonic to the 8th scale degree is always a perfect 8th or octave

Looking Ahead

Know your key signatures and intervals. Everything from here on in Theory relies on your command of this information. As we progress, you will build many scales (major, minor, Blues, harmonic minor, melodic minor, modes, etc.), and chords (triads, 7th chords, 9th chords, 11th chords, 13th chords, and others). You will use intervals to build all of these.

FRETBOARD LOGIC

Scales

In the next several Modules you will complete your knowledge of the five major and minor pentatonic scales as well as the major and natural minor scales built within them. Continue this process with the Pattern II major pentatonic shell.

Pattern II Major Pentatonic Scale

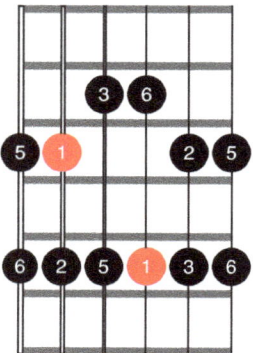

You can play the scale in any other key using the same approach; for example, for any key, locate the tonic on the 5th string with your second finger and follow the pattern. To build the major scale, add the 4th and 7th scale steps to each octave (in blue).

Pattern II Major Scale

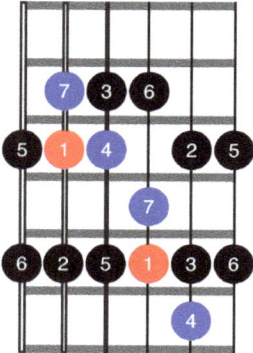

Add these scales to your practice routine and use strict alternate picking playing 8th notes.

Chords

In Level 1, you learned the basic major, minor, and sus4 "open chords", or "open-string voicings". Open string chords, or simply "open chords", are played in open position and normally include at least one open (unfretted) string. There are occasions where the character of a song calls for an open-chord sound but there may be a chord or two for which there is no open chord. In these cases you will need to play a barre chord on the chords that have no open chord.

Here are a couple progressions that require a mix of open chords and barre chords.

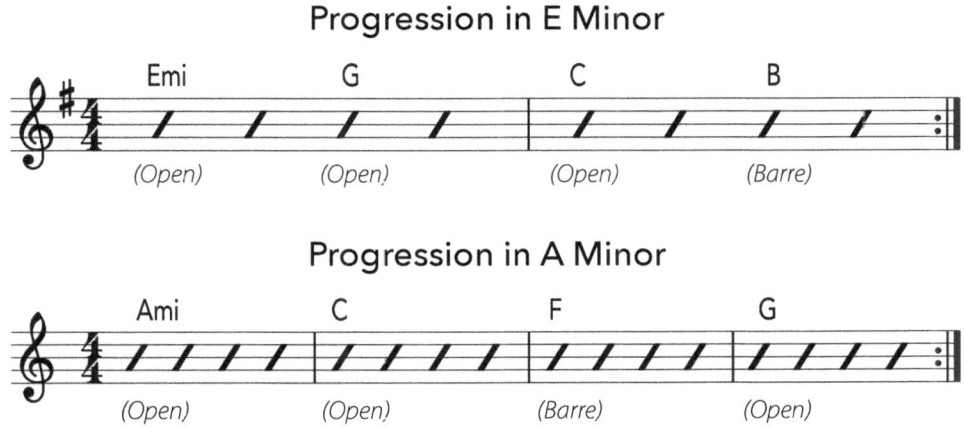

Intervals

Next is the study of interval shapes on the fretboard. This topic will be taught throughout Level 2. It is not a glamorous subject, but it is essential for really understanding the fretboard.

Guitarists benefit from the visual nature of the fretboard. We learn scales, arpeggios, chords, and the location of notes by using diagrams. The visual nature of the fretboard gives guitarists a huge advantage compared to learning other instruments. If you've played a brass or woodwind instrument, there is no visual equivalent to the fretboard. And even on a keyboard, while it's understandable in visual way, the patterns and fingerings change for every key. Think about how convenient it is that most of what we have learned about the fretboard is movable. All of the pentatonic, major, and natural minor scale shapes can be moved to any key by simply moving to the right place on the neck.

Recognizing visual shapes is key to learning intervals on he fretboard. They will be introduced gradually, so learning them will be a manageable process. Later in this course, your knowledge of intervals will be used to work in riffs, licks, and other kinds of guitar parts. All of the intervals introduced in the Theory Module have corresponding visual "shapes" on the neck.

In this Unit, you will learn shapes for minor and major 2nds and 3rds on a single string. Study the fretboard graphics below and memorize these interval shapes. We will be spending a lot of time learning about intervals throughout this program, so make sure that you spend some time to memorize these shapes.

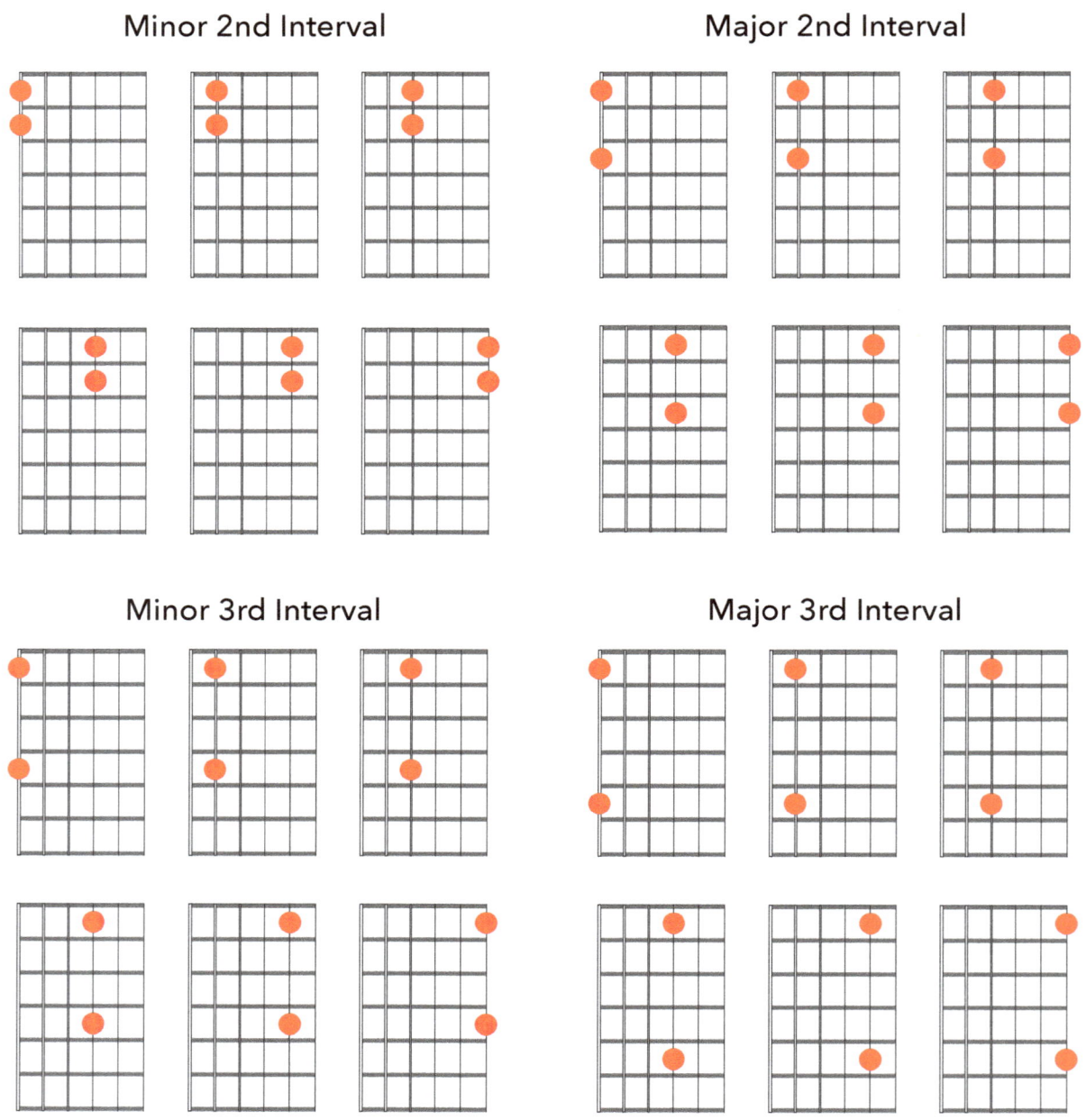

The Octave Shape Family tree

The ultimate goal of all the Fretboard Logic Modules is to provide an organized way to demystify the neck. You need a clear visual map so you can find or build any scale, arpeggio, or chord quickly and efficiently. You need to be self-reliant on the fretboard which means that you shouldn't have to rely on a book or website to help figure out how to play a scale, arpeggio, or chord. This is possible through the use of the Octave Shape system you have learned from the very beginning of this program. This system of organization is the foundation of the entire Fretboard Logic curriculum.

So far you see how the scales, arpeggios, and chords you have learned are built within the Octave Shapes. Know that ALL scales, arpeggios, and chords on the entire fretboard can be built within the five Octave Shapes. This means that we can build an "Octave Shape Family Tree", so to speak, that shows how all scales, arpeggios, and chords are organized within the five Octave Shapes. As you progress through the Fretboard Biology program you will build on the Family Tree structure.

Building the Family Tree

Imagine a real family tree with great-grandparents in the top position on the page, grandparents in the next tier below, parents in the next tier below, and the current generation at the bottom. You could say that each generation is a "derivative" of the previous generation who are, of course, derivatives of the generation before them. You have probably seen this kind of family tree before.

A Family Tree

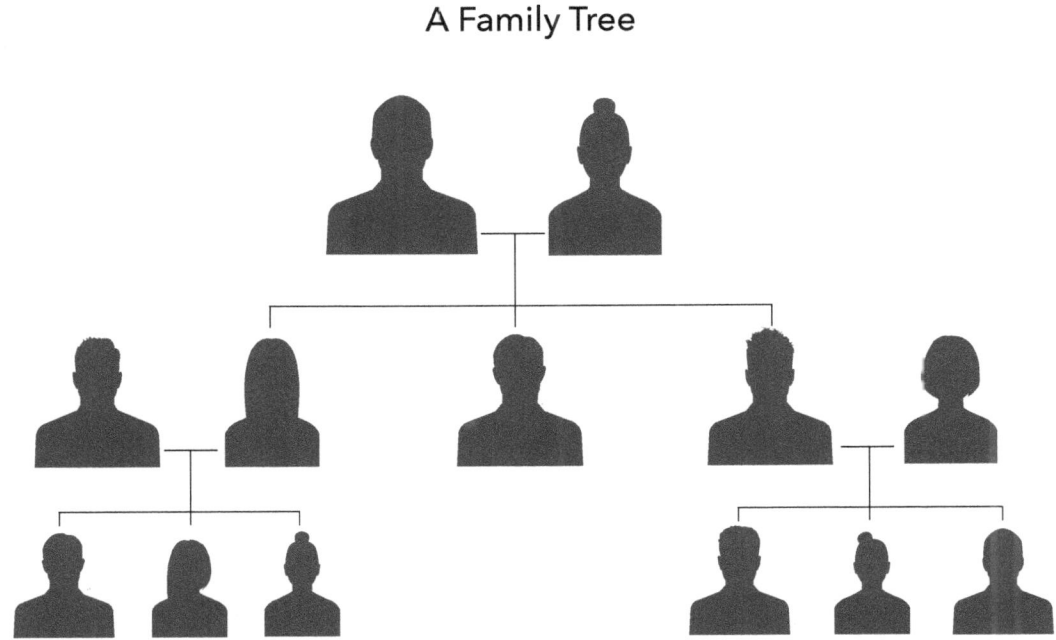

We can apply the same concept to the Octave Shape system. Think of an Octave Shape as the great-grandparent. Start by looking at Octave Shape I, or what we call Pattern I.

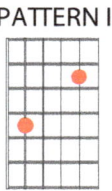

We can derive several scales, arpeggios and chords from this Octave Shape. Start with the major and minor pentatonic shells. Place those below the Octave Shape like you would in a family tree. Put major pentatonic to the left and minor pentatonic to the right. The illustration below shows the pentatonic scales as derivatives of the octave shape.

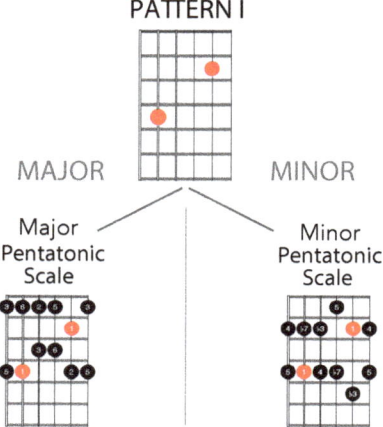

Both a major triad arpeggio and a minor triad arpeggio can be derived from this Octave Shape. Place those below the Octave Shape along side the pentatonic scales - the major triad arpeggio to the left and the minor triad arpeggio to the right.

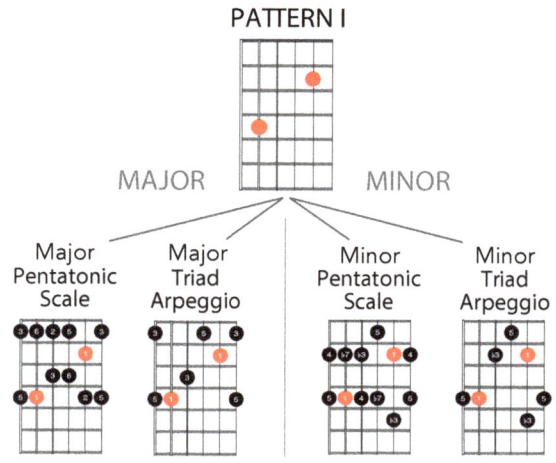

Both a major triad chord and a minor triad chord can be derived from this Octave Shape. Place those below the Octave Shape along side the pentatonic scales. Place the major triad chord to the left and the minor triad chord to the right.

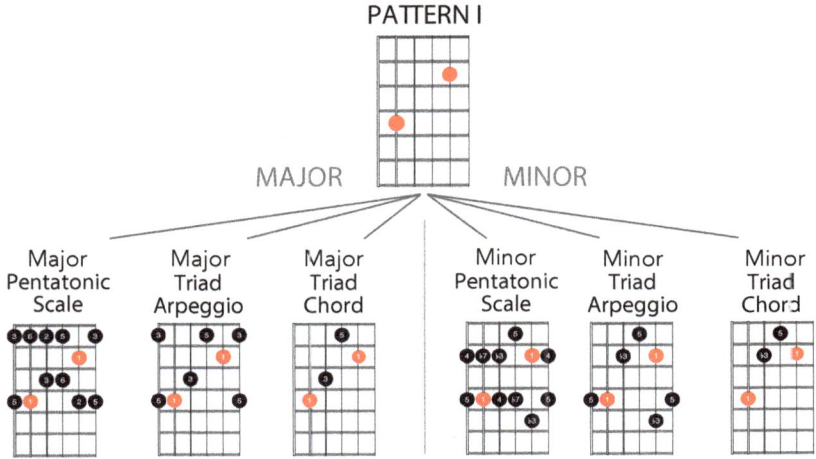

Look at what we've done so far. We've organized six derivatives below the original Octave Shape. Relating that to a family tree, we've established the equivalent of "the next generation". Let's keep going and see what can be derived from the major and minor pentatonic scales.

All of the major and minor scales can be derived from the pentatonic scales by simply adding a couple of notes to the pentatonic scale. In the case of the harmonic and melodic minor scales, other adjustments are made to the pentatonic scale.

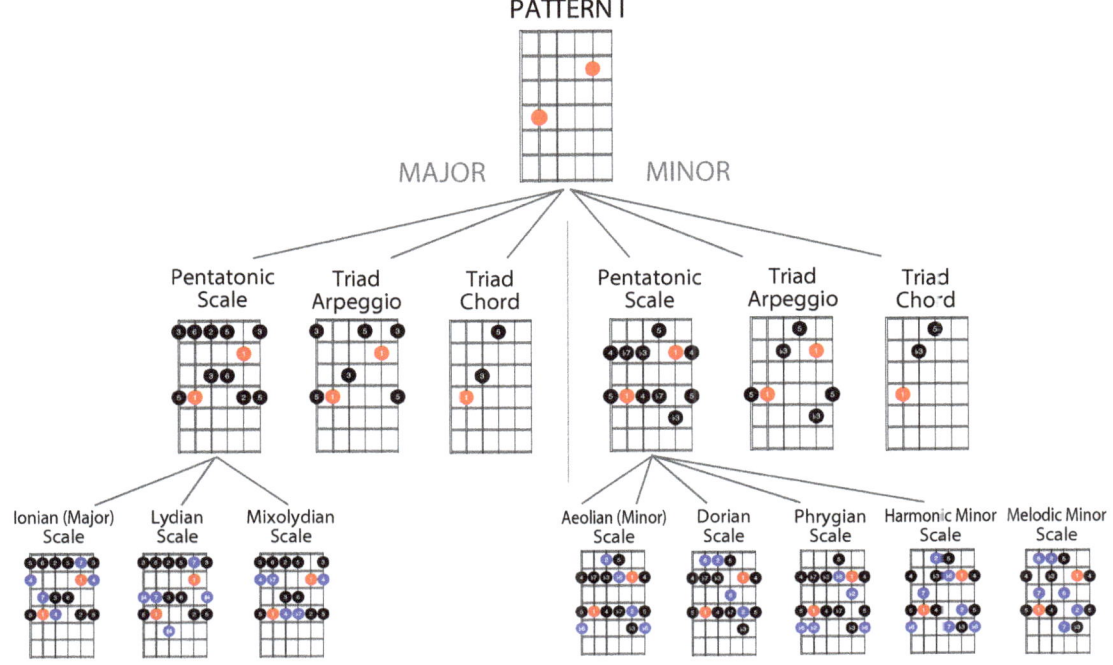

The Octave Shape Family Tree

The illustration below shows the vast number of scales, arpeggios, and chords that can be derived from each basic Octave Shape, in this case, Pattern I. Although a full discussion of each of the items shown on the Octave Shape Family Tree will take place in upcoming Units, let's take a look ahead to see where we are going. This is presented for you at this point so you can see the organizational system; don't feel responsible for learning all these scales, arpeggios, and chords yet.

As you examine the Pattern I Octave Shape Family Tree, notice the scales are highlighted in pink, the arpeggios in green, and the chords in yellow. At the top of the scales group is the pentatonic shell and below it are the seven-note scale derivatives. At the top of the arpeggios group are the triad arpeggios with the 7th arpeggio derivatives below. At the top of the chords group are the triad chords, the 7th chord derivatives are below them, and other derivatives are below them. Let's look more closely at each of these.

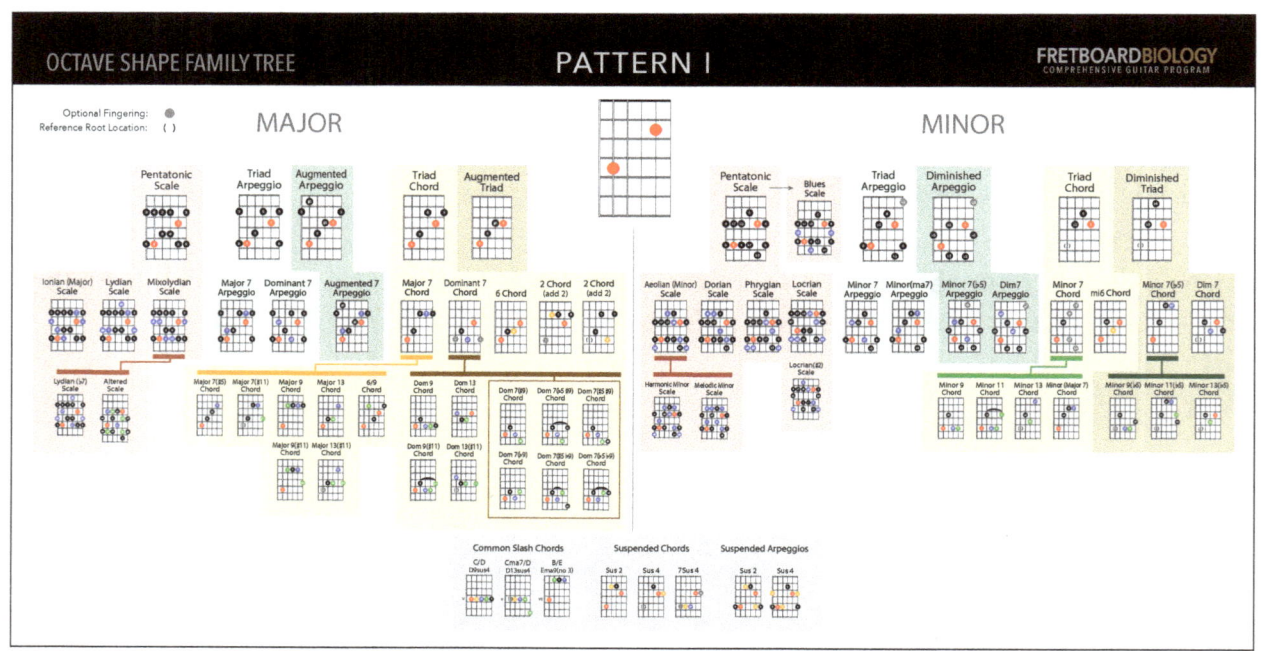

Scale Derivatives

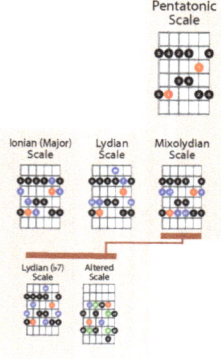

On the left half of the page is the major pentatonic scale. Below it are the scales derived from the pentatonic shells by adding two notes. These are the seven-note scales: Major, Lydian, Mixolydian. They are written below the pentatonic scale because they all are derived from the pentatonic scale. Below the Mixolydian scale are the "dominant sounding" scales that are derived from it: the Lydian (♭7) and the Altered scales. They are written below the Mixolydian scale because they are used over dominant 7th chords.

On the right side is the minor pentatonic scale. Below it are the scales derived from the minor pentatonic shell by adding one or two notes: the Blues scale (by adding one note) and the Natural Minor, Dorian, and Phrygian scales (by adding two notes).

Below the natural minor scale are the scales that are derived from it: the Harmonic Minor and Melodic Minor scales. They are written below the Natural Minor scale because they are the next generation of the thread.

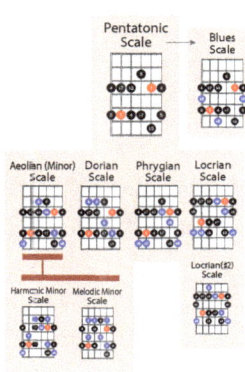

Arpeggio Derivatives

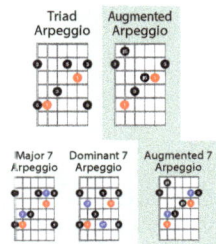

On the left side are the major triad arpeggio and the augmented triad arpeggio. Below the major triad arpeggio are the 7th-chord arpeggios derived from it: the major 7 and dominant 7 arpeggios. They are written below the major triad arpeggio because they are the next generation of arpeggios that have major 3rds.

On the right side is the minor triad arpeggio. Below it are the 7th-chord arpeggios derived from it: the minor 7 and minor(ma7) arpeggios. They are written below the minor triad arpeggio because they are the next generation of arpeggios that have minor 3rds. Also on the right side is the diminished triad arpeggio. Below it are the 7th-chord arpeggios we derive from it: the minor 7(b5) arpeggio and the diminished 7 arpeggio. They are written below the diminished triad arpeggio because they are the next generation.

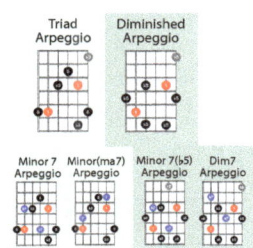

Chord Derivatives

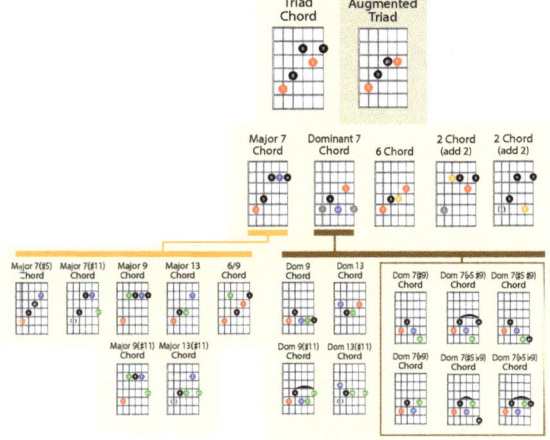

On the left side is the major triad chord. Below it are the 7th chords we derive from it: the major 7 and dominant 7 chords. They are written below the major triad chord because they are the next generation of chords that have major 3rds. Also on the left side is the augmented triad chord.

On the right side is the minor triad chord. Below it are the 7th chords derived from it: the minor 7 and minor 6 chords. They are written below the minor triad because they are the next generation of chords that have minor 3rds. Below the minor 7 chord are the chords derived from it. Also on the right side is the diminished triad chord. Below it are the 7th chords we derive from it: the minor 7(b5) and diminished 7 chords. They are written below the diminished triad because they are the next generation of chords that have a minor 3rd and diminished 5th. Below the minor 7(b5) chord are the chords derived from it. They are written below the minor 7(b5) because they are the next generation of the minor7(b5) chord.

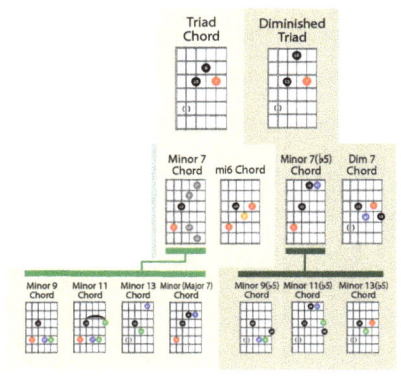

Suspended (Sus) and Slash Chords

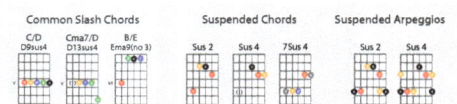

There are two categories of chords that don't fit neatly into either the Major quality side or the Minor quality side of the Family Tree.

The first of these is the suspended 4th chords, or "sus chords". These don't fit well into either side because they don't have a 3rd and can be used in either a major or minor context. There are other sus chords, such as the 7sus4, sus2, sus6/4, and others, that need to be included in the Family Tree as well.

The second category is what we call "slash chords". These are common and also don't have a 3rd to clearly define their quality. We have briefly discussed suspended chords in previous Units but we haven't discussed slash chords. There will be a thorough discussion about them in upcoming Units. For now, just know that they reside in their own area of the Family Tree along with sus chords in each of the Octave Shapes.

TECHNIQUE

In the Level 1 Technique Modules you learned various articulation devices like hammer-ons, pull-offs, slides, bends, and release bends. The Modules in Level 2 Technique will be focused on developing solid alternate picking in the following areas:

- Moving across the strings ascending and descending
- Dealing with 8th-note syncopation
- Playing 16th notes
- Dealing with 16th-note syncopation
- Playing 8th-note triplets
- Dealing with 8th-note triplet syncopation
- Playing 16th-note triplets
- Dealing with 16th-note triplet syncopation

Subdivisions - How Beats are Divided

In both the Technique and Improvisation Modules, you will learn alternate picking for several different subdivisions. The term subdivision is used to describe how a beat is divided. For example:

- Dividing a quarter-note beat into two equal parts results in an 8th-note subdivision.

$$♩ \div 2 = ♪♪ \text{ or } ♫$$

- Dividing a quarter-note beat into three equal parts results in an 8th-note triplet subdivision.

$$♩ \div 3 = \underbrace{♫♪}_{3}$$

- Dividing a quarter-note beat into four equal parts results in a 16th-note subdivision.

$$♩ \div 4 = ♪♪♪♪ \text{ or } ♬♬$$

- Dividing a quarter-note beat into six equal parts results in a 16th-note triplet subdivision.

$$♩ \div 6 = \underbrace{♬♬}_{3}\underbrace{♬♬}_{3} \text{ or } \underbrace{♬♬♬}_{6}$$

How to Approach Alternate Picking

There are two basic approaches to alternate picking. One way is literal and strict, meaning that all the rules about alternate picking are always adhered to. Another way is to think about the rules as general guidelines that can be varied in certain situations. This means that occasionally you might play two down strokes or two up strokes in a row. My opinion is that, as with most things related to technique, use the alternate picking rules in a strict way when practicing, but don't think about it too much when performing. With that as a starting point, let's begin.

Alternate Picking Ascending and Descending

By now you have dealt with the challenges of alternate picking when ascending or descending a scale, especially when the scale pattern has two notes on one string, three on the next string, two on the next, and so on. Before we move into the other aspects of alternate picking let's make sure you are clear about how to practice scales and arpeggios as you move across the strings ascending and descending, using eighth notes. We will use a scale you already know so you can check whether or not you are doing it right. Use the Pattern I F major scale, and use what you learn here as a guide for all of the other scales.

Pattern I F Major Scale

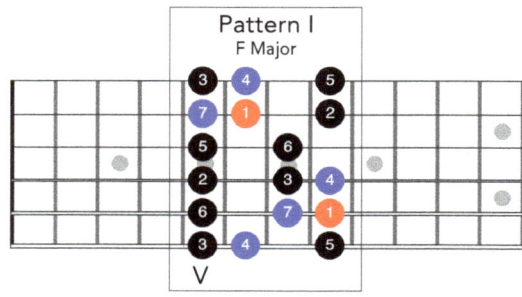

Ascending

1. Start on the tonic, F, on the 5th string with our 4th finger at the 8th fret with a down stroke.

2. This means the second note of the scale will be on the next string higher, the 4th string, with your 1st finger at the 5th fret with an up stroke. This is the first challenge: a new string higher with an up stroke.

3. Next, play the third note of the scale on the 4th string with your 3rd finger at the 7th fret with a down stroke.

4. And the fourth note of the scale will be on the same string with your 4th finger at the 8th fret with an up stroke.

Fretboard Biology — Level 2 • Unit 1: Technique

5. The next note of the scale is played on a new string, the 3rd string, with your 1st finger at the 5th fret with a down stroke.
6. The next note of the scale is also played on the 3rd string with your 3rd finger at the 7th fret with an up stroke.
7. The next note of the scale is played on a new string, the 2nd string, with your 1st finger at the 5th fret with a down stroke.
8. The next note of the scale is also played on the 2nd string with your 1st finger at the 6th fret with an up stroke.
9. The next note of the scale is also played on the 2nd string with your 4th finger at the 7th fret with a down stroke.
10. The next note of the scale is played on a new string, the 1st string, with your 1st finger at the 5th fret with an up stroke.
11. The next note of the scale is also played on the 1st string with your 2nd finger at the 6th fret with a down stroke.
12. The next note of the scale is also played on the 1st string with your 4th finger at the 8th fret with an up stroke.

Descending

1. Play the scale descending repeating on the 1st string with your 4th finger at the 8th fret with a down stroke.
2. The next note below is on the same string, the 1st string, played with your 2nd finger at the 6th fret with an up stroke.
3. The next note below is on the same string, the 1st string, played with your 1st finger at the 5th fret with a down stroke.
4. The next note descending is played on a new string, the 2nd string, with your 4th finger at the 8th fret with an up stroke. This is another challenge: a new string with an up stroke while descending.
5. The next note descending is also played on the 2nd string with your 2nd finger at the 6th fret with a down stroke.
6. The next note descending is also played on the 2nd string with your 1st finger at the 5th fret with an up stroke.
7. The next note descending is played on a new string, the 3rd string, with your 3rd finger at the 7th fret with a down stroke.
8. The next note descending is also played on the 3rd string with your 1st finger at the 5th fret with an up stroke.
9. The next note descending is played on a new string, the 4th string, with your 4th finger at the 8th fret with a down stroke.

10. The next note descending is played on the same string, the 4th string, with your 3rd finger at the 7th fret with an up stroke.
11. The next note descending is played on the same string, the 4th string, with your 1st finger at the 5th fret with a down stroke.
12. The last note, the tonic, is played on a new string, the 5th string, with your 4th finger at the 8th fret with an up stroke.

The challenge with using alternate picking comes from the asymmetry in the scale and arpeggio shapes; in other words, there are a different number of notes played on each string. Some strings have one note, some have two notes, and some have three. So why use alternate picking if it's so challenging? That is a good question and is open for debate, but many great guitarists argue that the consistency of the unbroken down-up-down-up picking pattern is essential to playing with great time. That is important. It is my strong opinion that you should make alternate picking your primary picking-hand approach.

RHYTHM NOTATION

Understanding rhythm notation is important to any musician's development. If you understand rhythm notation, you can read and write rhythm figures on a chart. This is critical skill for a literate musician.

So far in Theory the focus has been on the vertical axis of music, which involves the concept of pitches (notes) and how they function in melodies and chords. Pitch refers to how high or low a note is. Notes are placed vertically on the staff in a way that shows whether the note is high or low. The horizontal axis shows how music relates to time. This is referred to as "rhythm". Proper and clear rhythm notation is the focus of these Modules.

Pulse

An important aspect of rhythm is "pulse", which is normally felt as a pattern combining strong and weak beats.

Meter

A specific pattern of strong and weak beats is called "meter". Common popular music most often divides pulses into groups of four and sometimes into groups of three. Other combinations are less common.

Meter is divided into "measures". Measures are sometimes called "bars". Measures are separated from each other by barlines. Meter is the number of pulses (beats) within one measure of music.

Meter, Measures, and Bars

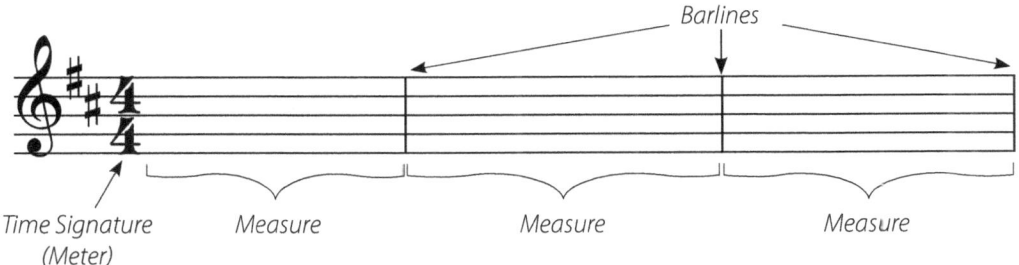

Music notation requires symbols to represent the duration of both sound and silence. In other words, every bit of time that passes in a piece of music must be notated, whether there is sound or silence. Notes represent sound while rests represent silence. The common symbols that represent sound and silence are listed in the chart below.

Symbols for Notes and Rests

SYMBOL	NOTES & RESTS
𝐨	Whole Note
𝅗𝅥	Half Note
♩	Quarter Note
♪	8th Note
𝅘𝅥𝅯	16th Note
▬	Whole Rest
▬	Half Rest
𝄾	Quarter Rest
𝄿	8th Rest
𝅀	16th Rest

This discussion will continue in the next Module. Study the concepts explained in this Module: meter, measures, bars, barlines, notes, and rests. Also familiarize yourself with the names of the kinds of notes and rests.

RHYTHM GUITAR

Folk Rhythm Guitar

Nearly every culture in the world has its own version of Folk music because it is the music of "the folk" - the common population. In Folk music, the lyrics are central to the music because they tell stories that describe life in the culture.

In the next few Units we will learn how to play guitar in American Folk music. Even if you aren't interested in playing Folk music, it is likely you will be called on at some point in your career to play or record acoustic guitar in a Folk style and the chords you will play will be the same open-string voicings you have learned in this course.

The main role of guitar in American Folk music is to accompany the singer or singers. Often the guitar is the only instrument. Everything you will learn in these modules works well when guitar is the only instrument but it works with a band, too. It is common for bass, drums, keyboards, and multiple guitars to provide the backing for the singers.

Typically most guitar students don't work very hard at playing open chords because they seem so simple—that is until they are in situations where they are under a microscope and realize they are not executing the chords as cleanly as they should. As you work through this Unit, check your ability to play these chords cleanly. Most guitarists think they are easy but they still deserve your attention.

Folk Rhythm Technique

Folk rhythm guitar parts require a solid knowledge of open-chord voicings. Guitarists playing Folk music should be competent with both strumming and basic fingerpicking. First, let's discuss strumming. You just studies alternate picking for an 8th-note subdivision in the Technique Module, so this will be fresh in your mind. The strumming patterns we use in this Module are based on an 8th-note subdivision.

Strumming open-voicing chords cleanly on an acoustic guitar is often taken for granted until performances are examined closely in the studio. Strive to play all the strings used in a specific voicing evenly. Take care to not let unused strings ring and don't let your fretting hand fingers interfere with open strings.

Whether playing alone with the singer or as part of a band, your strumming hand needs to play with authority, taking charge of the rhythm feel of the group. I suggest widening the path that your pick follows. It will help in a few ways:

- The pick attack is more even across all the strings if you strike the low strings from a slightly further distance on a down stroke and the high strings from a slightly further distance on an up stroke.

- You can play a stronger pulse when your pick motion is slightly exaggerated compared to where it might be played when strumming parts in other genres.
- You can play more forcefully and therefore louder if you have a wider pick path.

Here is a progression in 4/4 time using some common open chords. Play it two ways. First, play it alone with no band. Use a metronome as a click to practice keeping a steady beat. Record it and listen back. Listen for how strong your rhythm pulse is and whether you are playing the chords cleanly.

Next, play it with the backing track. When playing with the track or band, you have other instruments helping with the rhythm. Even so, be strong with your strumming hand pulse. You need to be in sync with the other instruments but the strumming guitar is still the central component of the rhythm section. Record it and listen back. Listen for how strong your rhythm pulse is and how cleanly you can play the chords.

Folk Rhythm Progression in G Major

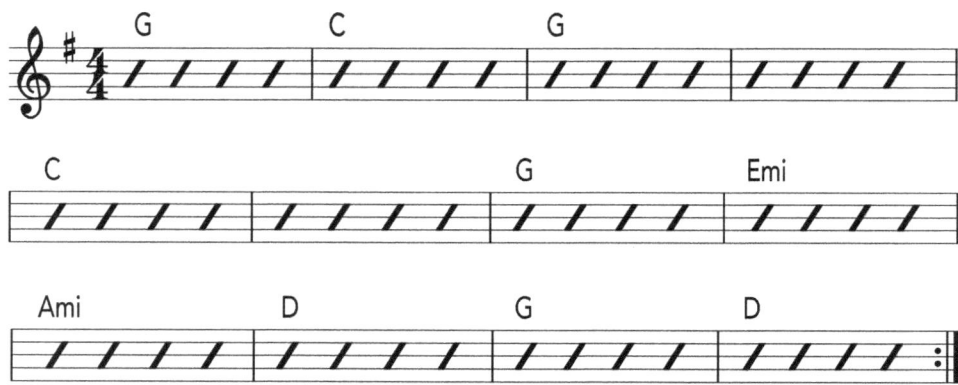

Some guitarists use a lighter pick to play strumming parts on an acoustic guitar. This reduces the resistance when making contact with the strings and reduces the harshness of the attack. It also has more of a brush sound. Experiment with different thicknesses of picks as well as the strength of your attack to see how these affect the sound of your guitar and the overall sound of the tune when playing with the backing track.

IMPROVISATION

In the Level 2 Improvisation Modules we will work through some of the different rhythm feels we encounter as soloists. It's important to practice soloing over a variety of grooves. Later in the Level we will begin the important study of "chord-tone soloing", which is the use of the notes of a chord to create lines in our solos.

In Level 1 Improvisation we focused on the following topics:

- Key-center soloing: Key-center soloing is where the source of notes for a solo is the scale of the song's key. With this approach the soloist isn't very specific about note choices. This is a nomadic way to solo; the soloist wanders around within a scale pattern. This can be pretty unsatisfying to both the listener and you.

- Storytelling in soloing: This is the idea that your solo needs to tell a story. It should have a beginning, middle, and end, and the listener should feel like they are being taken on a musical journey.

- Motif development: A musical motif is a musical statement. It should be both a melodic and rhythmic idea that is clear and can be remembered and restated.

- The five elements of contrast: These are: low to high, slow to fast, simple to complex, sparse to dense, and soft to loud. Using these helps us build intensity in our story.

These topics were introduced at the beginning because they are the most important things to know about playing a good solo. Everything else you learn just helps you tell a story better. These are the basic guiding principles of playing a good solo.

You should be comfortable soloing within each of the feels and subdivisions presented in the Technique Modules in Level 2. In the following Improvisation Modules you'll be given simple progressions with different feels and subdivisions. I suggest you first play some simple lines to get comfortable with the subdivision and the correct alternate picking as presented in the corresponding Technique Modules. After you are comfortable with the feel, practice all the elements of good storytelling we spent so much time with in Level 1. That is always important!

Here is a straight 8th-note groove in C minor. It's a two-bar phrase repeated over and over.

Progression in C Minor

This exercise focuses on your picking hand. Stay true to the 8th-note alternate-picking pattern. Practice playing with the track two different ways:

- First, just find a pattern of C minor pentatonic where you feel comfortable. Focus on your picking hand and play 8th-note lines to get comfortable with the 8th-note subdivision and how you fit into the groove.
- Second, create a solo of finite length. I suggest 16 bars to begin. That is eight times through the two-bar phrase. Either a clean or overdrive sound will work fine. Record it and listen back, checking for good time and feel and for how well you told a story. Follow the alternate-picking rules.

C Minor Pentatonic Scales

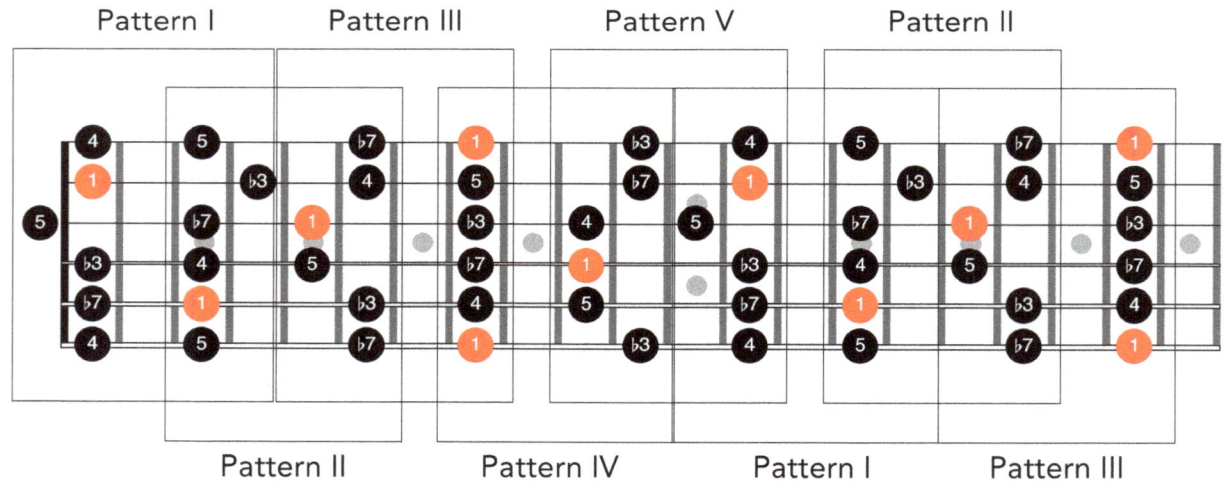

Level 2 Unit 1 • Example Solo

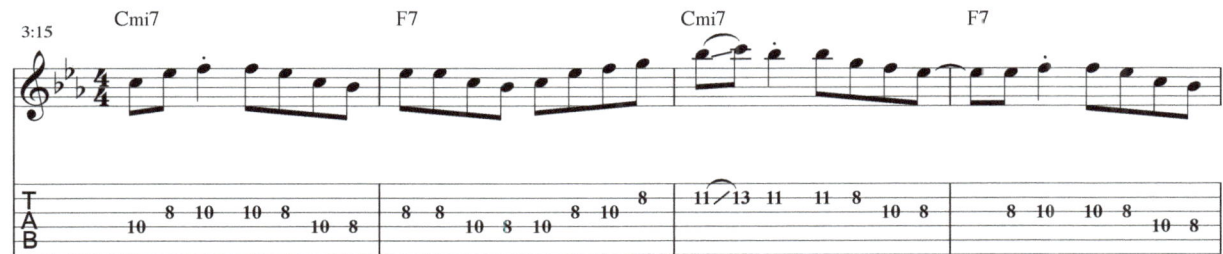

PRACTICE

Theory

- ❏ Go to the tabs below the Theory video on the website and complete the quiz.
- ❏ Spend time memorizing the quantity and quality of all the simple intervals.
- ❏ Memorize the intervals from the tonic to each scale degree of the major scale.

Fretboard Logic

- ❏ Learn the Pattern II major pentatonic scale and Pattern II major scales and add them to your practice routine.
- ❏ Practice the chord progressions, mixing open and barre chords, until you can perform them cleanly. Start by using a metronome until you can perform them cleanly, then play them along with the backing track.
- ❏ Memorize the minor 2nd, major 2nd, minor 3rd, and major 3rd intervals on a single string. Use the exercise in the tabs below the video to practice your recognition of intervals on the fretboard.
- ❏ Understand the Octave Shape Family Tree and how it organizes the fretboard for us.

Technique

- ❏ Practice playing the Pattern I F Major Scale ascending and descending with 8th notes using strict alternate picking.

Rhythm Notation

- ❏ Memorize the symbols used for common notes and rests.

Rhythm Guitar

- ❏ Practice Folk Rhythm Progression 1 with and without the backing track.

Improvisation

- ❏ Create a 16-bar solo using whichever patterns of the Cmi pentatonic scales you prefer. As always, record yourself and listen back.

UNIT 2

Learning Modules

> **Theory** - Measuring and Constructing Intervals

> **Fretboard Logic** - Pattern IV Major Pentatonic and Major Scales, Mixing Open and Barre-Chord Voicings, Intervals: 2nds and 3rds on Adjacent Strings

> **Technique** - Alternate Picking with a Syncopated 8th-Note Subdivision

> **Rhythm Notation** - Note Heads and Stems, Flags

> **Rhythm Guitar** - Folk Rhythm Guitar

> **Improvisation** - Soloing with a Straight 8th-Note Syncopation

> **Practice** - Continue Practice Routine Development

THEORY

Quantity is the general measurement of the distance between two notes and quality is the exact measurement. Half steps and whole steps can be grouped together to form bigger intervals, like perfect 4ths or minor 6ths, for example. The major scale provides a consistent and reliable pattern of intervals between from the tonic and each of the scale degrees that can be used for measuring intervals. It is time to make it work for us.

Like key signatures, intervals work from two different perspectives: you need to be able to look at an interval and identify it, and you need to know how to build an interval above or below a given note. We will start by learning how to measure an interval.

Interval Identification

Follow these easy steps to measure an interval:

1. Identify the key signature of the lower note of the interval you wish to measure. In this example, you see C and G above it. The key signature for C is no sharps or flats.

Identifying an Interval above C

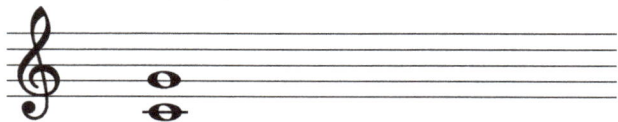

2. Determine the quantity of the distance between the C and G by counting the letters: It is a 5th.

Identifying an Interval above C

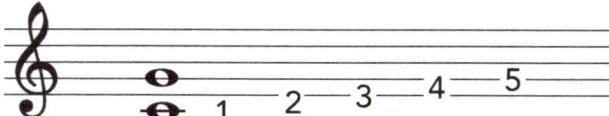

3. Compare the higher note in the interval to the note with the same letter in the major scale of the lower note: C to G is the same as C to G in the C major scale, which is a perfect 5th. Based on comparison, the interval is a perfect 5th.

C Major Scale

Fretboard Biology — Level 2 • Unit 2: Theory

Here are the steps so far: First, find the key signature of the lower note. Next, measure the quantity of the interval. Then compare the upper note to the note with the same letter in the major scale of the lower note.

Here is another with a slight variation.

1. Here is C and G♭ above it. The C major key signature is no sharps or flats.

Identifying an Interval above C

2. The quantity of the distance between the C and G♭ is a 5th. In the C major scale, the G is G natural.

Identifying an Interval above C

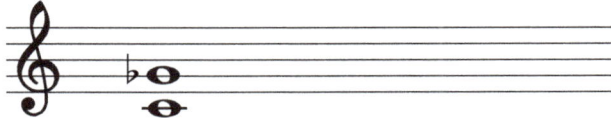

3. C to G natural is a perfect 5th, but the interval here is C to G♭. This is a half step smaller than C to G (the perfect 5th in the C major scale). The interval a half step smaller than a perfect 5th is a diminished 5th.

C Major Scale

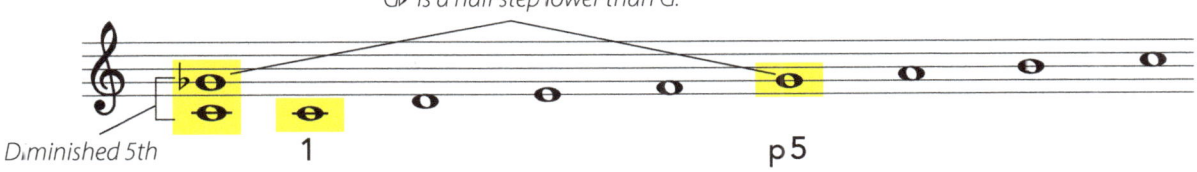

G♭ is a half step lower than G.

Diminished 5th   1   p5

Here is another example:

1. Here is a D and F natural above it. The D major key signature has two sharps: F# and C#.

Identifying an Interval above D

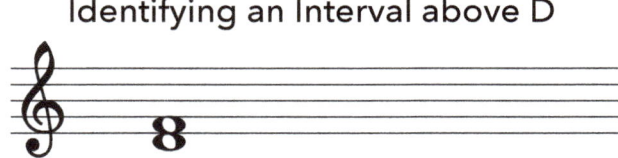

2. The quantity of the distance between the D and F is a 3rd. In the D major scale, the F is an F#. D to F# is a major 3rd, but the interval here is D to F natural.

Identifying an Interval above D

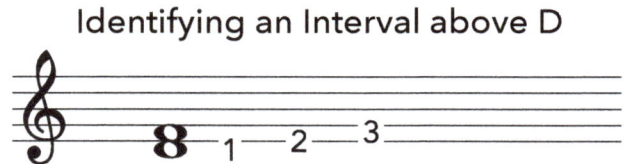

3. This is interval is a half step smaller than the major 3rd in the D major scale. The interval a half step smaller than major 3rd is a minor 3rd.

D Major Scale

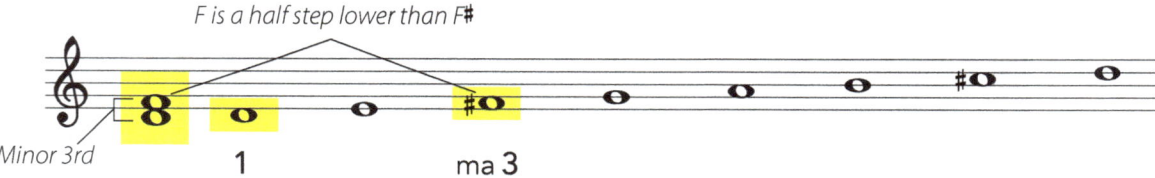

Here is another example:

1. Here is E♭ and A natural above it. The E♭ key signature has three flats: B♭, E♭, and A♭.

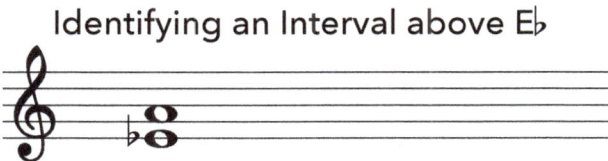

2. The quantity of the distance between the E♭ and A natural is a 4th. In the E♭ major scale, the A is A♭. E♭ to A♭ is a perfect 4th, but the interval here is E♭ to A natural.

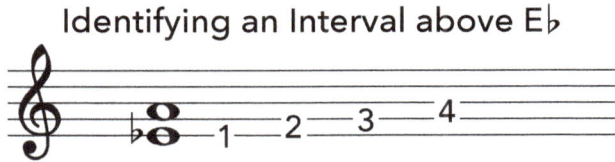

3. This is a half step larger than the perfect 4th in the E♭ major scale. The interval a half step larger than a perfect 4th is an augmented 4th.

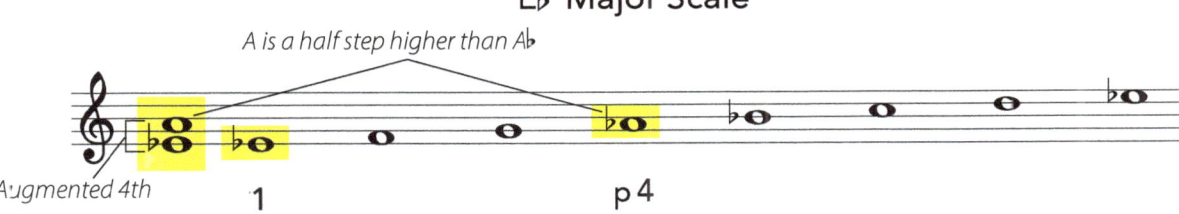

Interval Construction

Next, learn to do the opposite: Instead of identifying existing intervals, learn how to build an interval. There are a few easy steps:

1. Begin with the lower note of the interval you wish to build and identify its key signature. Here is a C, and you want to build a major 3rd above it. The key signature for C major is no sharps or flats.

Constructing a Major 3rd Interval above C

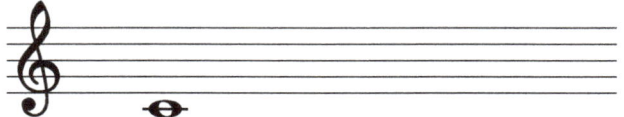

2. Determine the note for the quantity: a 3rd. Count C, D, and E. It is some kind of E.

Constructing a Major 3rd Interval above C

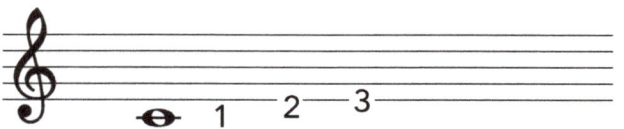

3. You want to build a major 3rd above C, and it is some kind of E. In the C major scale, the 3rd is major and it is E natural. Therefore, E natural is a major 3rd above C.

C Major Scale

Here are the steps for building an interval so far. First, find the key signature of the note you want to build above. Next, count up to the desired quantity. Then, compare the upper note you have just written to the note with the same letter in the major scale of the lower note. Then, if necessary, make an adjustment to create the interval you want to build.

Here is another example:

1. Here is a C again, but this time you want to build a minor 3rd above it. The key signature for C is no sharps or flats.

Constructing a Minor 3rd Interval above C

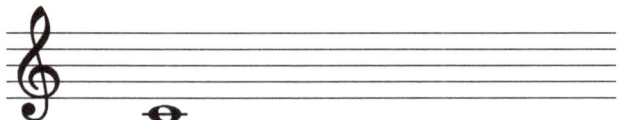

2. Determine the letter of the note for the quantity you want, which is a 3rd. Count C, D, and E. It is some kind of E.

Constructing an Interval above C

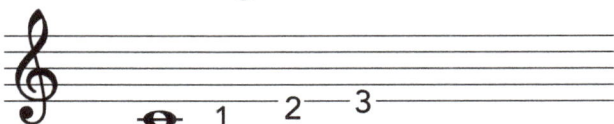

3. You are building a minor 3rd above C. In the C major scale, the 3rd is major and it's E natural. But you want a minor 3rd so you need to lower the E a half step by applying a flat, and the result is a minor 3rd. Therefore, E♭ is a minor 3rd above C.

C Major Scale

Place a flat before the E so it is a half step lower than E natural.

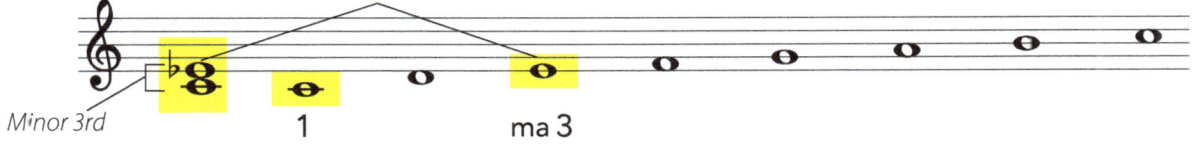

Here is another example:

1. Build a minor 6th above D. The key signature for D is two sharps: F♯ and C♯.

Constructing a Minor 6th Interval above D

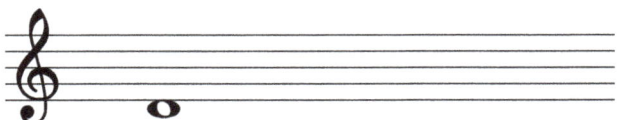

2. Determine the letter of the note for the quantity you want, which is a 6th. Count D, E, F, G, A, and B. It is some kind of B.

Constructing an Minor 6th Interval above D

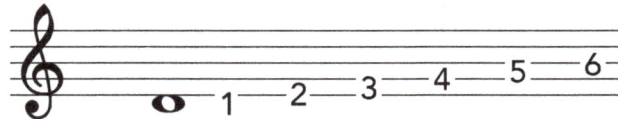

3. You want to build a minor 6th above D, and you know it is some kind of B. In the D major scale, the 6th is major and it's B natural. But you want a minor 6th so if you lower the B a half step by applying a flat, the result is a minor 6th. Therefore B♭ is a minor 6th above D.

D Major Scale

Place a flat before the B so it is a half step lower than B natural.

Here is another example:

1. Build a major 7th above A♭. The key signature for A♭ is four flats: B♭, E♭, A♭, and D♭.

Constructing a Major 7th Interval above A♭

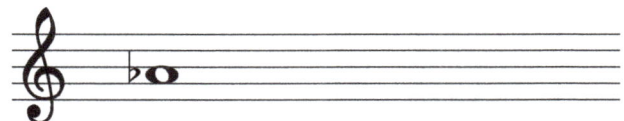

2. Determine the letter of the note for the quantity you want, which is a 7th. Count A, B, C, D, E, F, and G, so you know it is some kind of G.

Constructing a Major 7th Interval above A♭

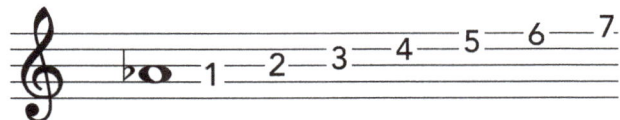

3. You want to build a major 7th above A♭, and you know it is some kind of G. In the A♭ major scale, the G is G natural. The G natural we have written on the staff is already a major 7th, no adjustment with a sharp or flat needed. Therefore, G is a major 7th above A♭.

A♭ Major Scale
Needs to be the same

You must practice building intervals until it is automatic. Soon, when you learn to build and identify chords, it will require building two, three, and more intervals above a root note.

You have learned the two most important foundational topics in Theory: key signatures and intervals. Everything about scales and chords you learn from this point forward relies on your command of this information. Take your time and learn this well!

FRETBOARD LOGIC

Scale

In Unit 1 you learned the Pattern II major pentatonic shell and the major scale built within it. Continue this process with the Pattern IV major pentatonic shell.

Pattern IV Major Pentatonic Scale

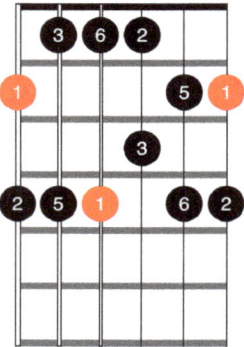

To build the major scale add a perfect 4th and a major 7th scale degrees in each octave (in blue). This is movable to any key.

Pattern IV Major Scale

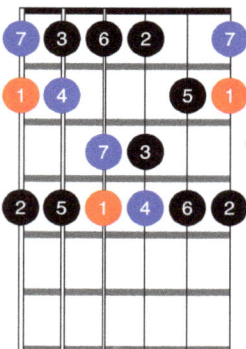

Add this scale to your practice routine and use strict alternate picking playing 8th notes.

Chords

In Unit 1 you played progressions that require a mix of open-string voicings and barre chords. Here are a couple more in this Module. Practice playing these progressions with a metronome at a comfortable tempo.

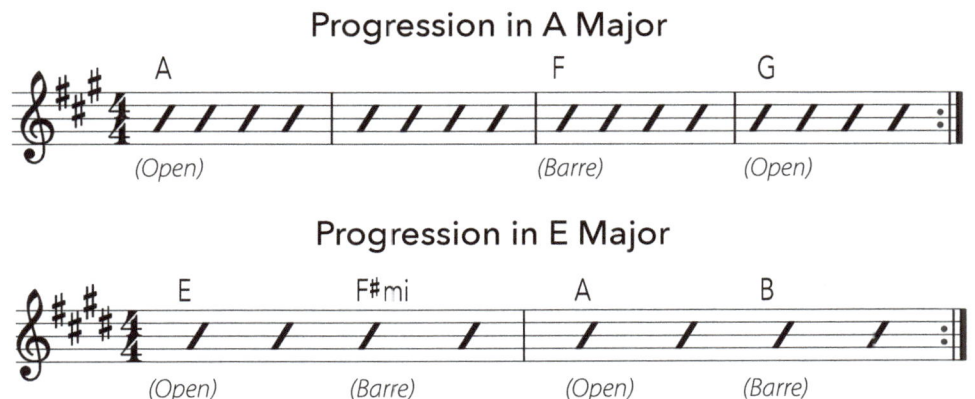

Interval Shapes on the Fretboard

Let's continue our study of interval shapes on the fretboard. As mentioned before, because we guitarists benefit from the visual nature of the fretboard, knowledge of the basic interval shapes is helpful to build scales, arpeggios, and chords. You will learn all interval shapes gradually over the next few Modules. In the last Unit you learned shapes for minor and major 2nds and 3rds on one string. In this Unit you will learn shapes for minor and major 2nds and 3rds on the adjacent bottom four strings.

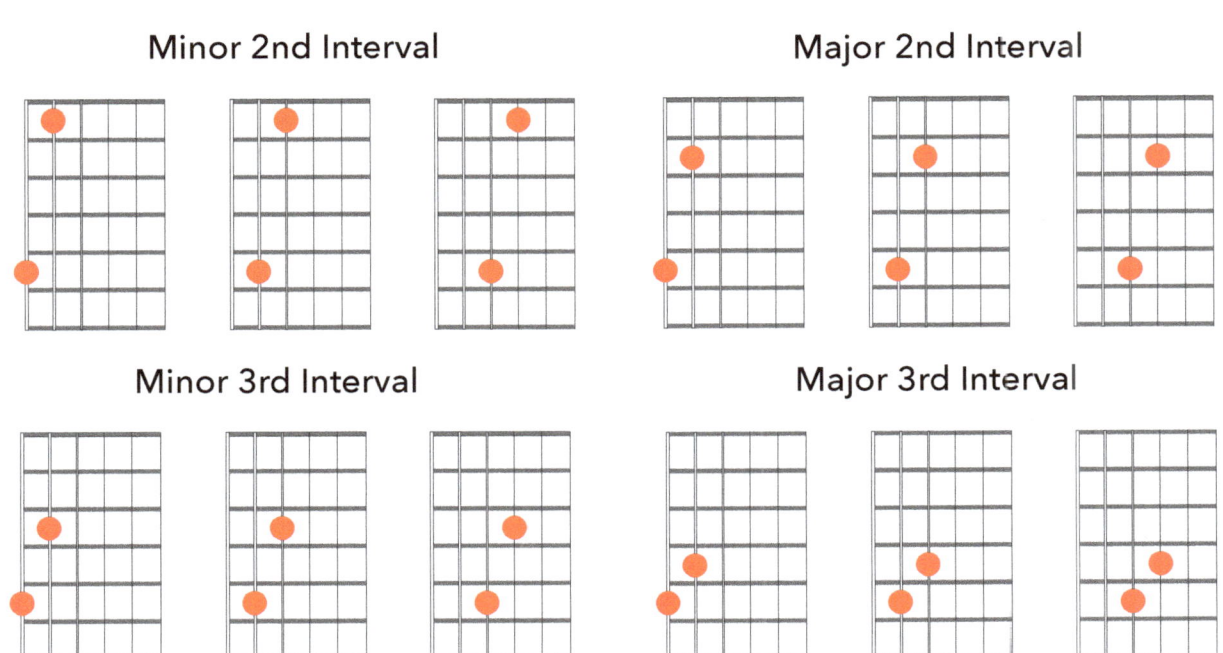

TECHNIQUE

Syncopation

"Syncopation" is where accents are shifted from a place in a measure that is usually strong to a place that is usually weak. Let's take a look at how to play syncopated rhythms using alternate picking.

Quarter-Note Syncopation

Quarter-note syncopation is where accents are shifted from beat one or three to beat two or four. Because quarter notes are almost always played with down strokes, quarter-note syncopation will be played with down strokes.

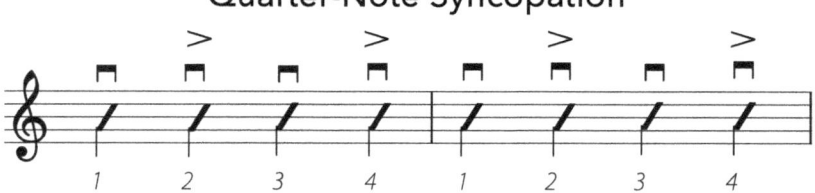

Quarter-Note Syncopation

(NOTE: This accent symbol (>) means to place more weight on the attack it's written above. In quarter note syncopation, more weight is placed on the notes on beats 2 and 4.)

Eighth-Note Syncopation

In 8th-note syncopation, some accents are shifted from the beat to the "and" (the up beat). Accents are shifted from 1, 2, 3, or 4 to the "and" of the 1, the "and" of the 2, the "and" of the 3, or the "and" of the 4. With an 8th-note alternate-picking pattern, attacks that are on the beat are played with down strokes, and attacks played on the "and", the up beats, are played with up strokes. For example, if a measure of music is all 8th notes, the pattern and articulation would be simple: a continuous down-up-down-up alternate-picking pattern. Here is an example of 8th-note syncopation.

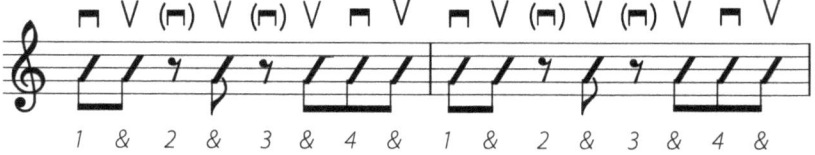

8th-Note Syncopation

(⊓) - *Indicates that the stroke movement is made without picking a string.*

RHYTHM NOTATION

In the last Module the topic of rhythm notation was introduced. We discussed meter, measures, barlines, notes, rests, and the symbols that represent them. Let's continue with our study and introduce a few new terms.

Note Heads and Stems

A "note head" is the roundish part of a note symbol that is placed on a line or space. Note heads are hollow or solid depending on their value (duration). A whole note or whole rest represents the longest duration we can write. Half notes and rests, quarter notes and rests, and so on, are shorter in duration. Whole and half notes have a hollow note head. All notes of shorter duration than a whole note have what is a called a "stem".

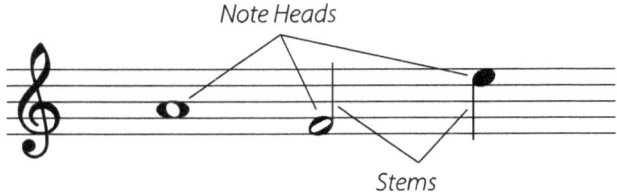

Here are some rules about stems:

- Stems are approximately one octave in length.
- Stems extend upward and are connected to the right side of the note head if the note head is below the middle line of the staff.
- Stems extend downward and are connected to the left side of the note head if the note head is above the middle line of the staff.
- If a note head is on the middle line, the stem can go either way, but there are other considerations which will be presented in a later Unit.

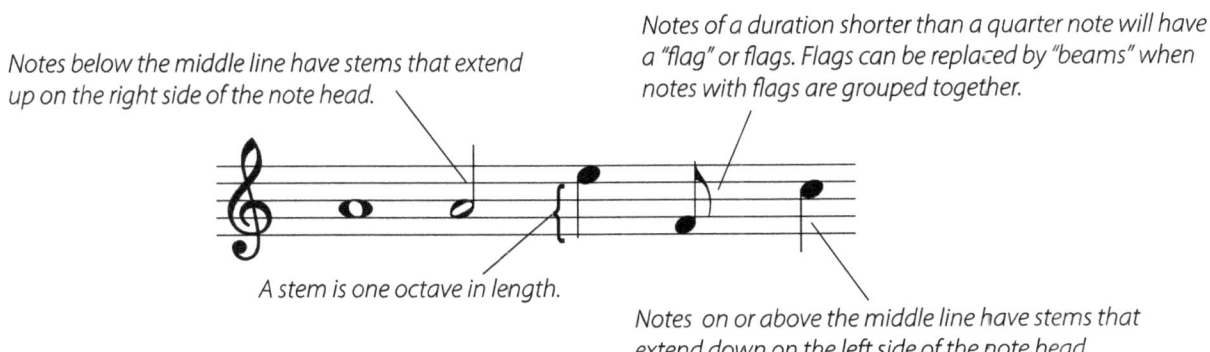

Notes below the middle line have stems that extend up on the right side of the note head.

Notes of a duration shorter than a quarter note will have a "flag" or flags. Flags can be replaced by "beams" when notes with flags are grouped together.

A stem is one octave in length.

Notes on or above the middle line have stems that extend down on the left side of the note head.

Flags

Flags are attached to the right side of a stem. An 8th note has one flag and is half the value (duration) of a quarter note. A 16th note has two flags and is half the value of an eight note. A 32nd note has three flags and is half the value of a 16th note and so on.

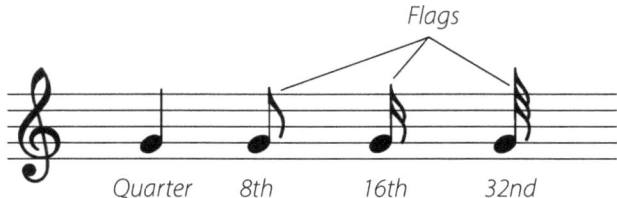

It has been my experience that the clearer the notation and organization of a written piece of music, the better the performance is. Consider this: When music is memorized, 100% of the musician's attention can be used for the performance. When music is read, a considerable percentage of the musician's attention is going to deciphering what is written, which means the performance suffers to some degree. This issue can be mitigated if the notation is clear. As you learn more about Rhythm Notation, you will learn how to organize music on the page as well. Keep in mind when notating music: written music should "look the way it sounds" both melodically and rhythmically.

RHYTHM GUITAR

In the last Unit you began your study of Folk rhythm guitar. The content in this series of Folk Rhythm Guitar Modules will serve you well. Even if you are not playing "Folk music", at some point in your career you will be asked to play or record acoustic guitar.

In the last Rhythm Guitar Module you learned that guitarists playing Folk music should be competent in two skills: strumming and basic fingerpicking. You learned some basic strumming in the last Unit. This unit has another progression to practice strumming using open voicing chords. Fingerpicking is introduced in the next Module.

In the last Unit you played an example in 4/4 time. This example is in 3/4 time. The strumming pattern you use here is based on an 8th-note subdivision. Here is progression in G major for you to practice.

Folk Rhythm Progression in G Major

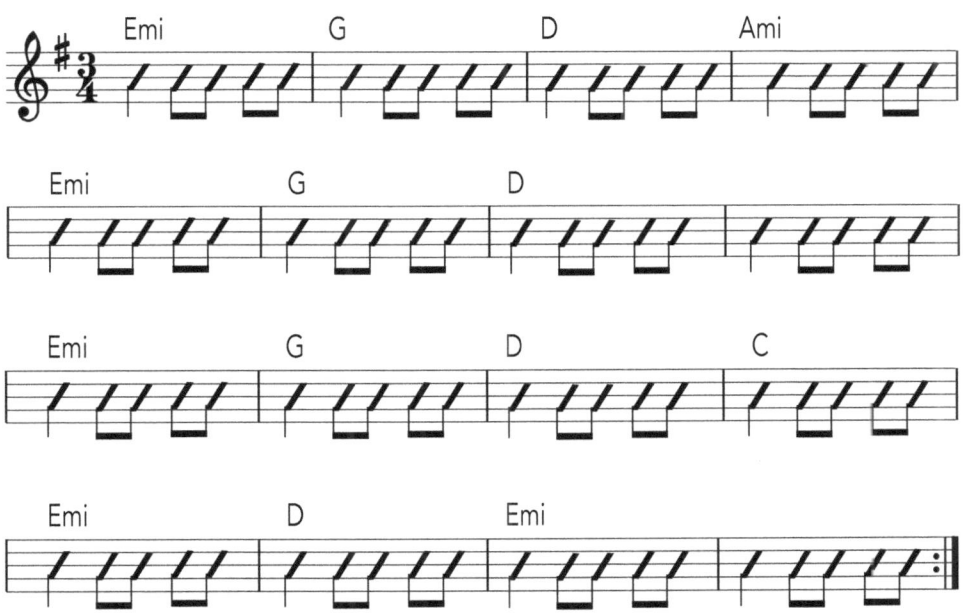

First, play this progression with no backing track, but use a metronome to keep a steady beat. Next, play it with the backing track. With a band, you have other instruments helping with the rhythm. Regardless, keep a strong pulse with your strumming hand. You need to be in sync with the other instruments, but the guitar is still the central component of the rhythm section in Folk music. Record it and listen back. Listen for how strong your rhythm pulse is and how cleanly you can play the chords.

IMPROVISATION

In Unit 1 you practiced soloing with basic 8th-note subdivisions. Dividing a quarter-note beat into two equal parts results in 8th-note subdivisions. In the Unit 2 Technique Module, 8th-note syncopation was introduced, so here is another progression with an 8th-note feel, but this time play some syncopated rhythms. This means that you will be shifting at least some of the accents and attacks from the beats to the "ands".

This is a straight 8th-note groove in the key of A major. It is a two-bar phrase repeated over and over. Like the last one, this exercise is about staying true to the 8th-note alternate-picking pattern.

Progression in A Major

Practice playing with the track two different ways:

- First, find a pattern of A major pentatonic scale you're comfortable with. Focusing on your picking hand, play 8th-note lines to get comfortable with the 8th-note subdivision and how you fit into the groove. Include some syncopation and, of course, stay true to the alternate-picking pick-direction rules.

- Second, create a solo of finite length, perhaps 16 bars to begin which is eight times through the two-bar phrase. Use either a clean or overdrive sound. Record it and listen back to check for good time and feel and to see how well you told a story.

A Major Pentatonic Scales

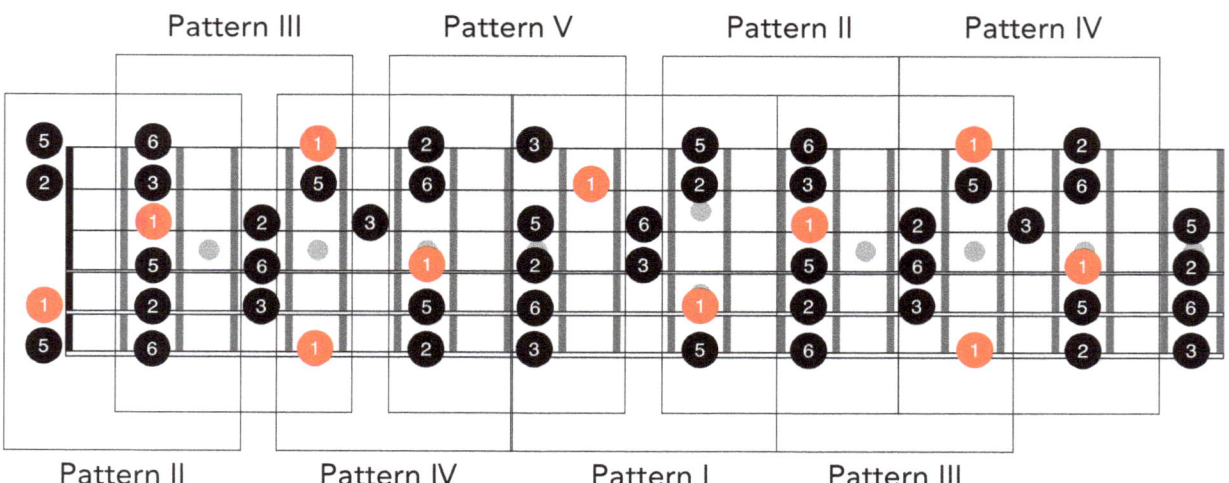

Level 2 Unit 2 • Example Solo

PRACTICE

Theory

- ❑ Go to the tabs below the Theory video on the website and complete the quiz.
- ❑ Practice measuring and constructing intervals until you are comfortable with those processes.

Fretboard Logic

- ❑ Learn the Pattern IV major pentatonic scale and Pattern IV major scales and add them to your practice routine.
- ❑ Practice the chord progressions, mixing open and barre chords, until you can perform them cleanly. Start by using a metronome until you can perform them cleanly, then play them along with the backing track.
- ❑ Memorize the minor 2nd, major 2nd, minor 3rd, and major 3rd intervals on the adjacent bottom four strings. Use the exercise in the tabs below the video to practice your recognition of intervals on the fretboard.

Technique

- ❑ Practice playing with a syncopated 8th-note pattern using strict alternate picking.

Rhythm Notation

- ❑ Learn how to write and recognize note heads, stems, and flags.

Rhythm Guitar

- ❑ Practice Folk Rhythm Progression 2 with and without the backing track.

Improvisation

- ❑ Create a 16-bar solo using whichever patterns of the A major pentatonic scales you prefer. As always, record yourself and listen back.

UNIT 3

Learning Modules

> **Theory** - Major, Minor, Augmented, and Diminished Triad Formulas, Suspended 4th formula

> **Fretboard Logic** - Pattern V Major Pentatonic and Major Scales, Introduction to Triad Super Shapes, Intervals: 4ths and 5ths on Adjacent Strings

> **Technique** - Alternate Picking with a 16th-Note Subdivision

> **Rhythm Notation** - Meter and Time Signatures

> **Rhythm Guitar** - Folk Rhythm Guitar, Introduction to Fingerpicking

> **Improvisation** - Soloing with a Straight-16th Note Subdivision

> **Practice** - Continue Practice Routine Development

THEORY

Triads

In this Unit you will learn to use intervals to build chords. The first type of chord you will construct is a three-note chord called a "triad". A triad is just two intervals built above a note we call the root. The root is the name of the chord.

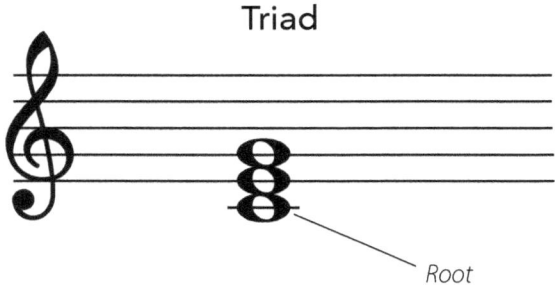

The simplest way to think of a triad is as two intervals built above a root: a 3rd and a 5th. There are three components to a triad: the root, the 3rd, and the 5th.

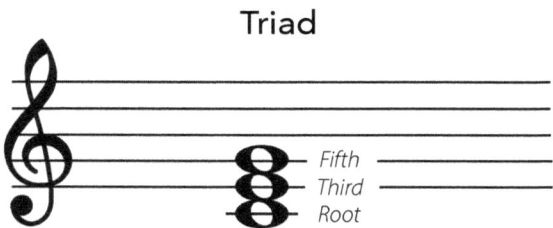

The 3rd can be either a major 3rd or a minor 3rd, and the 5th can be a perfect 5th, a diminished 5th, or an augmented 5th. The quality of the 3rd and 5th affects the personality of each triad. There are four triad types and they each use a unique combination of these intervals. We use a familiar term, "quality", to name each of the four types of triads: major, minor, augmented, and diminished.

Triad Formulas

Here are the interval formulas for each type of triad:

Major Triad

A major triad has a major 3rd and a perfect 5th.

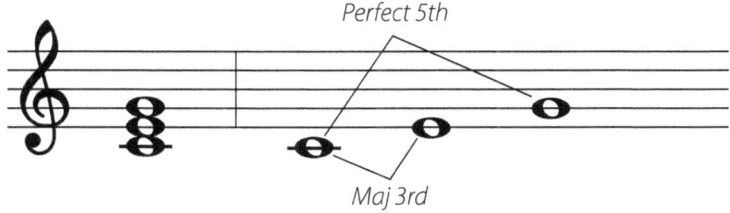

Minor Triad

A minor triad has a minor 3rd and a perfect 5th.

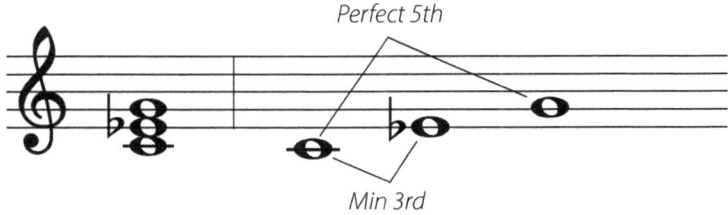

Augmented Triad

An augmented triad has a major 3rd and an augmented 5th.

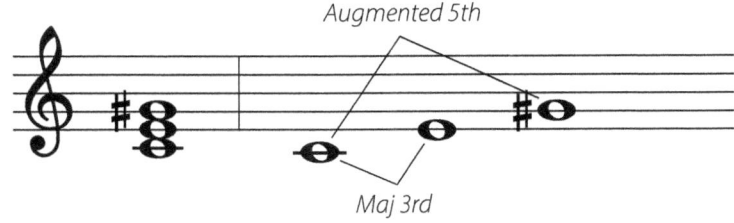

Diminished Triad

A diminished triad has a minor 3rd and a diminished 5th.

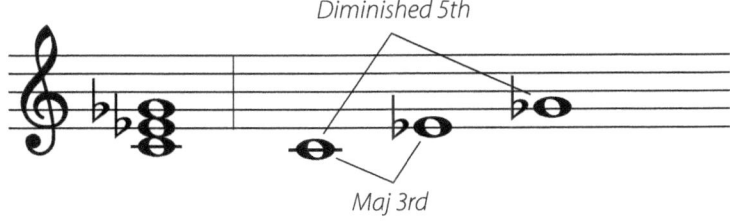

A suspended 4th chord is another three-note chord although traditionally it isn't called a triad. A suspended 4th chord consists of a root with a perfect 4th and perfect 5th above it. In a suspended 4th chord, the perfect 4th replaces the major 3rd when used in a major context and replaces the minor 3rd when used in a minor context. The word "suspended" is abbreviated to "sus" in the chord symbol and when speaking. Sometimes, but not always, the sus4 chord is followed by a major chord in a major context or a minor chord in a minor context.

Sus4 Chord

A sus4 chord has a perfect 4th and a perfect 5th.

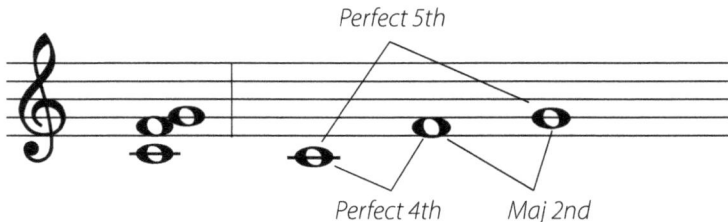

It should be clear why you learned intervals first: A triad is just two intervals built above a root. It is important to address the dual meanings for some terms. The terms major, minor, augmented, and diminished have meanings when referring to intervals. Now you are learning that these same terms have different (but related) meanings when referring to triads. Triads are named major, minor, augmented, and diminished according to the interval formula for each one. Triads will be discussed in greater detail in the next couple of Units, but start by learning some important definitions. Some of these will be familiar to you:

Root

The root is the fundamental note of a chord. Chords are named according to their roots. For example, if the root is C, it is a C chord; if the root is D, it is a D chord, and so on. This is similar to our discussion about scales and keys: The tonic is the fundamental note of a scale and key. Keys and scales are named according to their tonics.

Chord

A chord is three or more notes played simultaneously.

Triad

A three-note chord.

Arpeggio

The notes of a chord are played melodically; that is, one note after another rather than simultaneously.

Chord Tones

The notes of a chord are called "chord tones", and they have names: root, 3rd, and 5th. It should be noted that the chord tones of a triad are a 3rd apart from each other.

Suspended 4th Chord or Sus4

A three-note chord where a note a perfect 4th above the root replaces the 3rd.

Root-Position Chord

A root-position chord has the root as the lowest note. There are instances where, for musical reasons, a chord tone other than the root is played as the lowest note of the chord. In these cases it is called an "inverted chord" or simply "an inversion".

Inverted Chord

An inverted chord has a chord tone other than the root as its lowest note.

You learned about key signatures and intervals in earlier Units. Your study of key signatures helped you understand intervals because you used the major scale and key signatures to help measure intervals. Now you are relying on your knowledge of intervals to help build chords.

You are still in the foundational phase of learning Theory. Knowing the triad formulas is as critical to your development as is knowing key signatures and intervals. Make sure you know these triad formulas really well before moving on because the next Units will be about identifying and building triads.

FRETBOARD LOGIC

Scales

You have learned four of the five major pentatonic shells so far, plus the major scales built within each of them. Complete the process by learning the Pattern V major pentatonic shell.

Pattern V Major Pentatonic Scale

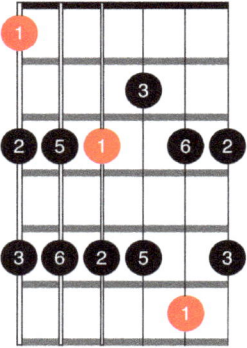

Add a perfect 4th and major 7th (in blue) to create a Pattern V major scale. This is movable to any key by sliding to the right place on the fretboard.

Pattern V Major Scale

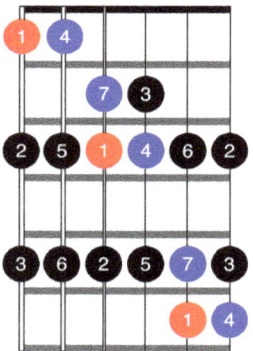

Add this scale to your practice routine and use strict alternate picking playing 8th notes.

Chords

The Patterns II and IV major and minor barre chord shapes are triads, even though five strings are played in the Pattern II barre chord and all six strings in the Pattern IV barre chord. A triad has only three components: a root, a 3rd, and a 5th. They are triads because some chord tones are played in multiple octaves.

Often rhythm guitar parts call for triad shapes that use only three strings. Many of these three-string shapes are based on our Patterns II and IV barre chords, which you already know. You can find these three-string voicings by isolating three-string sets of notes inside these barre-chord shapes.

Patterns II & IV Barre Chords

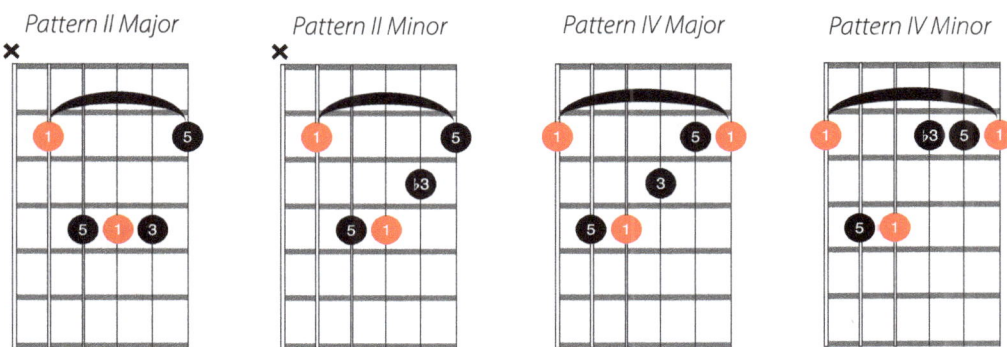

Super Shapes

A Super Shape is made up of all the notes of a triad that can be located in a region of the neck. These three-string triad shapes are useful for rhythm guitar parts because you can move from one chord to the next without moving your fingers very far.

There are three major Super Shapes and three minor Super Shapes that are movable to any position on the fretboard. We will start by looking at the three major Super Shapes.

Major Super Shape I

The first super shape is based on the Pattern IV major barre chord. It is divided into four three-string sets:

- String set 1-2-3
- String set 2-3-4
- String set 3-4-5
- String set 4-5-6

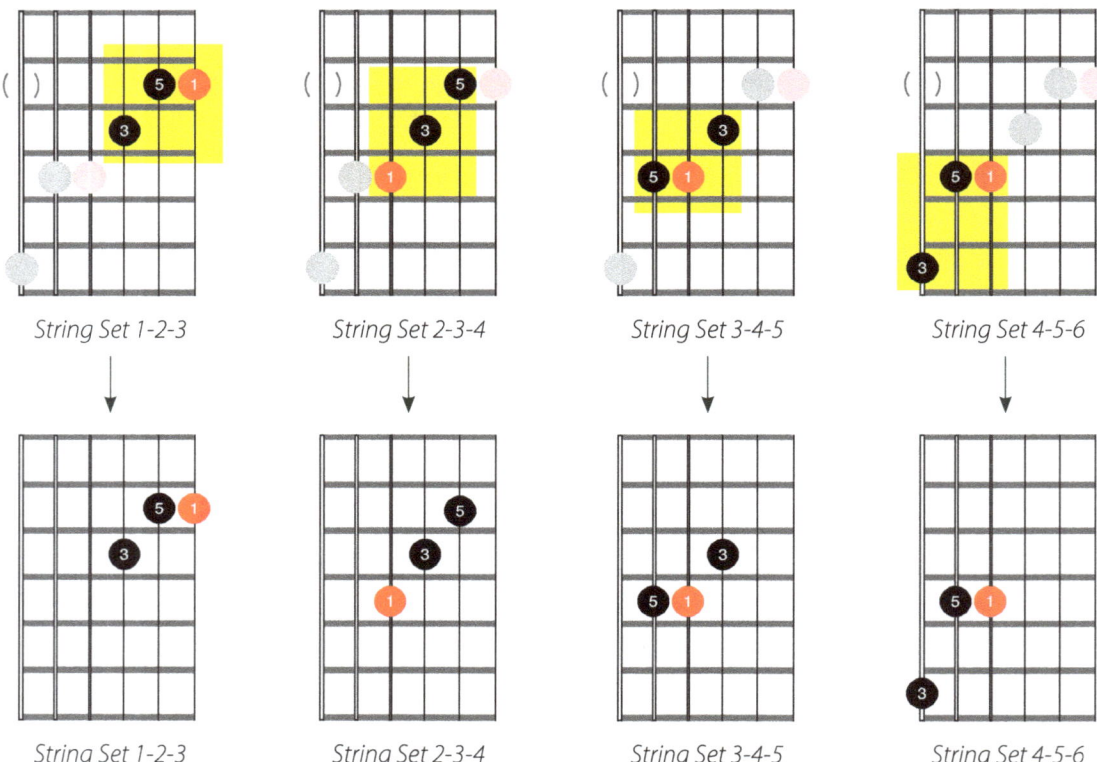

Major Super Shape I
(Based on Pattern IV triad shape.)

String Set 1-2-3   String Set 2-3-4   String Set 3-4-5   String Set 4-5-6

Only string sets 1-2-3 and 2-3-4 are practical for most parts. The 3-4-5 string set is sometimes practical but the string set 4-5-6 is usually impractical. These lower sets are somewhat impractical because the register is so low they sound muddy. Note that the set using the 4-5-6 strings uses a note slightly out of the Pattern IV region.

Major Super Shape II

The next super shape is based on the Pattern I major triad shape. Again, we divide this super shape into four three-string sets:

- String set 1-2-3
- String set 2-3-4
- String set 3-4-5
- String set 4-5-6

Major Super Shape II
(Based on Pattern I triad shape.)

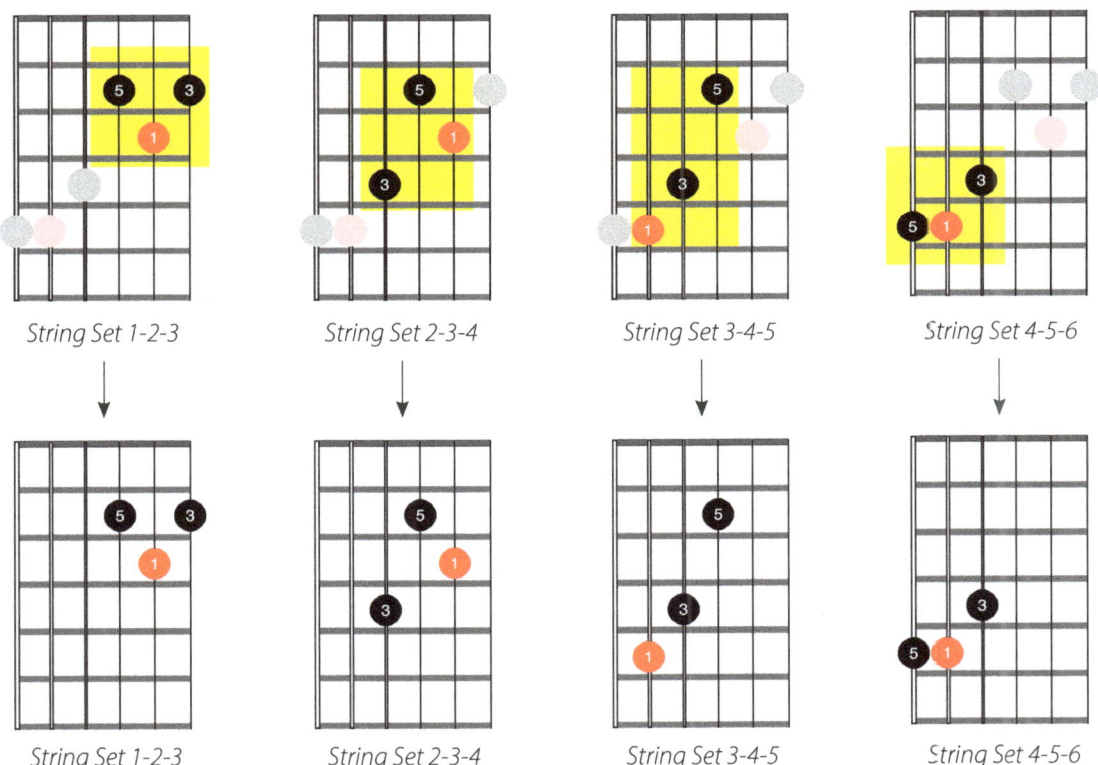

Note that only string sets 1-2-3 and 2-3-4 are practical for most parts. The 3-4-5 string set is sometimes practical but the string set 4-5-6 is somewhat impractical.

Major Super Shape III

The next super shape is based on the Pattern II major barre chord, but we borrow a little bit from the Pattern III area. We divide this super shape into four three-string sets:

- String set 1-2-3
- String set 2-3-4
- String set 3-4-5
- String set 4-5-6

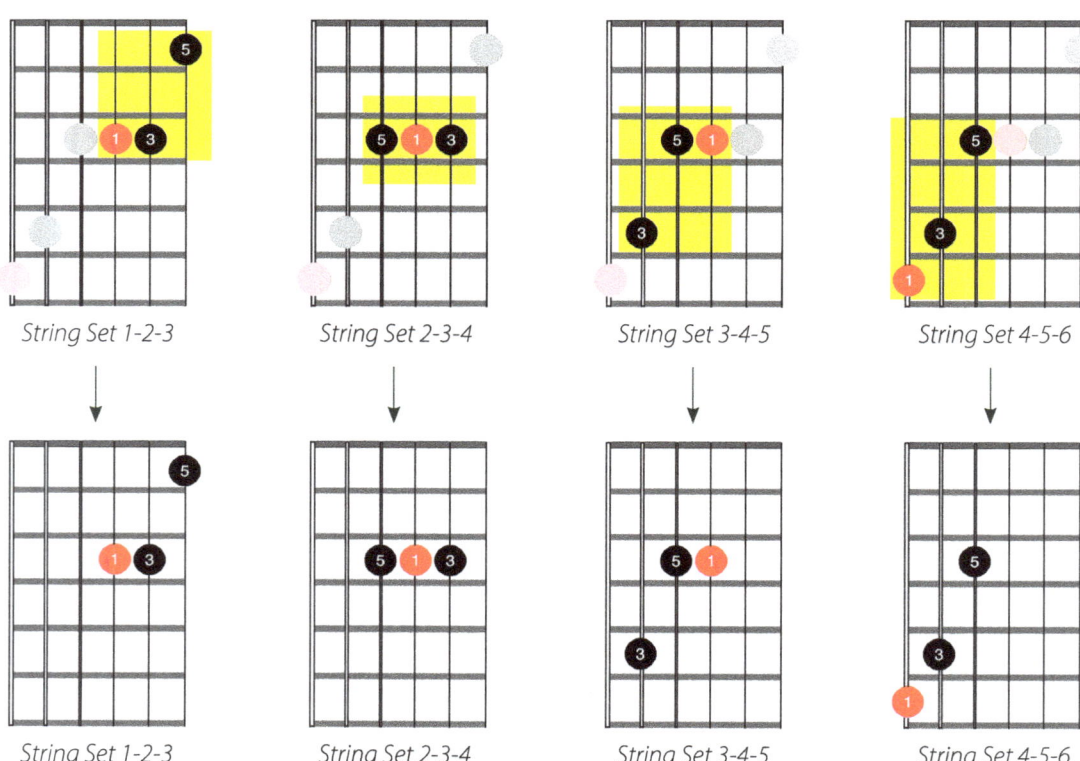

Major Super Shape III
(Based on Pattern II triad shape.)

String Set 1-2-3   String Set 2-3-4   String Set 3-4-5   String Set 4-5-6

String Set 1-2-3   String Set 2-3-4   String Set 3-4-5   String Set 4-5-6

Again, note that only string sets 1-2-3 and 2-3-4 are practical for most parts. The 3-4-5 string set is sometimes practical but the string set 4-5-6 is usually impractical. String sets 3-4-5 and 4-5-6 use notes out of the Pattern II area and partially in the Pattern III area.

Learning "super shapes" is manageable because you already know the bigger shapes so well (that is, the Patterns IV, I, II, and III Octave Shapes and major barre chords). For now, practice each of these three major super shapes by just playing each three-string set of a super shape in order. Pick any root you like and start with one super shape, then move to the next super shape, and then the next. Later, we will learn the minor super shapes.

Interval Shapes on the Fretboard

Continue your study of interval shapes on the fretboard. So far, you have learned shapes for minor and major 2nds and 3rds on one string and on adjacent bottom four strings.

This Unit introduces shapes for perfect 4ths and 5ths, augmented 4ths, and diminished 5ths on adjacent strings in the bottom four-string region of the neck. The reason for only looking at the bottom four strings right now is because the relationships change when dealing with the line between the 2nd and 3rd strings. You will learn the shapes for the top strings in a later Unit.

Perfect 4th Interval

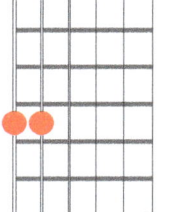 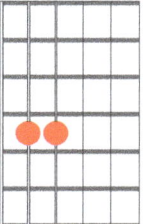 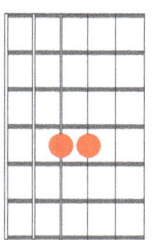

Augmented 4th Interval

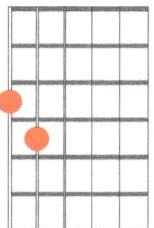 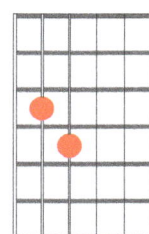 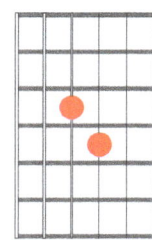

Diminished 5th Interval

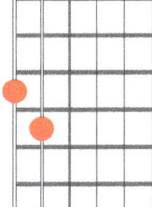 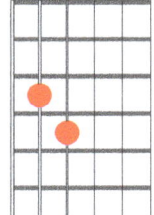 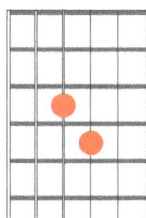

Perfect 5th Interval

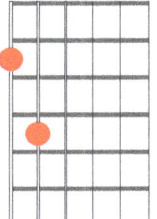 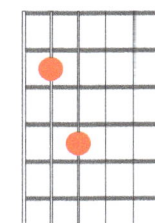 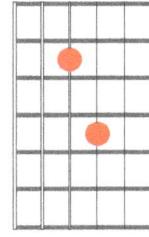

TECHNIQUE

We've learned about alternate picking for 8th notes. Here are the rules for alternate picking with 16th-notes:

- An attack on the beat is played with a down stroke
- An attack played on the "e", which is the second 16th note, is played with an up stroke
- An attack played on the "and", the third 16th note, is played with a down stroke
- An attack played on the "a", the fourth 16th note, is played with an up stroke

16th Note Picking Pattern

If a measure of music is made up of all 16th notes, the pattern is continuous down-up-down-up alternate picking. Practice playing this constant 16-note pattern with the metronome clicking on the quarter note, just playing one note. For every click you will play a down-up-down-up motion. Gradually increase the tempo as you get more comfortable.

Next, practice the Semi-Chromatic Exercise introduced in Level 1 with 16th notes with the metronome clicking on the quarter note. Because 16th notes are usually physically faster, keeping steady is more important and slightly more challenging, making alternate picking even more important.

RHYTHM NOTATION

As you learned in the Rhythm Notation Module for Unit 1, rhythm is a pulse, which is felt as a pattern of strong and weak beats. The specific pattern is called "meter". The meter of a song is shown at the beginning of the music in the form of a time signature, which you learned about in Level 1. The time signature, similar to a key signature, informs the performer how the information on the page is to be read.

A time signature is written on the staff just after (to the right of) both the clef sign and key signature. A time signature has two numbers, one placed above the other. The top number indicates the number of beats (which are the pulses) each measure contains. The bottom number indicates which note symbol (half, quarter, 8th, or 16th) represents one beat.

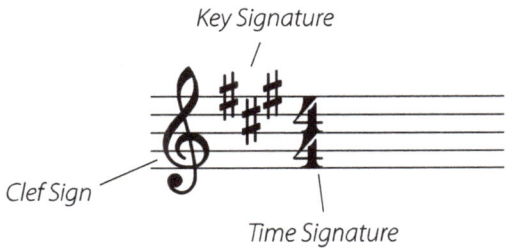

The most common top number is "4", indicating four beats or pulses per measure. It is also common to see these numbers on top: 2, 3, 6, and 12. Theoretically, a measure could have any number of beats but numbers other than 2, 3, 6, 12 or 5, 7, 9, 11, and 13 are impractical and rare.

The bottom number tells the musician what symbol represents one beat (pulse). It is an actual note value, so only a few numbers are possible. The most common bottom number is "4", meaning that a quarter note represents one beat. 8 and 2 are also common.

Here are some very common time signatures: 4/4, 3/4, 2/2, 6/8, and 12/8.

Common Time Signatures

2 = half note is one beat   4 = quarter note is one beat   8 = 8th note is one beat

In 4/4 time there are four beats per measure and a quarter-note represents one beat.

4/4 Time

In 3/4 time there are three beats per measure and a quarter-note represents one beat.

3/4 Time

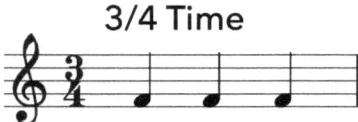

In 2/2 time there are two beats per measure and a half-note represents one beat.

2/2 Time

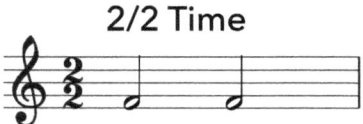

In 6/8 time there are six beats per measure, and an 8th-note represents one beat.

6/8 Time

In 12/8 time there are twelve beats per measure, and an 8th-note represents one beat.

12/8 Time

There are styles of music that use time signatures that are rare in popular Western music. Although these time signatures are less common, they are important to know: 2/4, 5/4, 6/4, 7/4, 3/8, 4/8, 5/8, 7/8, 9/8, 11/8, 13/8.

The same rules apply to these time signatures: The top number is the number of beats per measure and the bottom number is the note value that represents one of those beats.

Common Time Signatures

RHYTHM GUITAR

Guitarists playing Folk music should be competent in two skills: strumming and basic fingerpicking. You learned about strumming in folk music in the last two Units. Now the focus is on fingerpicking. This Unit will introduce several fundamental concepts and techniques, which can be developed and expanded with deeper study. The concepts explained here provide a foundation for more in-depth study of fingerpicking.

Fingerpicking

Fingerpicking parts can serve several accompaniment functions simultaneously:

- Provide the bass line
- Provide the harmony (or chord structure)
- Provide the groove

They can be played with fingernails, fingerpicks, a thumbpick and bare fingers, or with both bare thumb and fingers. If you fingerpick with fingernails, they will require grooming and maintenance.

Thumbpicks and fingerpicks require significant practice in order to make a consistent and pleasant tone. For introduction purposes, use bare thumb and fingers.

Your picking-hand fingers are labeled as follows:

T: Thumb

1: Index finger

2: Middle finger

3: Ring finger

The 4th finger is normally not used.

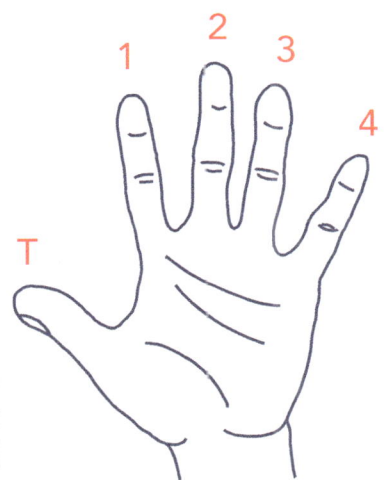

Good fingerpicking requires good time, controlled dynamics, and an even and consistent attack. It's important to have independence and control of your thumb and fingers.

The following examples and exercises focus on a couple of patterns that are adjusted slightly for individual chord voicings. The way you play each pattern will vary slightly depending on the string on which the root is played. In these examples the root is played at the beginning of each arpeggiated sequence.

Basic Fingerpicking Pattern

Begin with the most basic pattern. You will play a four-note sequence, which starts by playing the root with the thumb and then each finger in order: Thumb (T), then the index finger (1), then the middle finger (2), then the ring finger (3): T – 1 – 2 – 3.

- Hover your picking hand over the strings with your thumb right above the area of the 6th, 5th, and 4th strings. Your thumb plays the root on those strings.
- Keep your 1st, 2nd, and 3rd fingers loosely together as a kind of "claw" even though your fingers will move independently.
- For now, use them on two different three-strings sets: 4-3-2 and 3-2-1 .
- On string set 4-3-2, your 1st finger plays the 4th string, your 2nd finger plays the 3rd string, and your 3rd finger plays the 2nd string.
- On string set 3-2-1, your 1st finger plays the 3rd string, your 2nd finger plays the 2nd string, and your 3rd finger plays the 1st string.

First, learn to play this fingerpicking pattern with chords with roots on the 5th string, like A, Ami, and C.

5th String Roots: String Set 4-3-2

The first example is for an open A chord. Your thumb is assigned to the root on the 5th string and your other fingers are assigned to the string set 4-3-2.

Open A Chord

The same goes for an open Ami chord: your thumb is assigned to the root on the 5th string and your other fingers are assigned to the string set 4-3-2.

Open Ami Chord

Adapt this pattern for an open C chord, which also has a 5th-string root. Your thumb is assigned to the root on the 5th string and your other fingers are assigned to the string set 4-3-2.

Open C Chord

5th String Roots: String Set 3-2-1

Switch the string set for your fingers. This next example is also for chords with roots on the 5th string, like A, Ami, and C. Your thumb is still assigned to the root on the 5th string, but for this one, your other fingers are assigned to the string set 3-2-1. The first example is for an open A chord.

Open A Chord

The next example is for an open Ami chord.

Open Ami Chord

Adapt this pattern for an open C chord, which also has a 5th-string root.

Open C Chord

4th String Roots: String Set 3-2-1

This next example is for chords with roots on the 4th string, like D and Dmi. Your thumb is assigned to the root on the 4th string and your other fingers are assigned to the string set 3-2-1. Practice the pattern on an open D chord.

Open D Chord

Now practice it on an open Dmi chord.

Open Dmi Chord

6th String Roots: String Set 4-3-2

Next, learn to play this fingerpicking pattern with chords that have roots on the 6th string, like E, Emi, and G. Your thumb is assigned to the root on the 6th string and your other fingers are assigned to the string set 4-3-2. Begin with an open E chord.

Open E Chord

Now, play it on an open Emi chord.

Open Emi Chord

Now apply it to an open G chord.

Open G Chord

6th String Roots: String Set 3-2-1

Move on to another string set; string set 3-2-1. Your thumb is assigned to the root on the 6th string and your other fingers are assigned to the string set 3-2-1. Begin by learning this for an open E chord.

Open E Chord

Now play it on an open Emi chord.

Open Emi Chord

And finally, play it on an open G chord.

Open G Chord

It is important for you to practice these fingerpicking examples for each individual chord before switching between chords in a progression. Practice it on each chord so you develop a feel for the thumb motion and establish the required muscle memory. After you get the pattern under you fingers, practice these patterns on each chord for a minute or so daily using a metronome.

Another Option

The pattern can be modified for your 1st, 2nd, and 3rd fingers so you have another option. In this pattern your fingers attack the strings in this order: Thumb, 1st finger, 2nd and 3rd fingers together, then 1st finger again. This new pattern can be applied to string set 4-3-2 as well as string set 3-2-1: T – 1 – 2&3 – 1

Open A Chord

Let ring   *Let ring*

Practice this alternative pattern with all the open-string chords and both string sets. There are many different fingerpicking patterns but the ones in this Module are a great place to start building independence in your picking hand.

Having a fundamental knowledge of fingerpicking is essential to playing Folk guitar. It is also incredibly valuable for other styles, so practice it and enjoy! In the next Module you will learn to fingerpick with alternating bass.

IMPROVISATION

In Units 1 and 2 you practiced soloing with a basic 8th-note subdivision. Remember: If you divide a quarter-note beat into two equal parts the result is an 8th-note subdivision. In the Technique Module of this Unit, alternate picking for 16th-note subdivisions is introduced.

Here is a straight 16th-note groove in B minor (Dorian) It is a two-bar phrase repeated over and over. The minor pentatonic or Blues scales work well over this.

Progression in B Minor

This exercise is about keeping your picking hand true to the 16th-note alternate-picking pattern. Practice playing with the track two different ways:

- First, find a pattern of B minor pentatonic or the Blues scale you are comfortable with. Focus on your picking hand and play 16th-note lines to get comfortable with the 16th-note subdivision and how you fit into the groove. Stay true to the alternate-picking pick-direction rules.
- Second, create a solo of finite length and, like before, I suggest 16 bars to begin, eight times through this two-bar phrase. Either a clean or overdrive sound will work fine. Record it and listen back, checking for good time and feel and for how well you told a story.

B Minor Pentatonic Scales

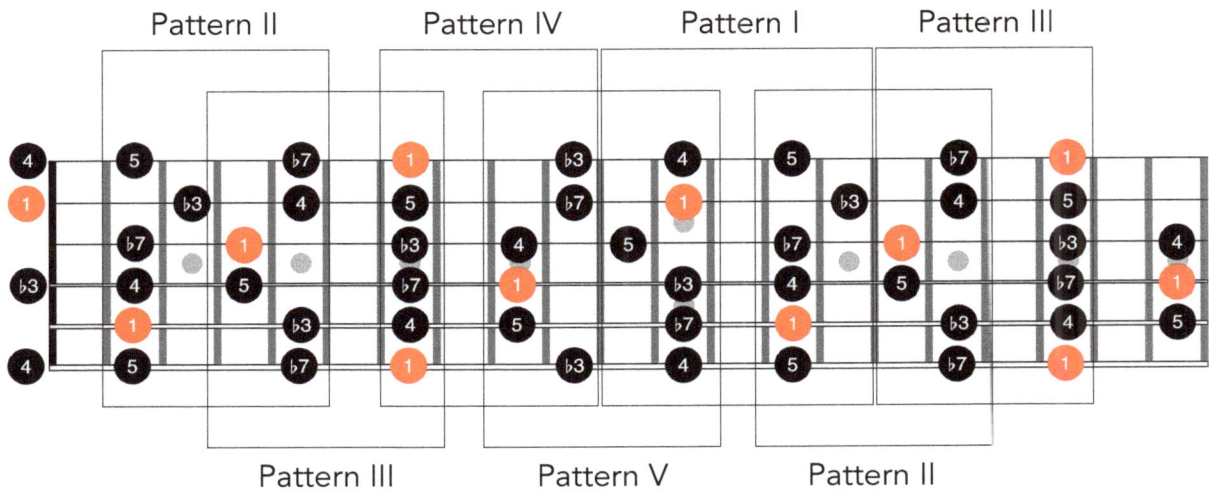

Level 2 Unit 3 • Example Solo

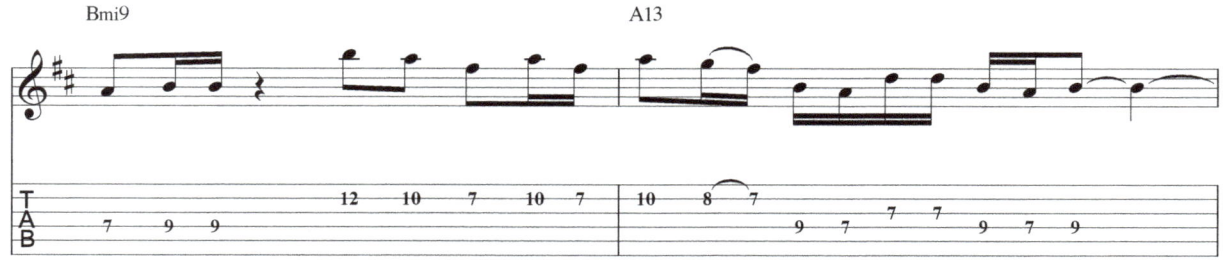
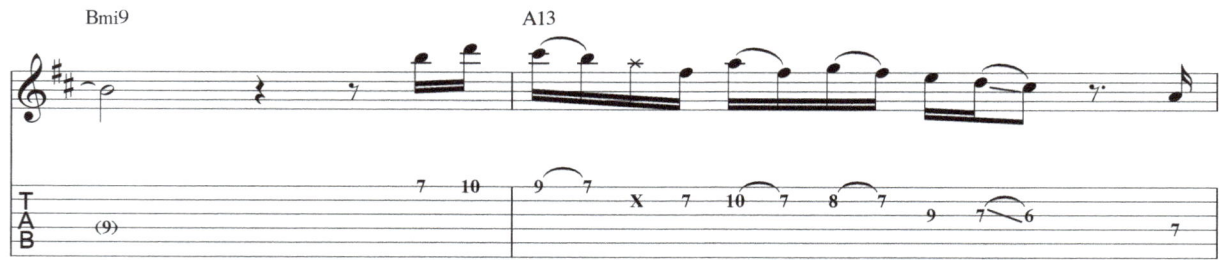

PRACTICE

Theory

- ☐ Go to the tabs below the Theory video on the website and complete the quiz.
- ☐ Memorize the interval formulas for major, minor, augmented, and diminished triads as well as suspended 4th chords.

Fretboard Logic

- ☐ Learn the Pattern V major pentatonic scale and Pattern V major scales add them to your practice routine.
- ☐ Learn the three major super shapes and the triads within each of them.
- ☐ Memorize the perfect 4ths, augmented 4th, diminished 5th, and perfect 5th intervals on adjacent bottom four strings. Use the exercise in the tabs below the video to practice your recognition of intervals on the fretboard.
- ☐ Look at how the new information from this Unit relates to the everything else in the Octave Shape Family Tree.

Technique

- ☐ Practice playing with a syncopated 16th-note pattern using strict alternate picking.

Rhythm Notation

- ☐ Learn how to properly recognize and write various time signatures.

Rhythm Guitar

- ☐ Learn and practice the basic fingerpicking patterns.

Improvisation

- ☐ Create a 16-bar solo using whichever patterns of the B minor pentatonic scales you prefer. As always, record yourself and listen back.

UNIT 4

Learning Modules

> **Theory** - Analyzing Triads, Chord Symbols

> **Fretboard Logic** - Pattern I Minor Pentatonic and Natural Minor Scales, Triads and Triad Super Shapes, Intervals: 6ths on Adjacent Strings

> **Technique** - Alternate Picking with a Syncopated 16th-Note Subdivision

> **Rhythm Notation** - Note and Rest Values

> **Rhythm Guitar** - Folk Rhythm Guitar, Alternating Bass Fingerpicking

> **Improvisation** - Soloing with a Syncopated 16th-Note Subdivision

> **Practice** - Continue Practice Routine Development

THEORY

In the last Unit you learned how to use your knowledge of intervals to construct and analyze chords; specifically, triads and sus4 chords. Here is a review:

Analyzing Triads

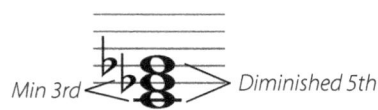

To study chords, you need to first learn to analyze triads. If you see a triad on the staff or know the notes in your head or on the fretboard, you should how to identify and name the triad. To analyze and label an existing triad, first determine the qualities of the 3rd and 5th. Then, compare the intervals with the four triad quality formulas.

Here are the steps:

1. Measure the interval from the root to the 3rd and determine if it is a major 3rd or a minor 3rd.

2. Measure the interval from the root to the 5th and determine if it is a perfect 5th, a diminished 5th, or an augmented 5th.

The results:

- If the 3rd is major and the 5th is perfect, it matches the interval formula for a major triad.

- If the 3rd is minor and the 5th is perfect, it matches the interval formula for a minor triad.

- If the 3rd is major and the 5th is augmented, it matches the interval formula for an augmented triad.
- If the 3rd is minor and the 5th is diminished, it matches the interval formula for a diminished triad.
- If the chord you are analyzing contains a 4th and not a 3rd, then it is a sus4 chord and not a triad.

Think about it this way: In previous Units where you learned about intervals, you measured (or analyzed) a single interval above a note. With triads, you are measuring two intervals above a note and matching the combination of two intervals with the triad formulas.

Here are a few for practice:

What is this Triad?

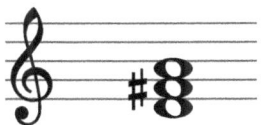

Start by identifying the root. In this example the root is D, therefore, we know that the triad is some kind of D chord.

Next, measure the interval between the root (D) and the 3rd (F#) to the determine quality of the 3rd. It is a major 3rd. You know that because you know key signatures: In a major scale the 3rd is major and in the key of D the 3rd is F#. This triad has a major 3rd.

What is this Triad?

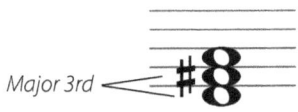

Next, measure the interval between the root (D) and the 5th (A) to determine the quality of the 5th. The quality of the 5th between D and A is a perfect 5th. You know that because you know key signatures: In a major key the 5th is perfect, and in the key of D the 5th is A, therefore, this triad has a perfect 5th.

D Major Triad

Finally, compare the intervals in this triad with the formulas for major, minor, augmented, and diminished triads. This triad has a major 3rd and a perfect 5th, so it is a major triad; a D major triad.

Here is another triad. Start by identifying the root. The root is F so you know that this is some kind of F chord.

What is this Triad?

Next, measure the interval between F and A♭ to determine the quality of the 3rd. The interval between F and A♭ is a minor 3rd. You know this because you know that in a major scale the 3rd is major and in the key of F the major 3rd is A. This example has A♭, so it is a minor 3rd above F.

What is this Triad?

Next, measure the interval between the root (F) and the 5th (C) to determine the quality of the 5th. The interval between F and C is a perfect 5th. A major scale has a perfect 5th. C is the 5th scale degree of F, therefore this triad has a perfect 5th.

Finally, compare the intervals in this triad with the formulas for major, minor, augmented, and diminished triads. This triad has a minor 3rd and a perfect 5th, so it is a minor triad; an F minor triad.

F Minor Triad

Here is another triad to analyze: Start by determining the root which is A, therefore we know that this is some kind of A chord. Next, measure the interval between A and C#

What is this Triad?

to determine the quality of the 3rd. It is a major 3rd. In the key of A major the 3rd of the scale is C# therefore this triad has a major 3rd.

What is this Triad?

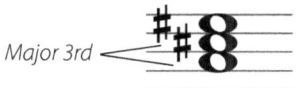

Next, measure the interval between A and E# to determine the quality of the 5th. It is an augmented 5th because the key of A has a perfect 5th, E. Therefore, this triad has an augmented 5th.

Finally, compare the intervals in this triad with the formulas for all of the triads. This triad has a major 3rd and an augmented 5th making it an A augmented triad.

A Augmented Triad

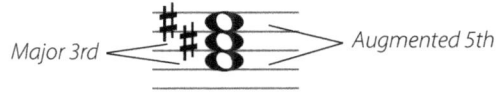

Here's another triad. Start by determining the root. The root is G so this is some kind of G chord.

What is this Triad?

Next, measure the interval between G and B♭ to determine the quality of the 3rd. It is a minor 3rd. The key of G has a major 3rd, which is B. This triad has B♭ so it's a minor 3rd.

What is this Triad?

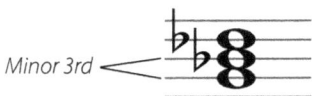

Next, measure the interval between G and D to determine the quality of the 5th. It is a diminished 5th. The key of G has a perfect 5th, which is D and D♭ is half step lower, so it's a diminished 5th. This triad has a diminished 5th.

Finally, compare the combination of intervals to the interval formulas for triads. This triad has a minor 3rd and a diminished 5th, therefor it is a G diminished triad.

G Diminished Triad

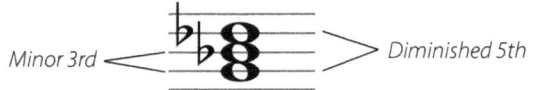

Here's one more. The root is B so this is some kind of B chord.

What is this Triad?

Next, measure the intervals and compare them to the triad interval formulas. The interval between B and E is not a third. It is a perfect 4th. Major scales have a perfect 4th, and the 4th degree of the B major scale is an E. So instead of having a major or minor 3rd, this chord has a perfect 4th.

What is this Triad?

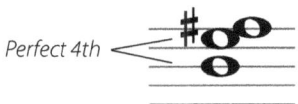

Next, determine quality of the interval between B and F♯. It's a perfect 5th because in the key of B the 5th scale degree is F♯. This triad has a perfect 5th.

Finally, compare the combination of intervals in the chord to the formulas for the four triads. It doesn't match any of them but it does match the formula for a suspended 4th chord. This is a Bsus4 chord.

B Suspended 4 Triad

Chord Symbols

A "chord symbol" is a shorthand way to notate a chord instead of writing the individual notes on the staff. Chord symbols are things like G, Dmi, D+, E7, or Ama7.

There are many styles of writing chord symbols around the world. In fact, a style in one part of the world may contradict a style in another part of the world – this true even within the United States – so it is best to use symbols that are universally understood.

In my career performing with musicians from around the world I have seen some pretty interesting ways musicians write chord symbols. As a result, I have been involved in some musical train wrecks where a musician played what they thought the chord symbol meant, only to learn that the person writing the music intended for something completely different to be played.

There has never, to my knowledge, been a gathering of composers, arrangers or copyists who came together to agree on a worldwide, standardized system. But through the emergence of notation software like Finale and Sibelius and the proliferation of instructional material, magazines and websites, some people have claimed their way to write chord symbols as "the way".

I am not convinced there is a universally-accepted method for writing chord symbols, but I will present some best practices. What I present in this program is based on my experience and what I know to be the best way to avoid disasters created by misunderstanding. I am certain if you use the chord symbols I present here, musicians from anywhere on the planet will know what you mean.

Much later in the Fretboard Biology course, there will be an entire Unit dedicated to the complexity and diversity of chord symbol notation.

We begin with triads and what I believe to be the best triad chord symbols. Here is an outline about writing chord symbols for triads.

Major Triads

Major triads are best labeled with the letter name only, as in "C". Writing "C major", "CMaj", or "CMa" is redundant and clutters a chord chart. It is basically unnecessary. Using an upper case "M" or the triangle symbol is unclear and could confuse the reader, as these symbols have different meanings in different regions of the world. *C is best.*

Minor Triads

Minor triads are best labeled with the letter name, as in "C", plus "mi". Writing "C minor" or "Cmin" is more than you need and, again, clutters a chord chart. Also, using an upper case "M" or lower case "m" is unclear and could confuse the reader. Using a dash, as in "C-", is also common and universally accepted as an efficient and clear way to write C minor. ***Cmi is best.***

Augmented Triads

Augmented triads are best labeled with the letter name and "+", as in "C+". Writing "C augmented" or "Caug" clutters a chord chart. Writing "C(#5)" is sometimes acceptable, but "(#5)" should be reserved for chords with 7ths. This will be covered in more detail in later Units. ***C+ is best.***

Diminished Triads

Diminished triads are best labeled with the letter name and "°", as in "C°". Writing "C diminished" or "C dim" clutters a chord chart. ***C° is best.***

Suspended 4th Chords

Suspended 4th chords are best labeled with the letter name of the root and "sus" or "sus4". Writing "C suspended 4th" clutters a chord chart. ***Csus is best.***

Power Chords

A power chord is really just a dyad consisting of a root and 5th. It doesn't have a major or minor quality itself, but a quality can be implied by the context in which it's used. The power chord is usually labeled as a "5" chord. For example a G power chord would be labeled "G5". We will talk more about these in a later Unit.

Now that you know how to write chord symbols, go to the Triad Analysis Exercise on the website and work through the exercises. Repetition and persistence is the way! Don't skip on this important skill. The better you get at analyzing triads and writing and recognizing chord symbols, the better you'll be at looking at a chart and quickly understanding what is happening from a Theory standpoint.

A Look Ahead

Let's take a look into the future to see how the process you just learned for analyzing triads will help you analyze other types of chords. Learning triads requires analyzing two intervals above a root and comparing them to the triad interval formulas. You'll soon study chords with more than three notes. You will learn that analyzing 7th chords requires analyzing three intervals above the root and comparing them to the different 7th-chord interval formulas. Learning 9th chords requires analyzing four intervals above the root and comparing them to the different 9th-chord interval formulas. This is also true for 11th and 13th chords, analyzing five and six intervals above the root, respectively.

When you know key signatures you can learn intervals. And when you know intervals, you can learn about chords. Much of Theory is about knowing interval formulas for chords and scales. So know your key signatures and intervals!

You need to know key signatures from two perspectives:

- When you see a key signature on the page you need to know what key it represents.
- When you write a song in a key you should know how to write the key signature on the staff.

Likewise, you need to know intervals from two perspectives:

- When you see two notes on the page you need to be able to identify the interval between them.
- When you are writing music on the staff you should know how to write the interval.

The same is true, of course, with triads. You need to know them from two perspectives:

- When you see a triad written on the staff, you need to be able to identify and label it properly.
- When we are writing music, you need to be able to build and write a triad correctly. You will learn to do that next.

FRETBOARD LOGIC

Scales

You have now learned all of the five major pentatonic shells and the major scales built within each of them. In the next few Units you will learn the rest of the minor pentatonic shells and the natural minor scales built within them. In this Unit you will learn the Pattern I minor pentatonic shell.

Pattern I Minor Pentatonic Scale

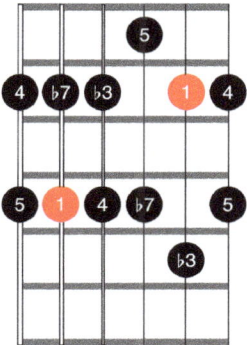

This is movable to any key. Next, add a major 2nd and a minor 6th (in blue) making it a Pattern I natural minor scale. Add this scale to your practice routine and use strict alternate picking, playing 8th notes.

Pattern I Natural Minor Scale

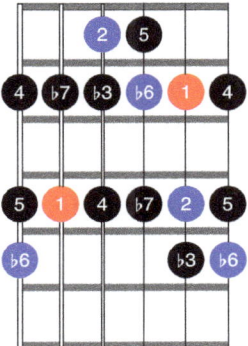

There are two more minor pentatonic shells along with the corresponding natural minor scales left to learn.

Chords

In the last Unit you learned three super shapes for major triads. Each super shape can be divided into four three-string triad voicings.

The Patterns II and IV major and minor barre chord shapes are triads, even though five strings are played in the Pattern II barre chord and all six strings in the Pattern IV barre chord. A triad has only three components: a root, a 3rd, and a 5th. They are triads because some chord tones are played in multiple octaves.

In the last Module we discussed how often a rhythm guitar part calls for triad shapes that use only three strings. The good news is that some of these three-string shapes are based on our Patterns II and IV barre chords, which you already know. These three-string voicings can be found by isolating three-string sets of notes inside these barre-chord shapes.

Barre Chords

Pattern IV Major *Pattern IV Minor* *Pattern II Major* *Pattern II Minor*

Super Shapes

As discussed in the last unit, a Super Shape is made up of all the notes of a triad that can be located in a particular region of the neck. Three-string triad shapes are useful for rhythm guitar parts because they are efficient and allow you to move from one chord to the next without moving your fingers very far.

In the last unit we explored the three major Super Shapes. In this unit, we will explore the three minor Super Shapes. Remember that these are movable for any root.

Minor Super Shape I

The first super shape is based on the Pattern IV minor barre chord. Divide this super shape into four three-string sets:

String set 1-2-3

String set 2-3-4

String set 3-4-5

String set 4-5-6

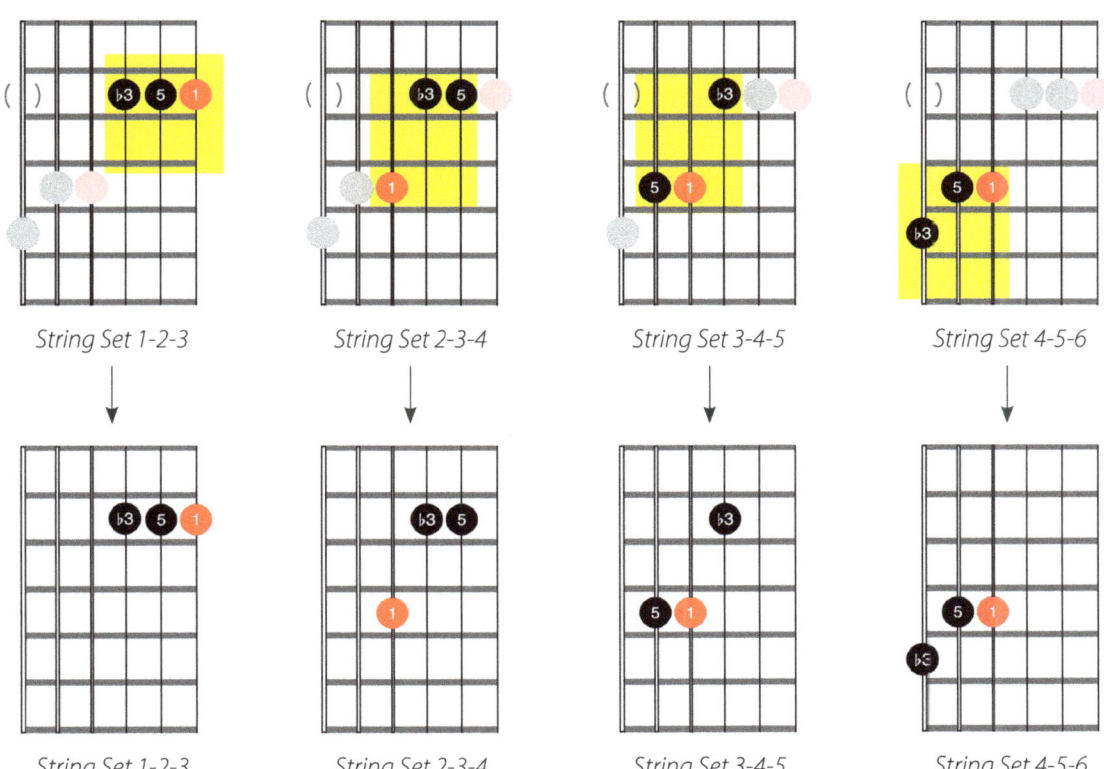

Only string sets 1-2-3 and 2-3-4 are practical for most rhythm guitar parts. The 3-4-5 string set is sometimes practical, but the string set 4-5-6 is usually impractical. These lower sets are impractical because the register is so low they sound muddy. Note that the set using the 4-5-6 strings uses a note slightly out of the Pattern IV region.

Minor Super Shape II

The next super shape is based on the Pattern I triad shape. Super shapes are divided into four three-string sets:

String set 1-2-3

String set 2-3-4

String set 3-4-5

String set 4-5-6

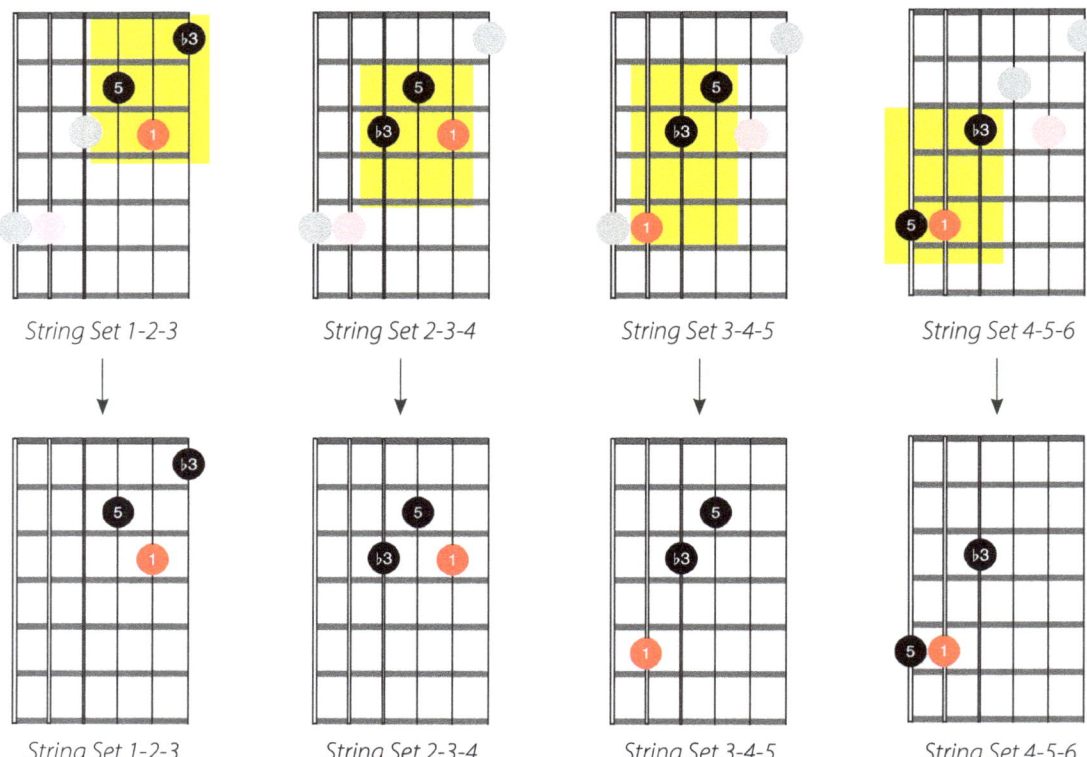

Minor Super Shape II
(Based on Pattern I triad shape.)

String sets 1-2-3 and 2-3-4 are practical for most parts. The 3-4-5 string set is sometimes practical, but the string set 4-5-6 is usually impractical.

Minor Super Shape III

The next super shape is based on the Pattern II minor barre chord but it borrows a little bit from the Pattern III area. Divide this super shape into four three-string sets:

String set 1-2-3

String set 2-3-4

String set 3-4-5

String set 4-5-6

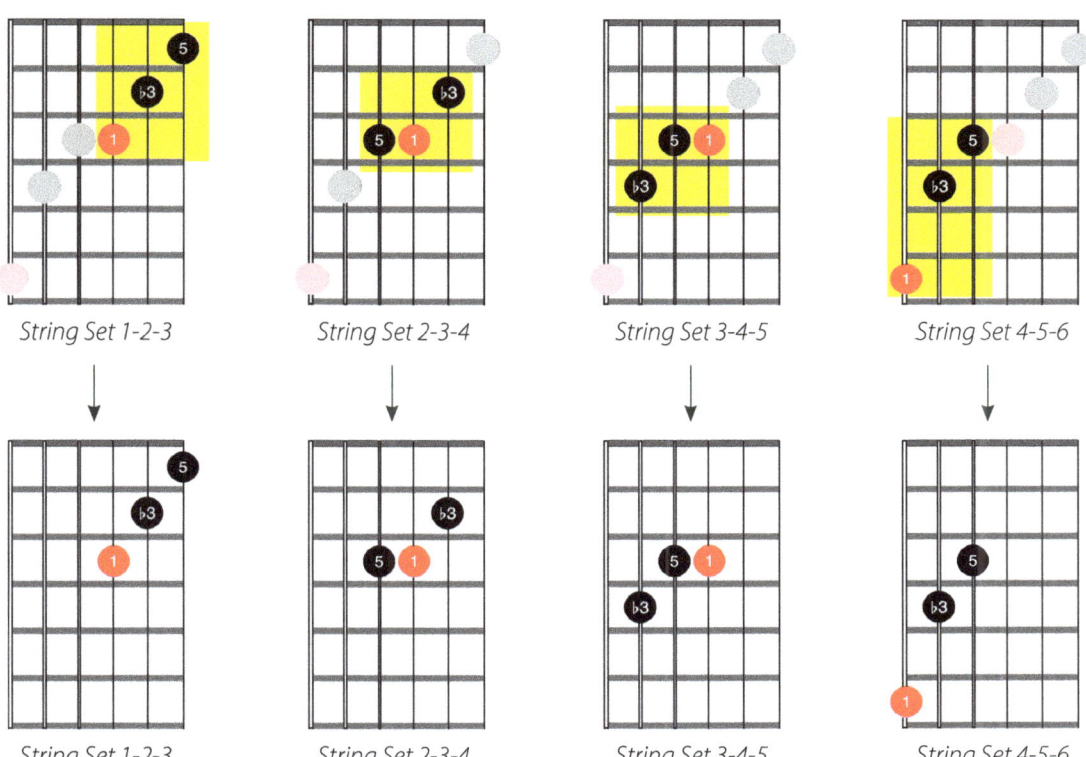

Minor Super Shape III
(Based on Pattern II triad shape.)

String Set 1-2-3   String Set 2-3-4   String Set 3-4-5   String Set 4-5-6

As before, only string sets 1-2-3 and 2-3-4 are practical for most parts. The 3-4-5 string set is sometimes practical, but the string set 4-5-6 is usually impractical. String sets 3-4-5 and 4-5-6 use notes out of the Pattern II area and partially in the Pattern III area.

Associating these super shapes with the Patterns IV, I, and II Octave Shapes and minor barre chords is best because you already know them so well. As in the last Unit, practice each of these three super shapes by just playing each three-string set of a super shape in order. Start with one super shape, then move to the next super shape, and then the next.

Interval Shapes on the Fretboard

Here are more interval shapes on the fretboard. So far you have learned shapes for minor and major 2nds and 3rds on one string and on adjacent strings. You have learned interval shapes for perfect 4ths and 5ths, augmented 4ths, and diminished 5ths on adjacent strings in the bottom four-string region of the neck.

Next look at minor and major 6th shapes on adjacent strings in the bottom four-string region of the neck. So far only intervals within the bottom four strings have been discussed because the shapes are different when crossing the line between the 2nd and 3rd strings. You will learn the shapes for the top strings in a later Unit.

Minor 6th Interval

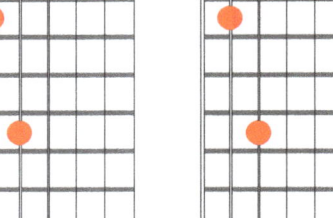
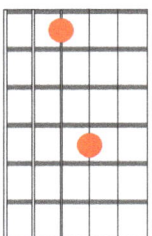

Major 6th Interval

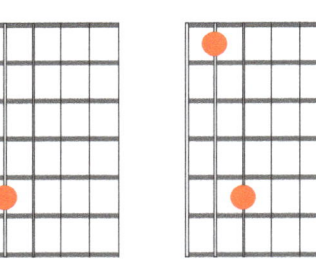
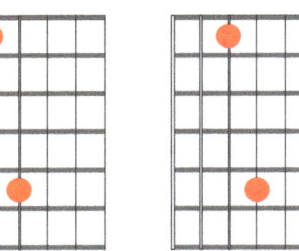

TECHNIQUE

In an earlier Module you learned that syncopation in music is where accents are shifted from a strong place in a measure to a place that is usually weak. You learned that when playing a syncopated rhythm, the assignment of down strokes and up strokes is the same, regardless of whether there is a note or rest.

In 16th-note syncopation, accents are shifted from the beat and the "and" (that is, from the up beats) to the second or fourth 16th note. If a measure of music is all 16th notes, the pattern and articulation would be simple: a continuous down-up-down-up alternate-picking pattern.

When playing a syncopated 16th-note rhythm, the assignment of down strokes to the beat and the "and", and up strokes to the "e" and the "a" is the same, regardless of whether there is a note or rest. Practice this pattern with the metronome set on the quarter note, slowly at first, and just play one note in the fretting hand. For every click you will have a down-up-down-up motion. You can gradually speed it up as you get more comfortable.

Because 16th notes are physically usually played faster, keeping steady is more important and slightly more challenging, making alternate picking even more important.

16th Note Syncopated Picking Pattern

RHYTHM NOTATION

In the last Unit you learned about meter and time signatures. In this Unit you will learn more detail about note and rest values. The word "value" refers to the duration of a note or rest. Some of this information was discussed in other Modules but here it is discussed in more detail.

Every bit of time that passes in a piece of music, including silence, must be represented with a symbol. Notes are used to represent sound and rests are used to represent silence.

4/4 time is very common and for now, it will be the starting point in the discussion about note and rest values. A measure in 4/4 times has four beats and has the capacity for one whole note.

A whole note or rest represents the duration of 4 beats.

Whole Notes and Rests

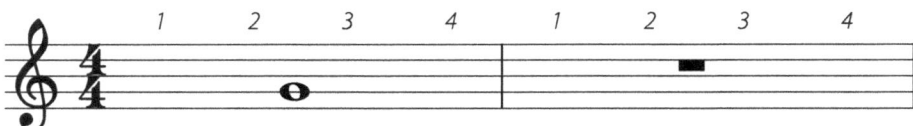

A half note or rest represents the duration of two beats in a 4/4 measure. A measure in 4/4 has the capacity for two half notes or rests.

Half Notes and Rests

A measure in 4/4 time has the capacity for four quarter notes. A quarter note or rest represents the duration of one beat in a 4/4 measure.

Quarter Notes and Rests

A measure in 4/4 time has the capacity for eight 8th notes. An 8th note or rest represents the duration of a half beat in a 4/4 measure.

Eighth Notes and Rests

A measure in 4/4 time has the capacity for sixteen 16th notes. A 16th note or rest represents the duration of a fourth of a beat in a 4/4 measure.

Sixteenth Notes and Rests

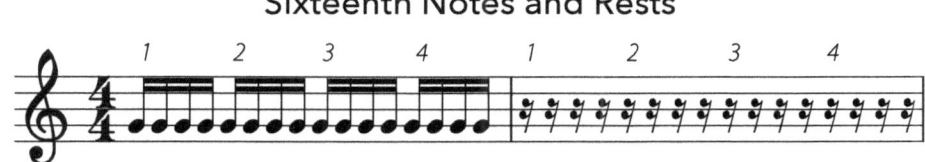

Note and Rest Values

The following graphic summarizes note and rest values that are the product of dividing a larger note by two.

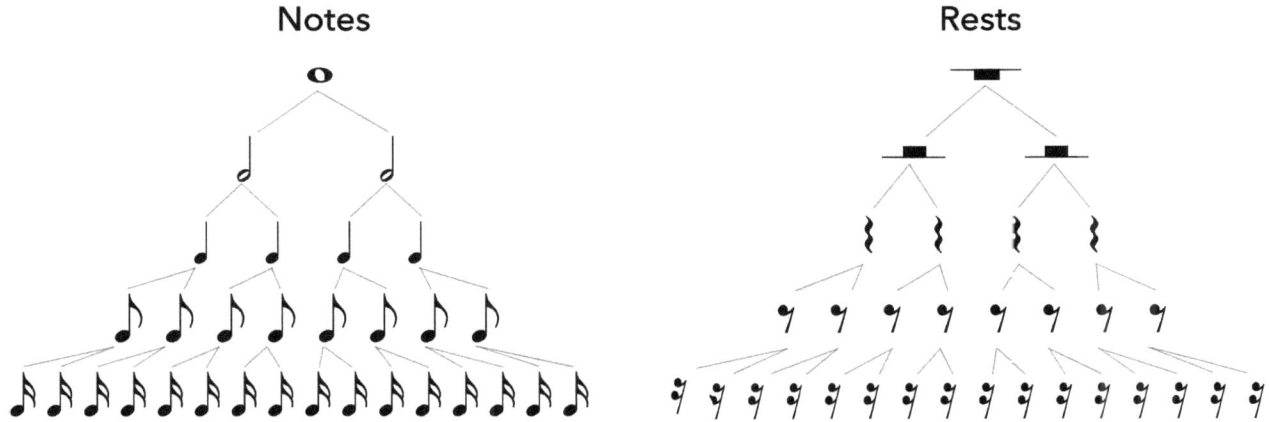

Triplets

Values created by dividing a note by three are called triplets. A whole note represents the duration of four beats in a 4/4 measure, but it can also be divided into three equal parts. These are called half-note triplets.

In other words, if a whole note or rest is divided by three the result is three half-note triplets or rests (under the triplet sign).

Whole Note or Rest Triplets

𝅝 ÷ 3 = 𝅗𝅥 𝅗𝅥 𝅗𝅥 (3)   ▬ ÷ 3 = ▬ ▬ ▬ (3)

A half note or rest represents the duration of two beats in a 4/4 measure. A half note or rest divided by three results in three quarter-note triplets or rests (under the triplet sign).

Half Note or Rest Triplets

𝅗𝅥 ÷ 3 = ♩ ♩ ♩ (3)   ▬ ÷ 3 = 𝄽 𝄽 𝄽 (3)

A quarter note or rest represents the duration of one beat in a 4/4 measure. A quarter note or rest divided by three results in three 8th-note triplets or rests (under the triplet sign).

Quarter Note or Rest Triplets

♩ ÷ 3 = ♫♪ (3)   𝄽 ÷ 3 = 𝄾 𝄾 𝄾 (3)

An 8th note or rest represents the duration of half a beat in a 4/4 measure. An 8th or rest divided by three results in three 16th-note triplets or rests (under the triplet sign).

Eighth Note or Rest Triplets

♪ ÷ 3 = ♬♬ (3)   𝄾 ÷ 3 = 𝄿 𝄿 𝄿 (3)

3/4 Time Signature

Examine how note and rest values appear in time signatures other than 4/4. A 3/4 time signature tells us there are three beats in a measure and the quarter note represents one beat.

Therefore, a 3/4 measure has the capacity for three quarter notes.

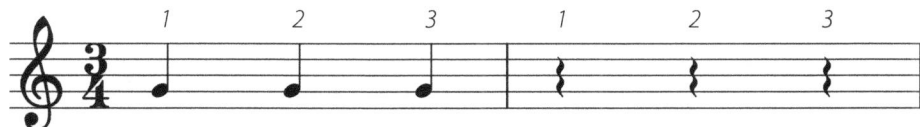

A 3/4 measure has the capacity for six 8th notes. They are usually grouped in pairs with beams.

A 3/4 measure has the capacity for 12 16th notes. They are usually grouped in three groups of four with beams.

6/8 Time Signature

A 6/8 time signature tells us there are six beats in a measure and the 8th note represents one beat.

Therefore a 6/8 measure has the capacity for six 8th notes. They are usually grouped together as two groups of three 8th notes beamed together.

They are sometimes grouped together as three groups of two 8th notes beamed together.

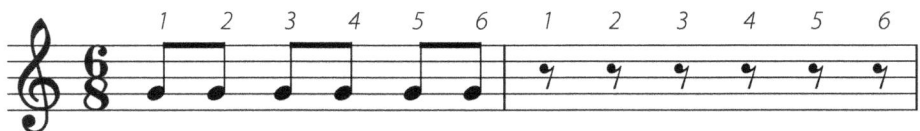

A 6/8 measure has the capacity for three quarter notes.

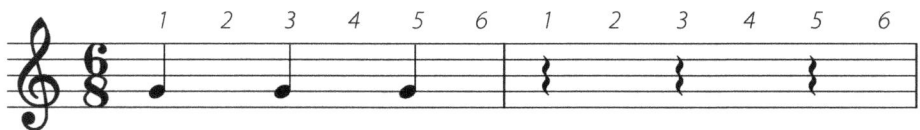

A 6/8 measure has the capacity for 12 16th notes.

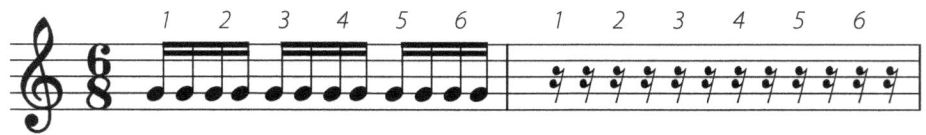

This same logic carries through for all time signatures. Smaller notes like 8th or 16th notes are usually grouped together in combination using beams as you just saw. Beaming will be discussed in more detail soon. For this Unit, know the values of notes and rests, whether they are the product of dividing a larger note by two or by three.

RHYTHM GUITAR

In the last Unit you started learning about fingerpicking. In this Unit you will learn another option: fingerpicking with alternating bass, a common pattern where the thumb alternates between the root and the 5th of the chord. This requires more thumb discipline than the fingerpicking patterns you learned before. Because the roots and 5ths are played on different strings for different chord voicings, the thumb has to be trained a specific pattern for each individual chord. Get comfortable with each chord before practicing progressions that combine open-chord voicings with alternating bass.

First, learn how to fingerpick with alternating bass with chords that have roots on the 5th string, like A, Ami, and C.

5th String Roots: String Set 4-3-2

The first example is for an open A chord. Your thumb is assigned to the root on the 5th string and alternates with the 5th of the chord on the open 6th string. For chords with the root on the 5th string, the 5th of the chord can be found on the 6th string at the same fret. Your other fingers are assigned to the string set 4-3-2.

Open A Chord

Next use this alternating bass pattern on an open Ami chord. Your thumb is assigned to the root on the 5th string and alternates with the 5th of the chord on the open 6th string. Your other fingers are assigned to the string set 4-3-2.

Open Ami Chord

Adapt this pattern for an open C chord, which also has a 5th-string root. But with a C chord your 3rd finger on your fretting hand will play the 5th of the chord on the 6th string, which is G, found at the 3rd fret. The 3rd finger on your fretting hand moves back and forth between the root and 5th.

Open C Chord

5th String Roots: String Set 3-2-1

Next switch the string set for your 1st, 2nd and 3rd fingers. This next set of examples is also for chords with roots on the 5th string, like A, Ami, and C. Your thumb is assigned to the root on the 5th string and the 5th of the chord is played on the open 6th string. For this one your other fingers are assigned to the string set 3-2-1.

The first example is for an open A chord.

Open A Chord

Next apply this to an open Ami chord.

Open Ami Chord

Adapt this pattern for an open C chord. Your thumb is assigned to the root on the 5th string and alternates with the 5th of the chord on the 3rd fret of the 6th string. Your other fingers are assigned to the string set 3-2-1.

Open C Chord

Let ring   *Let ring*

4th String Roots: String Set 3-2-1

This next example is used for chords with roots on the 4th string, like D and Dmi. For chords with the root on the 4th string, the 5th of the chord is played on the 5th string at the same fret. Practice the following pattern on an open D chord. This uses the string set 3-2-1. The thumb alternates between the root on the 4th string and the 5th of the chord on the open 5th string.

Open D Chord

Let ring   *Let ring*

Next, let's do it on an open Dmi chord.

Open Dmi Chord

Let ring   *Let ring*

6th String Roots: String Set 4-3-2

Next learn alternating bass for chords with roots on the 6th string. For an E chord, the root is played on the 6th string and the 5th is played on the 5th string at the 2nd fret. This example uses string set 4-3-2.

Open E Chord

Apply this to an Emi chord. The root is played on the 6th string and the 5th is played on the 5th string at the 2nd fret. This example also uses string set 4-3-2.

Open Emi Chord

6th String Roots: String Set 3-2-1

Next move your picking-hand fingers to string set 3-2-1. For this open E, again, the root is played on the 6th string and the 5th is played on the 5th string at the 2nd fret.

Open E Chord

Next apply this to an open Emi. Again, the root is played on the 6th string and the 5th is played on the 5th string at the 2nd fret.

Open Emi Chord

Alternating bass for the G chord is different. The root is played on the 6th string but the 5th of the chord is found on the open 4th string. Because the 4th string is used in the alternating bass pattern, use string set 3-2-1 for your other fingers.

Open G Chord

Another Option

You can also modify all of the exercises above for the other finger pattern we learned: T – 1 – 2&3 – 1.

Open A Chord

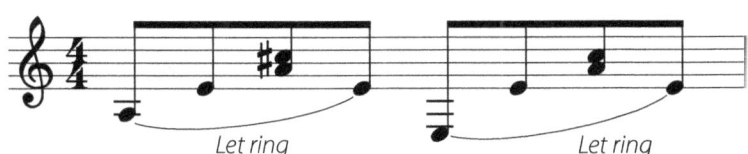

As always, practice working on each chord individually before you play progressions where your thumb is changing its pattern for each chord. In the next Module you will see a lot of progressions written for your practice. They can be used for practicing strumming or any of the fingerpicking patterns you learned.

IMPROVISATION

In the Technique Module for this Unit, 16th-note syncopation is introduced. Here is another progression with a 16th-note feel, but play some syncopated rhythms when you solo. You will be shifting at least some attacks from the beat and the "and", to the "e" and the "a".

This is a straight 16th-note groove in D. It is a two-bar phrase repeated as many times as you need.

Progression in D Major

This exercise is about keeping your picking true to the 16th-note alternate-picking pattern. Practice playing with the track in two different ways:

- First, just find a pattern of a D major pentatonic scale you feel comfortable playing (not the D major scale). Focusing on your picking hand, play 16th-note lines to get comfortable with the 16th-note subdivision and how you fit into the groove. Try including some syncopation and, of course, stay true to the alternate-picking pick-direction rules.
- Second, create a 32-bar solo – that is 16 times through this two-bar phrase. Pick a tone you like and begin. Record it and listen back; check for good time and feel and for how well you told a story.

D Major Pentatonic Scales

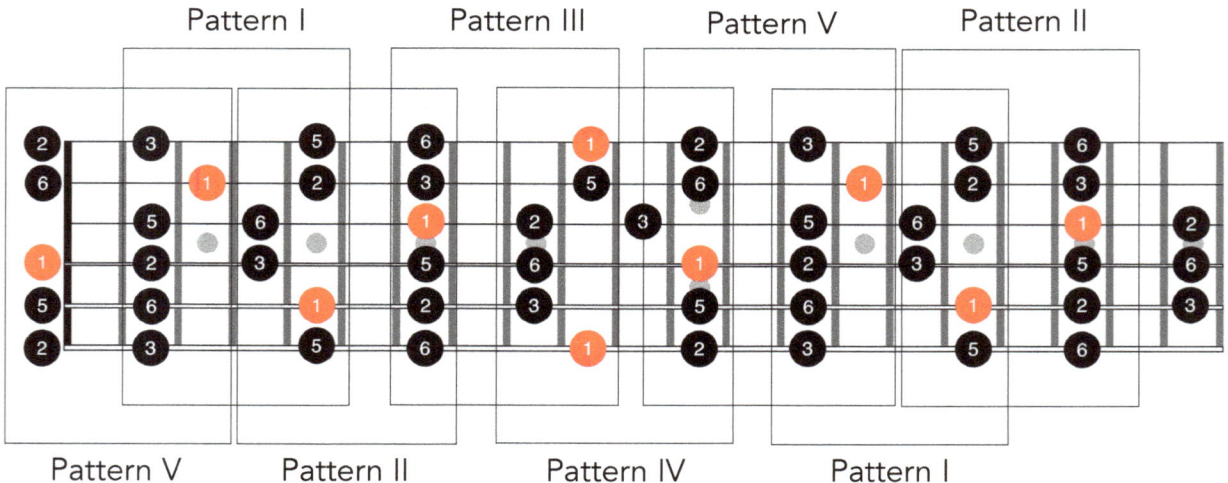

Level 2 Unit 4 • Example Solo

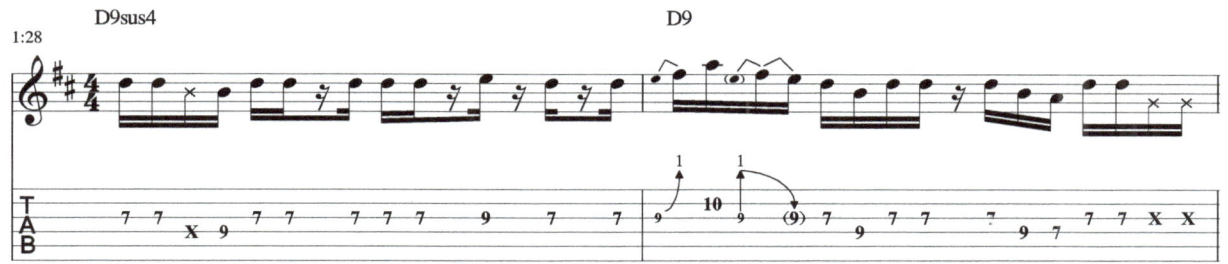

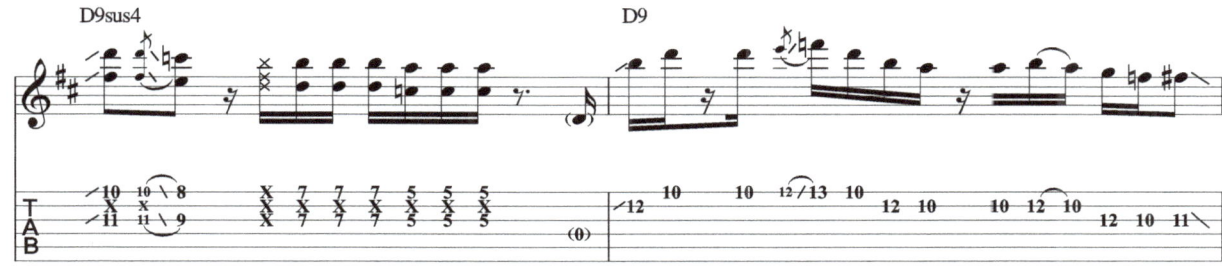

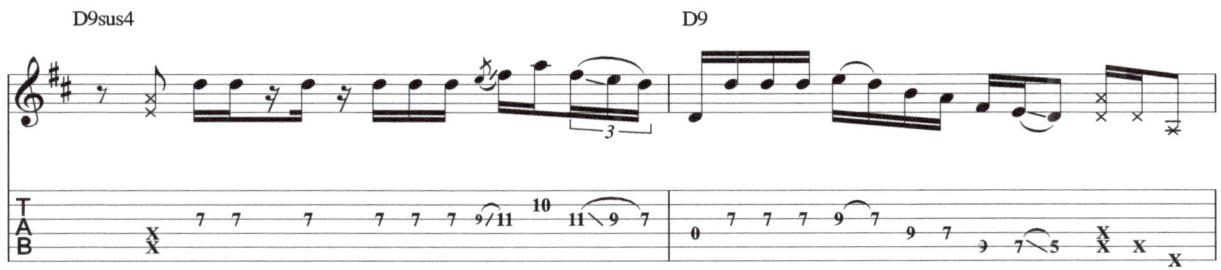

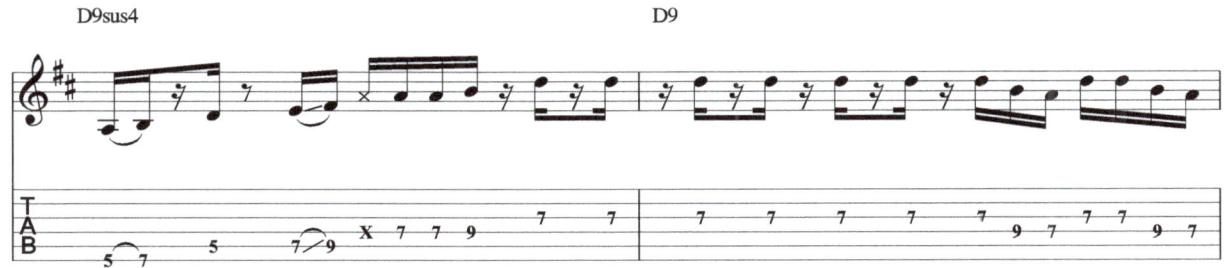

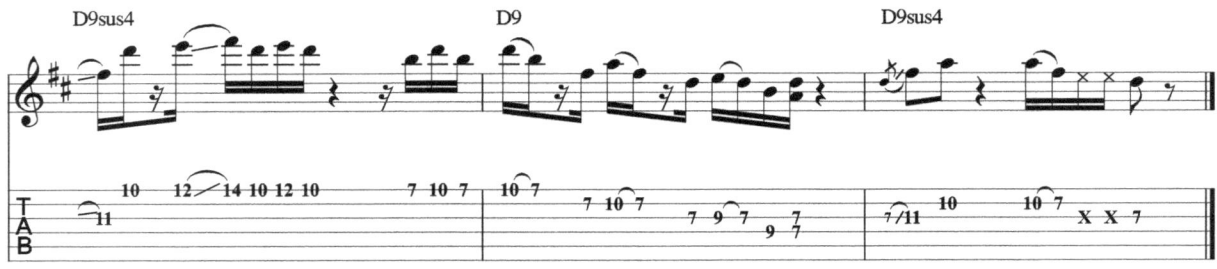

PRACTICE

Theory

- ☐ Go to the tabs below the Theory video on the website and complete the quiz.
- ☐ Learn how to analyze triads and practice analyzing them until you can do it very quickly.
- ☐ Learn and use recommended chord symbols.

Fretboard Logic

- ☐ Learn the Pattern I minor pentatonic scale and Pattern I natural minor scale, and add them to your practice routine.
- ☐ Learn the three minor super shapes and the three-string shapes within each of them.
- ☐ Memorize the major and minor 6th intervals on adjacent bottom four strings. Use the exercise in the tabs below the video to practice your recognition of intervals on the fretboard.
- ☐ Look at how the new information from this Unit relates to the everything else in the Octave Shape Family Tree.

Technique

- ☐ Practice playing with a syncopated 16th-note pattern using strict alternate picking.

Rhythm Notation

- ☐ Learn the values of notes and rests and how they relate to time signatures.

Rhythm Guitar

- ☐ Learn and practice the basic fingerpicking patterns with alternating bass.

Improvisation

- ☐ Create a 32-bar solo using whichever patterns of the D major pentatonic scale you prefer. As always, record yourself and listen back.

UNIT 5

Learning Modules

> **Theory** - Triad Construction

> **Fretboard Logic** - Pattern III Minor Pentatonic and Natural Minor Scales, Three-String Major Triad Shapes, Intervals: 6ths and 7ths on Non-Adjacent Strings

> **Technique** - Alternate Picking with 8th-Note Triplets

> **Rhythm Notation** - Dots and Ties

> **Rhythm Guitar** - Folk Rhythm Guitar Progressions

> **Improvisation** - Soloing with 8th-Note Triplets

> **Practice** - Continue Practice Routine Development

THEORY

You learned how to analyze triads. Next, learn to build the different qualities of triads: major, minor, augmented, and diminished. You will also learn to build suspended 4th chords.

Building Triads

Major Triad Construction

These are the steps to build a major triad:

1. Begin with the interval formula for the quality triad you want to build. A major triad requires a major 3rd and perfect 5th above the root.

Major Triad Formula: Major 3rd + Perfect 5th

2. Write the root on the staff. In this case, that is D.

D Major Triad

3. Write the note that a major 3rd above D the staff. In this case, that is F#.

D Major Triad

4. Write the note that is a perfect 5th above D on the staff. That is A.

D Major Triad

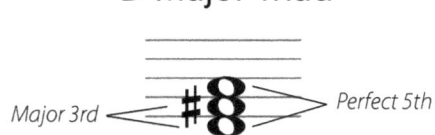

5. All together it is D – F# - A, a D major chord!

Minor Triad Construction

To build an E♭ minor triad. Follow the same steps.

1. To build an Eb minor triad, you need a minor 3rd above and perfect 5th above E♭.

Minor Triad Formula: Minor 3rd + Perfect 5th

2. Write the root on the staff. In this case, that is E♭.

E♭ Minor Triad

3. Write the note that is a minor 3rd above E♭ on the staff. In this case, that is G♭.

E♭ Minor Triad

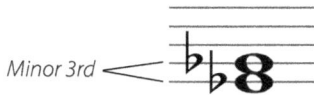

4. Write the note that is a perfect 5th above E♭ on the staff and that is B♭.

E♭ Minor Triad

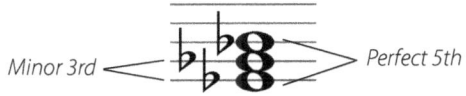

5. All together that is E♭ – G♭ - B♭, an E♭ minor chord.

Augmented Triad Construction

To build a C augmented triad, follow the same steps:

1. An augmented triad requires a major 3rd and an augmented 5th above the C.

Augmented Triad Formula: Major 3rd + Augmented 5th

2. Write the root on the staff. In this case, that is C.

C Augmented Triad

3. Write the note a major 3rd above C on the staff. In this case, that is E.

C Augmented Triad

4. Write the note an augmented 5th above C on the staff. In this case, that is G♯.

C Augmented Triad

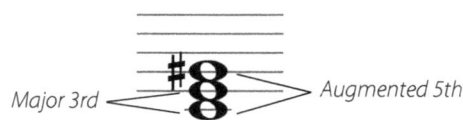

5. All together that is C – E – G♯m. A C augmented chord.

Diminished Triad Construction

To build an F diminished triad follow the same steps.

1. A diminished triad requires minor 3rd and diminished 5th above F.

Diminished Triad Formula: Minor 3rd + Diminished 5th

2. Write the root on the staff. In this case, that is F.

F Diminished Triad

3. Write in the note a minor 3rd above F on the staff. In this case, that is A♭.

F Diminished Triad

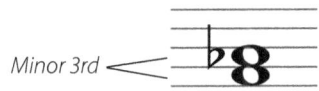

4. Write in the note a diminished 5th above F on the staff. In this case, that is C♭.

F Diminished Triad

5. All together that is F – A♭ - C♭, an F diminished chord.

Suspended Chord Construction

To build a suspended chord follow the steps:

1. An A suspended triad requires a perfect 4th and a perfect 5th above the A.

Suspended 4 (sus4) Triad Formula: Perfect 4th + Perfect 5th

2. Write the root on the staff. In this case, that is A.

A Suspended 4 Triad

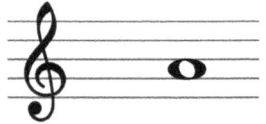

3. Write the note that is a perfect 4th above A on the staff. In this case, that is D.

A Suspended 4 Triad

4. Write the note a perfect 5th above A on the staff. In this case, that it is E.

A Suspended 4 Triad

5. All together that is A – D - E, an A suspended chord.

You can now build triads on the staff, but you should practice doing this in your head as well. Repetition and persistence is the way. You will find a Triad Construction Exercise on the website for this Module. Like triad analysis, triad construction is a very important skill.

Take another look into the future. Learning to build triads requires building two intervals above a root based on the triad interval formulas. Soon you will learn about construction chords with more notes. Constructing 7th chords requires building three intervals above the root based on their formulas. Chord construction relies on your knowledge of intervals and the triad interval formulas.

Internal Structure of Triads

Triads have an internal interval structure, too.

- A major triad has a major 3rd and a perfect 5th, but notice that the interval between the 3rd and the P5th is a minor 3rd. A major triad is a major 3rd and a minor 3rd, stacked.

Major Triad

- A minor triad has a minor 3rd and a perfect 5th, but notice that the interval between the 3rd and the P5th is a Major 3rd. A minor triad is a minor 3rd and then a major 3rd, stacked.

Minor Triad

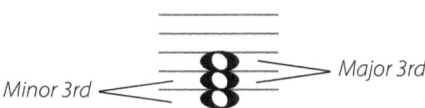

- An augmented triad has a major 3rd and an augmented 5th, but notice that the interval between the 3rd and the augmented 5th is a major 3rd. An augmented triad is a major 3rd and then another major 3rd, stacked.

Augmented Triad

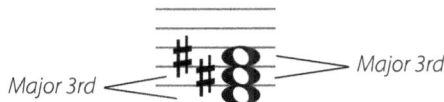

- A diminished triad has a minor 3rd and a diminished 5th, but notice that the interval between the 3rd and the diminished 5th is a minor 3rd. A diminished triad is a minor 3rd and then another minor 3rd, stacked.

Diminished Triad

Congratulations! You have accomplished something really significant. Understanding triad construction is a big deal. You have used your knowledge of key signatures to learn intervals. You have used your knowledge of intervals to learn and construct triads.

FRETBOARD LOGIC

Scales

There are two more minor pentatonic shells to learn as well as the natural minor scales built within them. In this Unit, you will learn the Pattern III minor pentatonic shell.

Pattern III Minor Pentatonic Scale

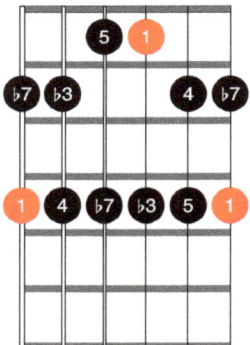

Of course, this is movable to any key, provided you know the notes of the 6th string, which is where our reference spot is in the scale pattern. Next, add a major 2nd and minor 6th (in blue) to make it a Pattern III natural minor scale.

Pattern III Natural Minor Scale

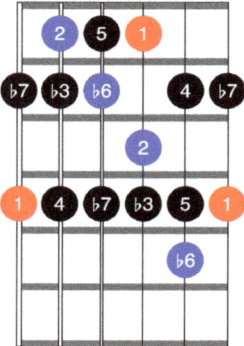

Add these scales to your practice routine and use strict alternate picking, playing 8th notes. There is one more minor pentatonic shell along with the corresponding natural minor scale left to learn. At that point you will know all five major pentatonic shells and corresponding major scales along with all five minor pentatonic shells and corresponding natural minor scales.

Chords

In the last two Units you learned three super shapes for major triads and three super shapes for minor triads. Each super shape can be divided into four three-string triad voicings. Know the material from the last two Units, because you will use three-string shapes in this Unit and beyond.

The most practical string sets are 1-2-3 and 2-3-4 because they are in the middle-to-high register where chords speak more clearly. String sets 3-4-5 and 4-5-6, which are in a lower register, tend to sound dark and muddy and are used far less frequently than the upper two string sets.

Many rhythm guitar parts call for three-string triad shapes so this system of super shapes is important. Another benefit is how efficient you can be with the movement on the fretboard. Strive to move your fingers as short a distance on the fretboard as possible.

Voice Leading

"Voice leading" is another concept you learn while learning the super shapes. It is discussed in more detail in a Unit coming soon but for now, know that voice leading is how the individual components (or voices) of each chord connect linearly when moving from chord to chord.

To begin, notice how far your hand moves when changing from chord to chord. Is it a short distance or a long distance. With smooth voice leading, your hand will move a short distance. As you work through the following material, the concept of voicing leading will be become clear and the advantages obvious.

Start by looking at the triads for the major super shapes. With your knowledge of the three-string shapes, you can work on some short chord progressions with the goal of being as efficient as possible. Look at this progression:

Progression in G Major

Using three-string triad shapes, you will learn to play this in six different ways. All six ways will require very little movement and as a result, your voice leading will be smoother.

Here is the first way:

- Start with string set 1-2-3 and play a G triad from the first super shape. The G triad's root is voiced on the 1st string at the 3rd fret in the first super shape.
- Next, find the closest possible way to play a string set 1-2-3 C triad. That comes from the third super shape. The root in the string set 1-2-3 voicing from the third super shape is voiced on the 3rd string, and C is found on the 5th fret of the 3rd string.
- Next, find the closest possible way to play a string set 1-2-3 D triad. That comes from the second super shape. The root in the string set 1-2-3 voicing from the second super shape is voiced on the 2nd string, and D is found on the 3rd fret of the 2nd string. You see how little you had to move.

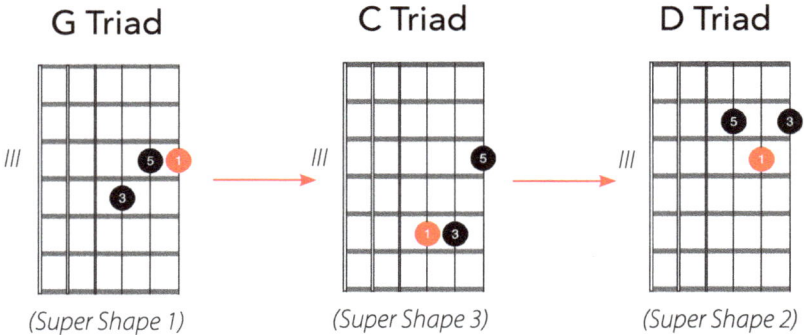

Here is the second way:

- Start with string set 1-2-3 and play a G triad from the second super shape. The root in the string set 1-2-3 voicing from the second super shape is voiced on the 2nd string, and G is found on the 8th fret of the 2nd string.
- Next, find the closest possible way to play a string set 1-2-3 C triad. That comes from the first super shape. The root in the string set 1-2-3 voicing from the first super shape is voiced on the 1st string, and C is found on the 8th fret of the 1st string.
- Next, find the closest possible way to play a string set 1-2-3 D triad. That comes from the third super shape. The root in the string set 1-2-3 voicing from the third super shape is voiced on the 3rd string, and D is found on the 7th fret of the 3rd string.

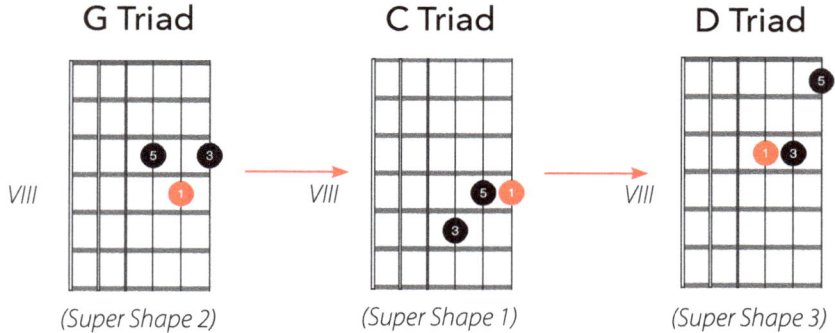

Here is the third way:

- Start with string set 1-2-3 and play a G triad from the third super shape. The root in the string set 1-2-3 voicing from the third super shape is voiced on the 3rd string, and G is found on the 12th fret of the 3rd string.
- Next, find the closest possible way to play a string set 1-2-3 C triad. That comes from the second super shape. The root in the string set 1-2-3 voicing from the second super shape is voiced on the 2nd string, and C is found on the 13th fret of the 2nd string.
- Next, find the closest possible way to play a string set 1-2-3 D triad. That comes from the first super shape. The root in the string set 1-2-3 voicing from the first super shape is voiced on the 1st string, and D is found on the 10th fret of the 1st string. Again, notice how little you had to move to play this progression.

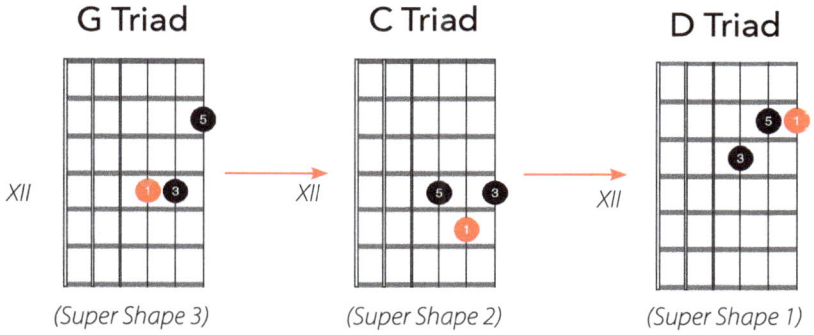

The three ways you just learned to play this mini-progression are voiced in a pretty high register and work well when the guitar needs to cut through a mix. Generally, these would be used in an arrangement where other instruments are filling out the middle register.

Next you will learn three more ways to play this mini-chord progression, but this time on string set 2-3-4. This places the guitar in the middle register. Generally, these would be used in an arrangement where the guitar needs to fill out the harmony, perhaps because there is no other chording instrument.

Here is the first way:

- Start with string set 2-3-4 and play a G triad from the first super shape. The root in the string set 2-3-4 voicing from the first super shape is voiced on the 4th string, and G is found on the 5th fret of the 4th string.
- Next, find the closest possible way to play a string set 2-3-4 C triad. That comes from the third super shape. The root in the string set 2-3-4 voicing from the third super shape is voiced on the 3rd string, and C is found on the 5th fret of the 3rd string.
- Next, find the closest possible way to play a string set 2-3-4 D triad. That comes from the second super shape. The root in the string set 2-3-4 voicing from the second super shape is voiced on the 2nd string and D is found on the 3rd fret of the 2nd string.

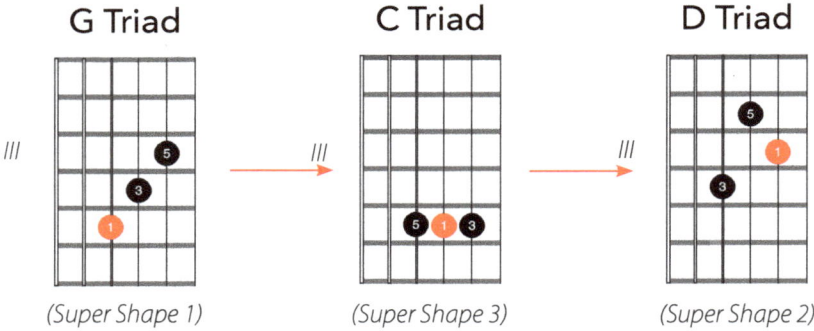

Here is the second way:

- Start with string set 2-3-4 and play a G triad from the second super shape. The root in the string set 2-3-4 voicing from the second super shape is voiced on the 2nd string, and G is found on the 8th fret of the 2nd string.
- Next, find the closest possible way to play a string set 2-3-4 C triad. That comes from the first super shape. The root in the string set 2-3-4 voicing from the first super shape is voiced on the 4th string, and C is found on the 10th fret of the 4th string.
- Next, find the closest possible way to play a string set 2-3-4 D triad. That comes from the third super shape. The root in the string set 2-3-4 voicing from the third super shape is voiced on the 3rd string, and D is found on the 7th fret of the 3rd string.

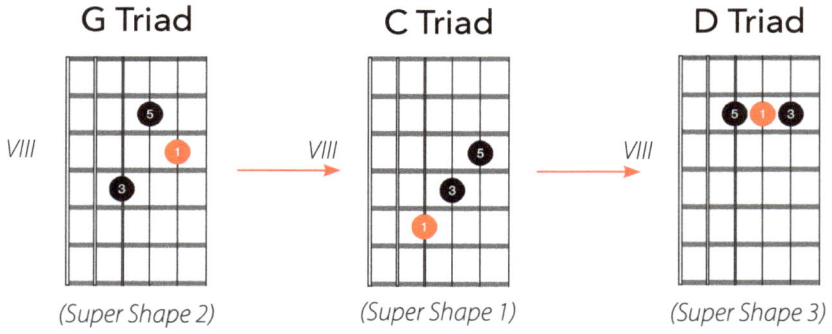

Here is the third way:

- Start with string set 2-3-4 and play a G triad from the third super shape. The root in the string set 2-3-4 voicing from the third super shape is voiced on the 3rd string, and G is found on the 12th fret of the 3rd string.
- Next, find the closest possible way to play a string set 2-3-4 C triad. That comes from the second super shape. The root in the string set 2-3-4 voicing from the second super shape is voiced on the 2nd string, and C is found on the 13th fret of the 2nd string.
- Next, find the closest possible way to play a string set 2-3-4 D triad. That comes from the first super shape. The root in the string set 2-3-4 voicing from the first super shape is voiced on the 4th string, and D is found on the 12th fret of the 4th string.

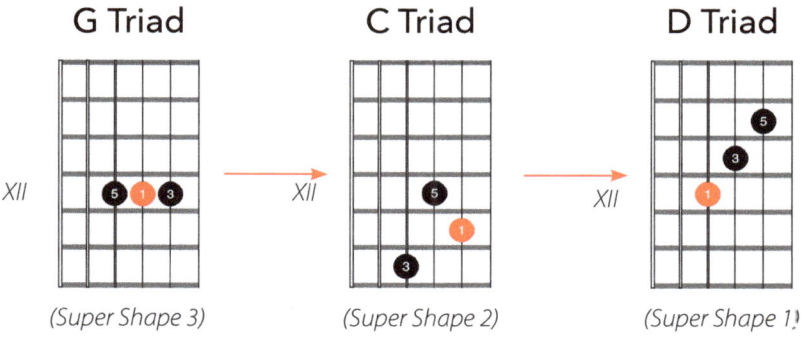

It is amazing how many classic rhythm guitar parts use these small shapes. Practice the examples and start using them in songs you already play. In the next Unit you will learn a simple progression with three-string minor triad shapes.

Interval Shapes on the Fretboard

So far you have learned many interval shapes in the bottom four-string region of the neck. Next look at the shapes for major and minor 6th and 7th intervals on non-adjacent strings in that same region. You learn the intervals in bottom four-string region first is because the interval shapes are different when crossing the line between the 2nd and 3rd strings. You will learn the shapes for the top strings in a later Unit.

Minor 6th Interval

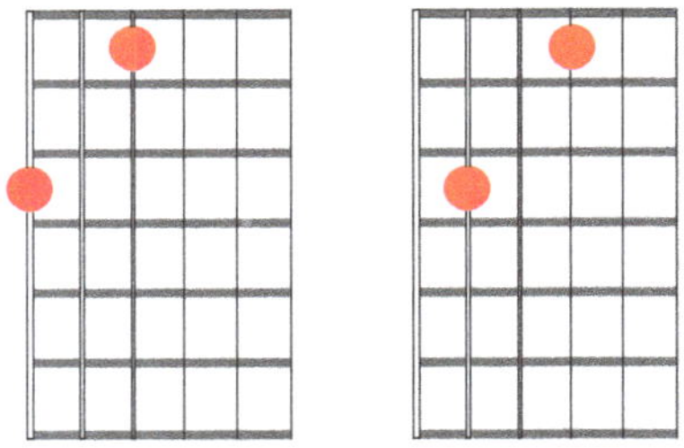

Major 6th Interval

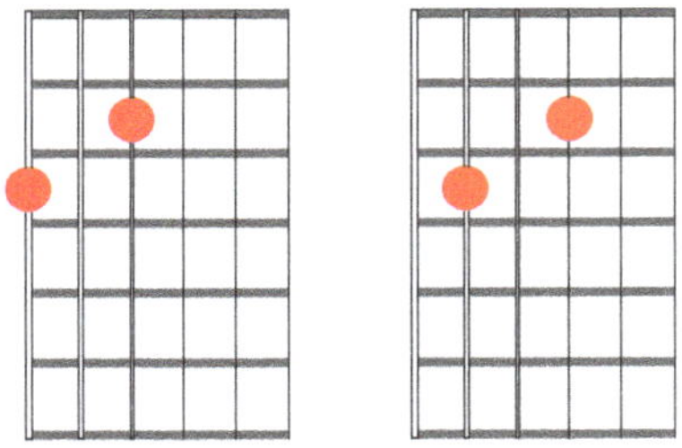

Minor 7th Interval

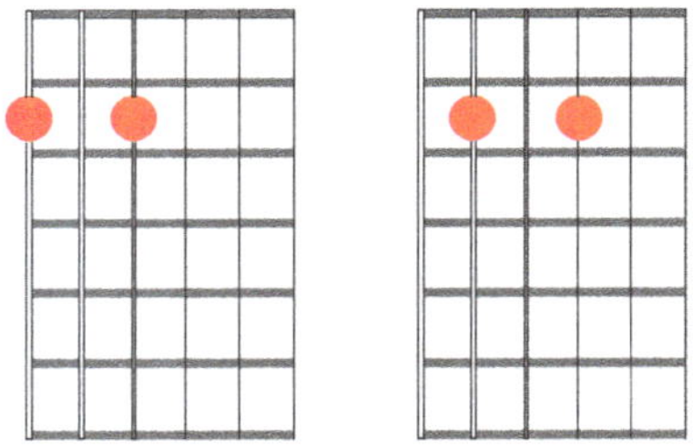

Major 7th Interval

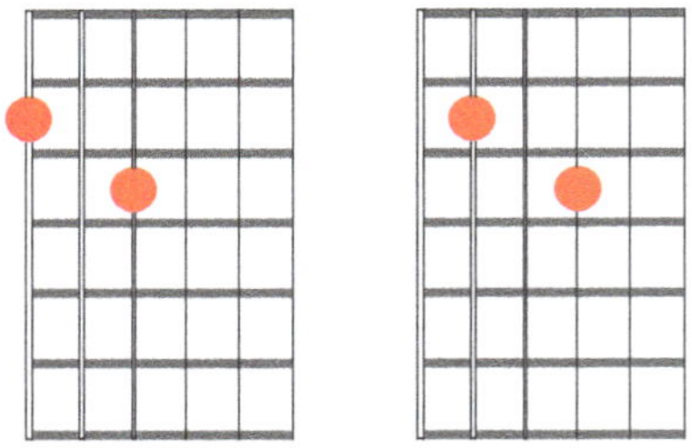

TECHNIQUE

You learned to apply alternate picking for 8th notes and 16th notes. In this Module, you will learn how to apply alternate picking to 8th-note triplets.

Just to review, a quarter note divided into two parts results in two 8th notes. A quarter note divided into three parts results in three 8th-note triplets. 8th-note triplets are notated with a "3" above or below the notes. There is a wide variety of ways triplets are written; sometimes the 3 is under or above a bracket or curved line, and sometimes the bracket or curved line is broken in the middle to make a place for the 3. Get used to seeing many different styles of triplet notation. One thing will be consistent, and that is the number 3.

When applying strict alternate picking to 8th-note triplets, the first 8th note is played with a down stroke, the second 8th note is an up stroke and the third 8th note is a down stroke. Next look at beat two. The last attack on the third 8th note of beat one was a down stoke so play the first 8th note of beat two with an up stroke, the second 8th note of beat two with a down stroke, and the third 8th note of beat two with an up stroke. Beat three is like beat one: down-up-down. Beat four is like beat two: up-down-up.

There are occasions playing rhythm guitar where I reverse the alternate-picking pattern because it allows me to make a strong accent on the back beats (beats two and four) with a down stroke. In these cases, play the first 8th note of beat one with an up stroke, the second 8th note of beat one with a down stroke, and the third 8th note of beat one with an up stroke.

The attack on the first 8th note of the second beat (where I want a strong accent) is a down stroke, the second 8th note is an up stroke, and the third 8th note is a down stroke. Beat three is like beat one: up-down-up. Beat four is like beat two: down-up-down. When the pattern is reversed this way, beats two and four start with a down stroke which facilitates a strong accent, reinforcing the back-beat in the groove.

In the Rhythm Guitar Modules you learned about Blues and the shuffle feel which is based on the 8th-note triplet. Having control of your pick direction is important to playing a shuffle groove with good time and feel.

RHYTHM NOTATION

In the last Unit you learned about note and rest values. In this Unit you will learn about ways to extend the duration of notes and rests. What if you write a song and the duration of a melody note is equal to a quarter note plus an 8th note? So far you have not learned a way to represent that duration of time. Whole, half, quarter, 8th, and 16th notes and rests, as well as half, quarter, 8th, and 16th triplets and rests represent only some of the durations of sound and silence.

"Dotted notes", "dotted rests", and "ties" are notation devices that provide notation solutions for values that aren't represented by the list we just mentioned.

Dotted Notes and Dotted Rests

A dot placed to the right of a note head or rest extends its duration by half of its value. For example, a dotted quarter note has a duration equal to a quarter note + 8th note.

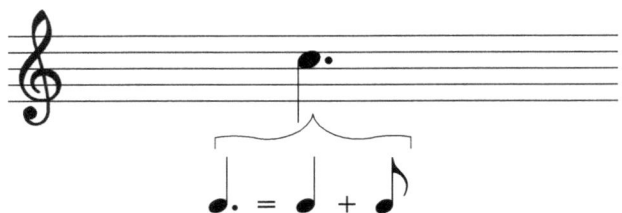

Here are some of the common dotted notes that you will see and their equivalent values:

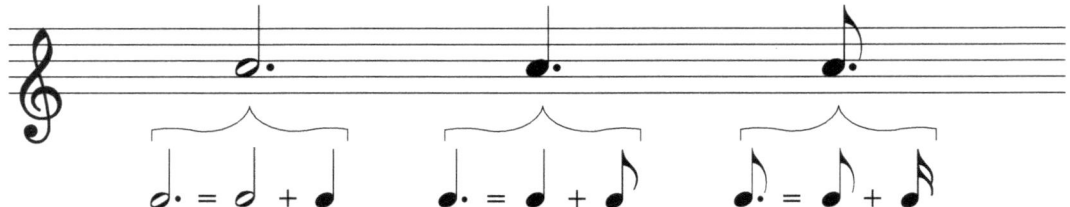

Ties

A tie is a curved line connecting two note heads of the same pitch. It extends the duration of the first note by the value of the second note. Ties don't actually touch the note head. Ties curve away from the direction of the stem of the first note in a tie situation.

Ties may be used "across bar lines" when the duration of a note extends beyond the end of a measure. Ties can also be used to facilitate proper grouping. This will be explained in more detail in the upcoming Module about grouping.

Ties and dots can solve some of the problems when trying to show that a note or rest fills an entire measure. For example, if a note needs to sustain through an entire measure in 3/4 time, a half note is too short, but a dotted half note has the same value as three quarter notes. Also, a half note tied to a quarter note has the same value as three quarter notes. Either is acceptable.

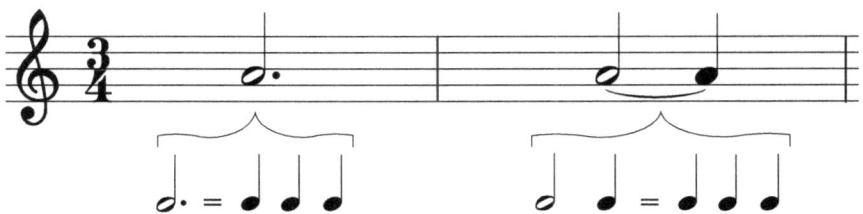

There is another interesting option. You have learned that in 4/4 time a whole note has the value of four beats. That is true, but regardless of the time signature, a whole note or whole rest fills an entire measure. For example, in 3/4 time, a whole note or rest represents the duration of three beats since there are three beats in a 3/4 measure.

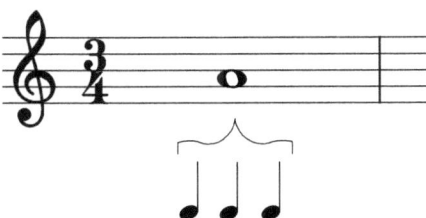

Here's another example; in 6/8 time, a whole note or rest represents the duration of six beats since there are six beats in a 6/8 measure.

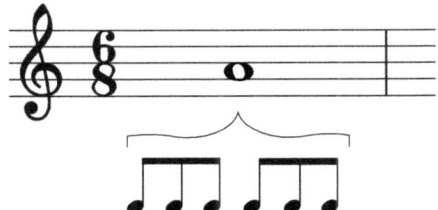

This is the same for any time signature: The duration of a whole note or whole rest is the entire measure—regardless of the time signature.

RHYTHM GUITAR

Over the past four Modules we have worked on Folk Rhythm Guitar. The primary role of guitar in American Folk music is to accompany a singer or singers. The guitar player is either strumming or fingerpicking. It is good to have some progressions to use to practice these skills.

This Module has a collection of progressions that range from short and simple to longer and more complex. There are no backing tracks to practice with because it is important that you be able to play alone. A full band with bass, drums, keyboards, and multiple guitars could be used for any of these, but the parts you need to play would be no different. Work on playing each of these progressions with the various strumming patterns provided as well as any of the fingerpicking patterns you learned. I also suggest playing with a metronome once you are comfortable with a part. You probably won't master all of the fingerpicking patterns before you need to move forward. Keep this material in your practice routine for awhile and chip away at the various fingerpicking patterns over time.

Here are some typical Folk strum patterns to use in the progressions. Be sure to follow the alternate-picking rules you learned for 8th-note subdivision: down strokes for the beat and up strokes for the "and". The pick direction is written in for each of the strum patterns.

Below are some chord progressions you can use to practice strumming and

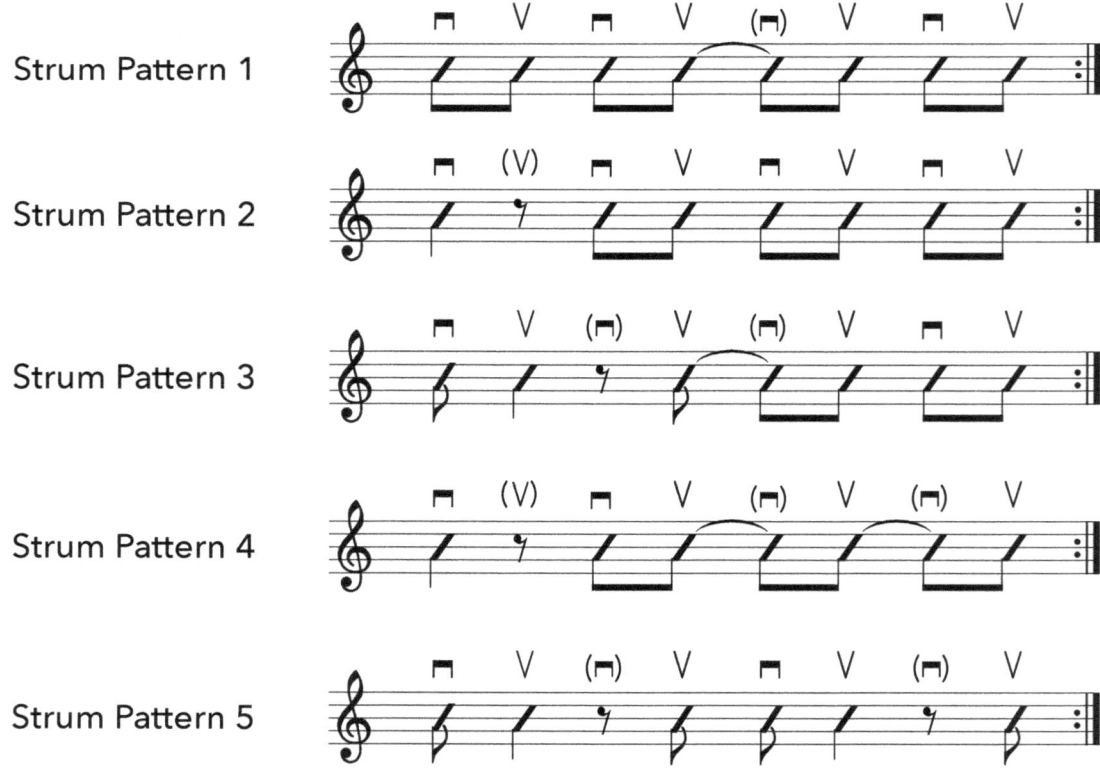

fingerpicking. The first few progressions are just two-chord exercises to help you practice adjusting your thumb pattern from chord to chord. As you look through the list of progressions you see they get longer and contain more chords. This increases the challenge for your picking hand thumb, which has to change its pattern for each chord. You can mix and match different fingerpicking patterns eventually. However, to start, I would use the same pattern throughout each progression with the thumb following either the first pattern you learned or the alternating bass you learned in the last Module. For strumming you might just want to move to the longer progressions.

All the material you learn in the Folk Rhythm Guitar Modules will have a lasting effect in so many areas of your playing. Practice with dedication and it will pay off.

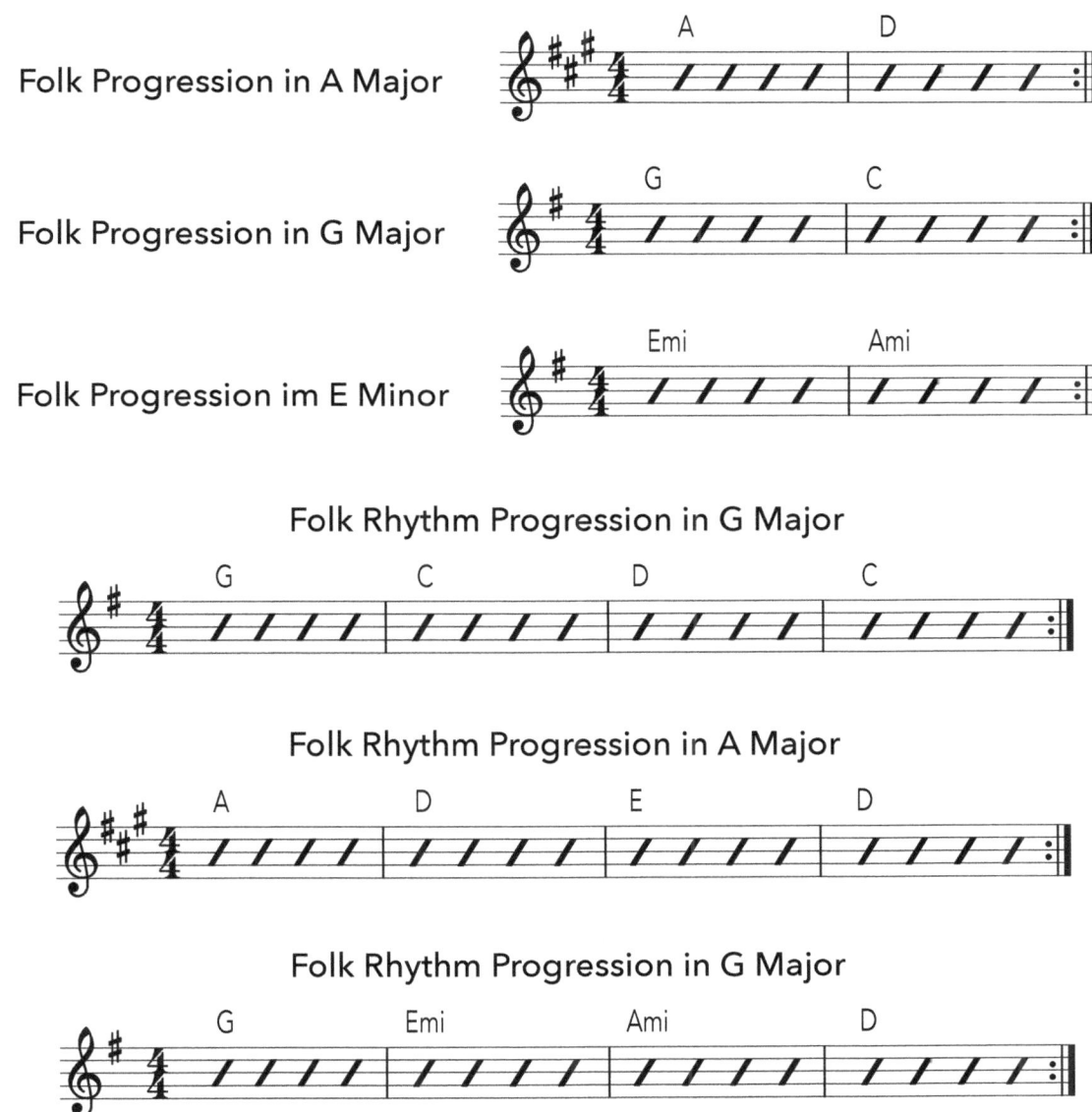

Folk Progression in E Major

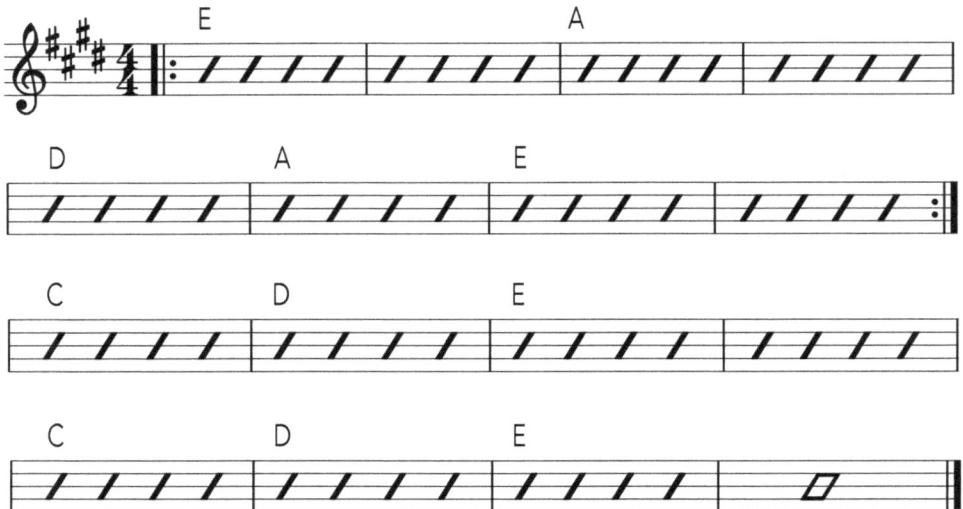

Folk Progression in G Major

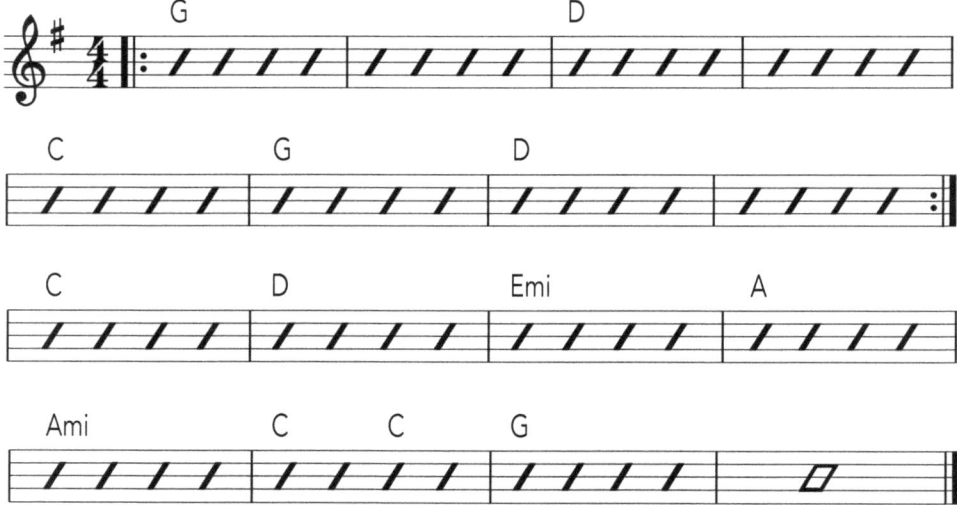

NOTE: For additional Folk rhythm progressions, please visit the Fretboard Biology website.

IMPROVISATION

So far you have been working on improvising with 8th- and 16th-note subdivisions. In the Technique Module for this Unit, alternate picking for 8th-note triplet subdivision is introduced.

Here is an 8th-note triplet groove in G minor. It is a two-bar phrase repeated multiple times.

Progression in G Minor

Stay true to the 8th-note triplet alternate-picking pattern. Practice playing with the track two different ways:

- First, find a pattern of G minor pentatonic or the G minor scale you feel comfortable playing. Focusing on your picking hand, play 8th-note triplet lines to get comfortable with the 8th-note triplet subdivision and how you fit into the groove. And, as we have been doing in all the Improvisation Modules, stay true to the alternate-picking pick-direction rules.

- Second, create a 16-bar solo which is eight times through this two-bar phrase. Either a clean or overdrive sound will work fine. Record it and listen back. Check for good time and feel and for how well you told a story.

G Minor Pentatonic Scales

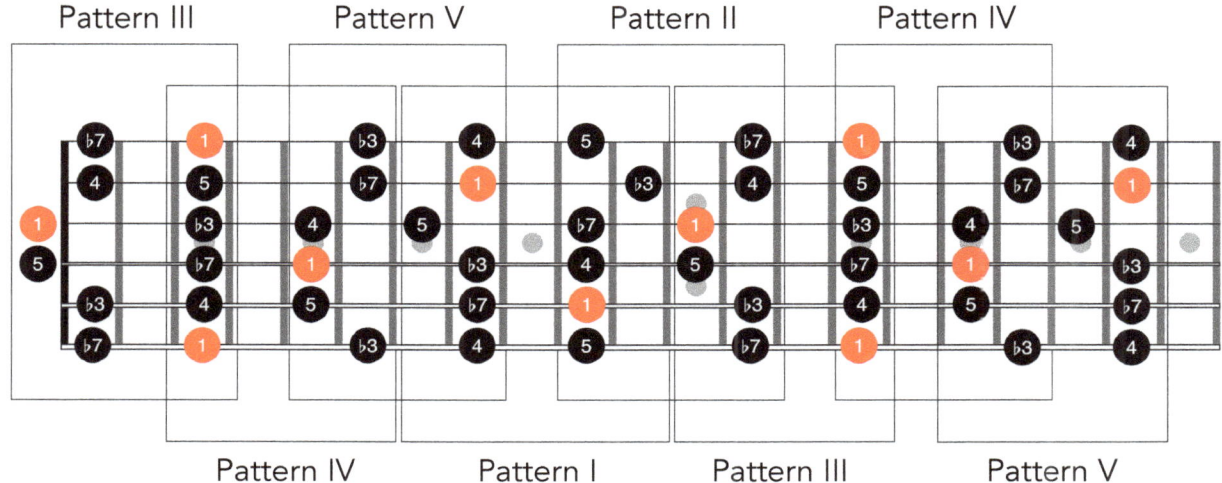

Level 2 Unit 5 • Example Solo

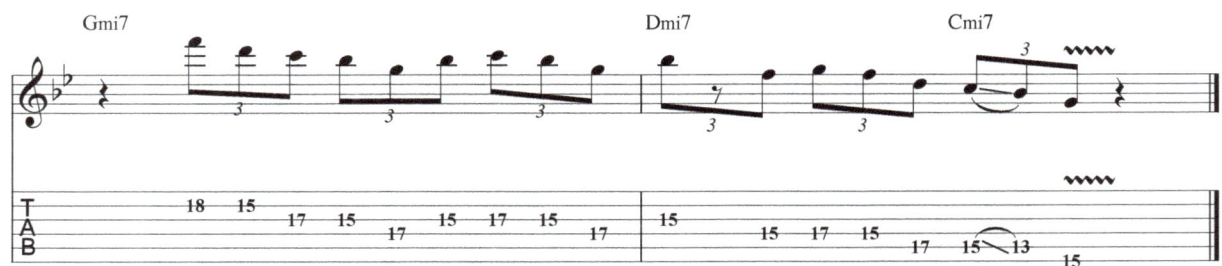

©2021 Fretboard Biology • fretboardbiology.com

PRACTICE

Theory

- ☐ Go to the tabs below the Theory video on the website and complete the quiz.
- ☐ Learn how to build triads and practice building them until you can do it very quickly.
- ☐ Practice using proper chord symbols.

Fretboard Logic

- ☐ Learn the Pattern III minor pentatonic scale and Pattern III natural minor scale, and add them to your practice routine.
- ☐ Memorize the major and minor 6ths and 7ths on non-adjacent bottom four strings. Use the exercise in the tabs below the video to practice your recognition of intervals on the fretboard.
- ☐ Look at how the new information from this Unit relates to the everything else in the Octave Shape Family Tree.

Technique

- ☐ Practice playing with an 8th-note triplet pattern using strict alternate picking.

Rhythm Notation

- ☐ Learn the uses of dots and ties.

Rhythm Guitar

- ☐ Learn and practice some basic strum patterns and progressions in folk guitar.

Improvisation

- ☐ Create a 16-bar solo with 8th-note triplets using whichever patterns of the G minor scales you prefer. As always, record yourself and listen back.

UNIT 6

Learning Modules

> **Theory** - Harmonizing the Major Scale with Triads

> **Fretboard Logic** - Pattern V Minor Pentatonic and Natural Minor Scales, Patterns I and III Major Triad Arpeggios, Three-String Minor Triad Shapes, Intervals: 2nds and 3rds on Top Three Strings

> **Technique** - Alternate Picking with Syncopated 8th-Note Triplets

> **Rhythm Notation** - Spacing and Grouping of Notes

> **Rhythm Guitar** - Classic Rock, Common Power Chords

> **Improvisation** - Soloing with Syncopated 8th-Note Triplets

> **Practice** - Continue Practice Routine Development

THEORY

The term "harmony", as in "harmony and theory", refers to chord progressions, and not vocalists singing the melody in harmony with one another. Understanding the harmony of a song helps us in soloing, playing chords, and with producing and arranging music. It is essential to understand harmonized major and minor scales in order to understand the "harmonic structure" of a song. It all starts by learning about harmonized scales. Here are two important definitions:

Harmonized Scale

The group of chords that result from building chords on each degree of a scale.

Diatonic Harmony

Chord progressions using chords built on each scale degree using only notes that are diatonic to the key.

The Harmonized Major Scale

Most scales can be harmonized and we will begin by harmonizing the major scale. The concept is simple: To harmonize a scale, build a chord on each degree of the scale. The chords are numbered based on the scale degree on which they are built using Roman numerals (I, II, III, IV, V, VI, VII).

A chord built on the 1st scale degree is called the I chord. To build the I chord, find the diatonic notes in the scale a 3rd higher and a 5th higher, and this forms a triad. Remember that a triad's quality is determined by the combination of qualities of the 3rd and the 5th. A chord built on the 2nd scale degree is called the II chord. A chord built on the 3rd scale degree is called the III chord, and so on with each note in the scale: IV, V, VI, and VII. The resulting seven chords are called the "harmonized scale".

The notes used to build each chord of a harmonized scale come from the key, the scale of the I chord. In other words, only "diatonic" notes are used. Diatonic means "of the scale". Again -- chord numbers are notated with Roman numerals which correspond to the scale degree on which the chord is built. When numbering chords with Roman numerals, an abbreviation for the quality is placed to the right of the Roman Numeral; "ma" for major triad, "mi" for minor triad, "+" for augmented, and "°" for diminished. We begin by harmonizing the C major scale and triads.

Here is the C major scale with the scale degrees numbered.

C Major Scale

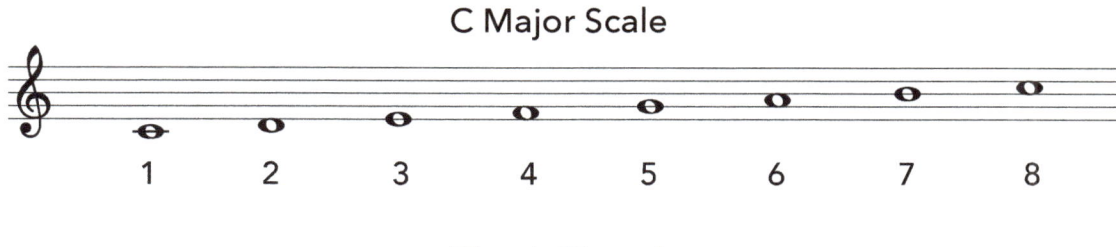

The I Chord

Start with the I chord. Find the 1st scale degree, C.

I Chord

Next, find the note that is a 3rd above C, and it has to be diatonic, meaning "from the key" we are in, which is C. That note is E. This the 3rd of the triad. Next, find the note that is a 5th above C, and it has to be from the C scale, too. That note is G. We call this the 5th of the triad.

I Chord

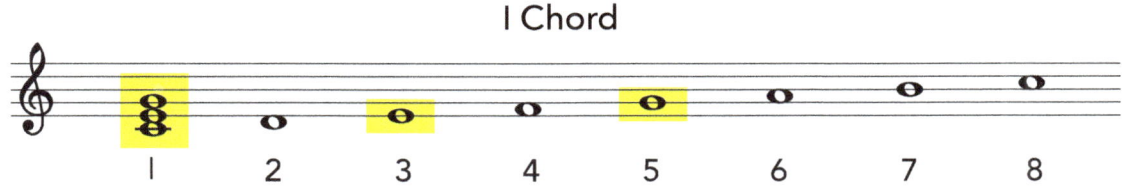

To determine the quality of the triad, analyze the two intervals and then compare them to the triad interval formulas. E is a major 3rd above C and G is a perfect 5th above C. The triad with a major 3rd and a perfect 5th is a major triad.

I Chord

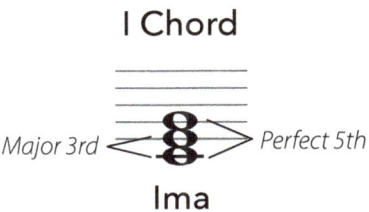

Ima

Conclusion: The I chord is major. It is labeled Ima.

The II Chord

Build the II chord. Start with the 2nd scale degree, which is D.

II Chord

Find the note that is a 3rd above D, and it has to be from the key we are in, which is C. That note is F. This the 3rd of the triad. Next, find the note that is a 5th above D, and it also has to be from the C scale. That note is A and this the 5th of the triad.

II Chord

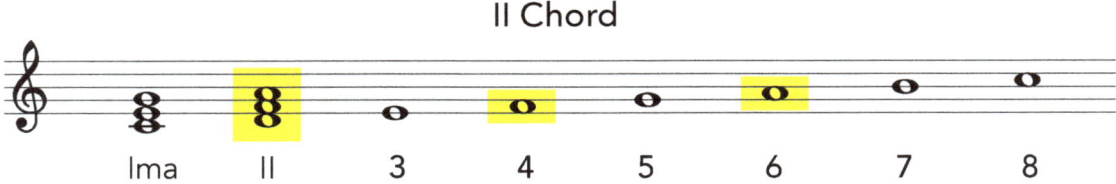

Analyze the intervals and then compare the two intervals to the triad interval formulas. F is a minor 3rd above D and A is a perfect 5th above D. The triad with a minor 3rd and a perfect 5th is a minor triad.

II Chord

Conclusion: The II chord is minor. It is labeled IImi.

The III Chord

Build the III chord. Start with the 3rd scale degree, which is E.

Find the note that is a 3rd above E from the key of C. It is a G. This the 3rd of the triad. Next, find the note that is a 5th above E from the key of C. That note is B. This is the 5th of the triad.

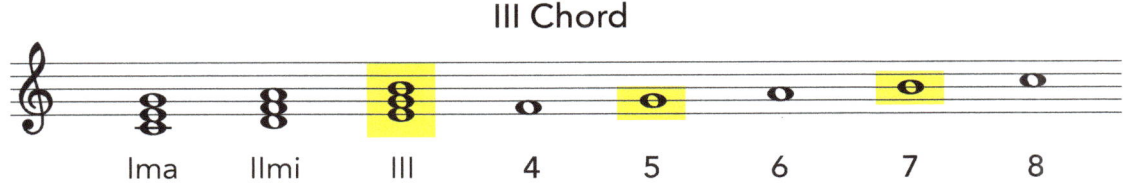

Analyze the intervals and then compare the two intervals to the triad interval formulas. G is a minor 3rd above E and B is a perfect 5th above E. The triad with a minor 3rd and a perfect 5th is a minor triad.

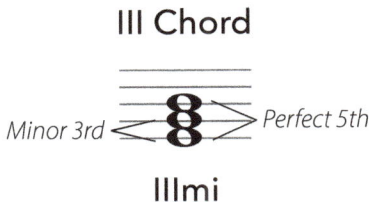

Conclusion: The III chord is minor. Label it IIImi.

The IV Chord

Build the IV chord. Start with the 4th scale degree, which is F.

IV Chord

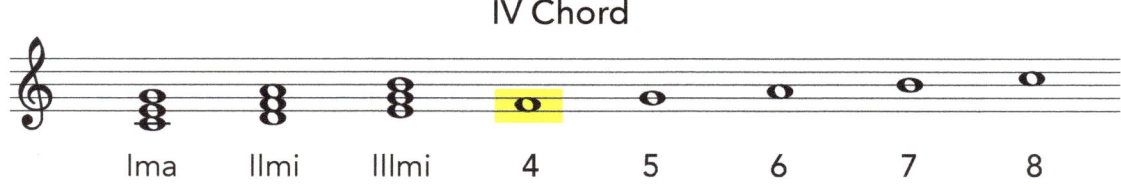

Find the note that is a 3rd above F from the key of C. It is A. It is the 3rd of the triad. Next, find the note that is a 5th above F, C. This the 5th of the triad.

IV Chord

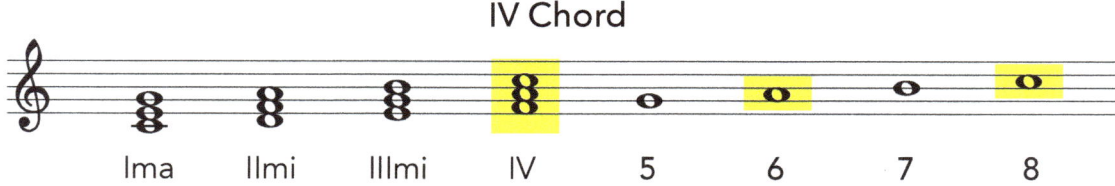

Analyze the intervals and then compare the two intervals to the triad interval formulas. A is a major 3rd above F and C is a perfect 5th above F. The triad with a major 3rd and a perfect 5th is a major triad.

IV Chord

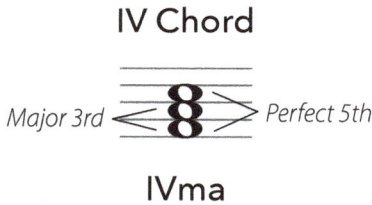

IVma

Conclusion: The IV chord is major. Label it IVma.

The V Chord

Build the V chord. Start with the 5th scale degree, G.

V Chord

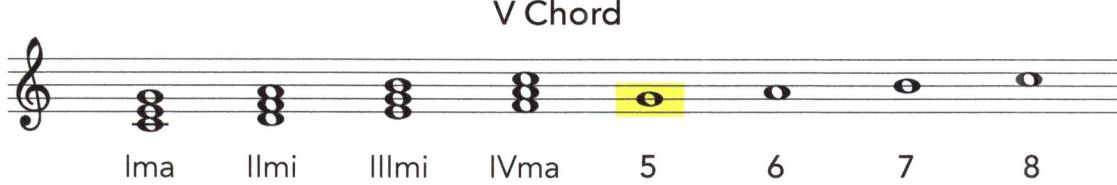

| Ima | IImi | IIImi | IVma | 5 | 6 | 7 | 8 |

Find the note a 3rd above G from the key of C. That note is a B. This the 3rd of the triad. Next, find the note a 5th above G from the C scale. That note is a D. This the 5th of the triad.

V Chord

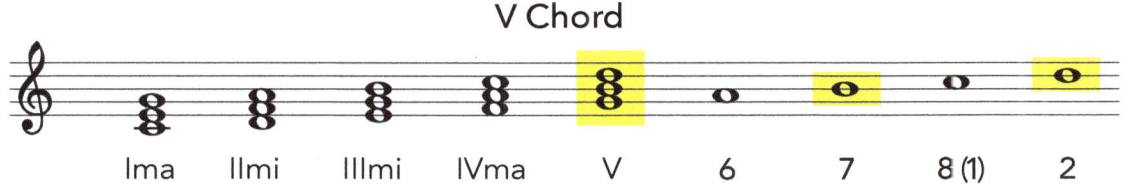

| Ima | IImi | IIImi | IVma | V | 6 | 7 | 8 (1) | 2 |

Analyze the intervals and then compare the two intervals to the triad interval formulas. B is a major 3rd above G and D is a perfect 5th above G. The triad with a major 3rd and a perfect 5th is a major triad.

V Chord

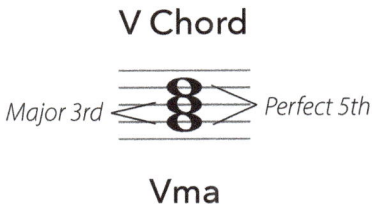

Major 3rd ⟵ ⟶ Perfect 5th

Vma

Conclusion: The V chord is major. Label it Vma.

The VI Chord

Build the VI chord. Start with the 6th scale degree, A.

VI Chord

Find the note that is a 3rd above A from the C scale. That note is C. This the 3rd of the triad. Next, find the note a 5th above A from the C scale. That note is E. This the 5th of the triad.

VI Chord

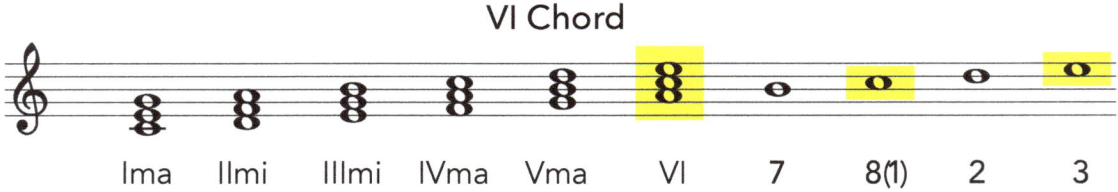

Analyze the intervals and then compare the two intervals to the triad interval formulas. C is a minor 3rd above A and E is a perfect 5th above A. The triad with a minor 3rd and a perfect 5th is a minor triad.

VI Chord

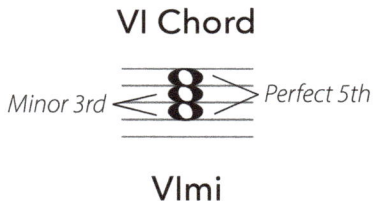

VImi

Conclusion: The VI chord is minor. Label it VImi.

The VII Chord

Last, build the VII chord. Start with the 7th scale, degree, B.

VII Chord

Find the note a 3rd above B from the key of C. That note is D. This the 3rd of the triad. Next, find the note a 5th above B from the C scale. That note is F. This the 5th of the triad.

VII Chord

Analyze the intervals and then compare the two intervals to the triad interval formulas. D is a minor 3rd above B and F is a diminished 5th above B. The triad with a minor 3rd and a diminished 5th is a diminished triad.

VII Chord

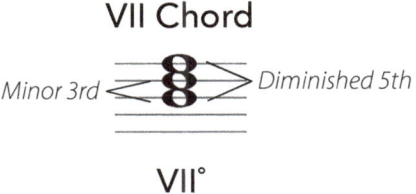

VII°

Conclusion: The VII chord is diminished. Label it VII°.

Here is the list of chords created by harmonizing the C major scale:
- The I chord is major
- The II chord is minor
- The III chord is minor
- The IV chord is major
- The V chord is major
- The VI chord is minor
- The VII chord is diminished

These chords are "diatonic" to the key of C major. If this process is repeated with the major scale in any other key, the result will be the same: The I chord will always be major, the II chord will always be minor, the III chord will always be minor, the IV chord will always be major, the V chord will always be major, the VI chord will always be minor, and the VII chord will always be diminished.

Memorize this. There is no other way around it. Here is a little trick that might help:
- I, IV and V are all major
- VII is diminished
- The rest are minor: II, III and VI

Harmonic Analysis

Soon you will learn about "harmonic analysis", which is a fancy term for analyzing a chord progression. Harmonic analysis is a critical skill for understanding what to play when improvising, playing chords, or arranging. To do this, you need to know the chords that are diatonic in any key.

Because key signatures determine the notes of every key and because the qualities of chords built on each scale degree are the same in all keys, any chord, I through VII, in any major key can be identified easily.

It is wise for you to quiz yourself on what the chords are in every key. Practice asking yourself questions like:

- What is the II chord in D?
- What is the V chord in E♭?
- What is the VII chord in B?
- What is IV chord in F?
- What is the III chord in G?

Do not skimp on practicing this skill, It is important. There is an exercise on the Fretboard Biology website to help you drill these until you can recite them quickly.

FRETBOARD LOGIC

Scales

There is one more minor pentatonic shell to learn, along with the natural minor scale built within it. This is an important milestone. In this Unit you will learn the Pattern V minor pentatonic shell.

Pattern V Minor Pentatonic Scale

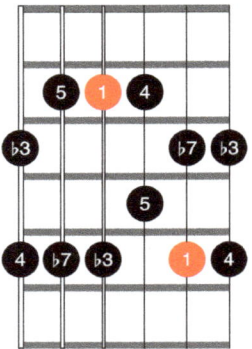

Like all the others, this is a movable pattern that can be played in any key. Next, add a major 2nd and a minor 6th (in blue), and the result will be a Pattern V natural minor scale. Add these scales to your practice routine and use strict alternate picking, playing 8th notes.

Pattern V Natural Minor Scale

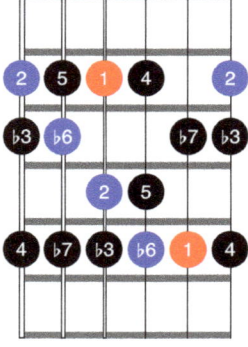

You know all five major pentatonic shells and corresponding major scales and all five minor pentatonic shells and corresponding natural minor scales. You now have access to every corner of the fretboard. The next topic in the next Unit related to scales shows how they all the shapes fit together so you can move smoothly between them and take full advantage of the range of the guitar.

Arpeggios

You have learned how to build chords in the Theory Modules. Now you'll learn about arpeggios. An arpeggio is a chord played as a melodic sequence of notes. In other words, instead of playing all of the notes of a chord simultaneously in a "block" format, the individual components – the chord tones – are played one at a time.

For example, a C major triad played as a block chord means all three chord tones, C, E, and G, are played simultaneously. To play C major triad as an arpeggio, play the chord tones one at a time. They can be played in any order and in multiple octaves as well.

You will recall two terms used early in the discussion of intervals:

- Harmonic interval: two notes played at the same time.
- Melodic interval: two notes played, one after the other.

Chords and Arpeggios

C triad played as a chord   C triad played as an arpeggio

Chords are usually played like a harmonic interval, where all the notes are played at the same time. They can be played like a melodic interval, where the notes are played one after another. When a chord is played like a melodic interval, it is an arpeggio.

Arpeggios play an important part in creating melodies because they outline a chord. They can be played regardless of whether the chord is being played by another instrument in the band. They are an essential part of learning to improvise over chord changes in any style from Blues to Jazz to Country to Rock. The study begins with learning triad arpeggios. A triad chord has a root, 3rd, and 5th. A triad arpeggios is exactly the same thing. There is no difference in their construction.

Arpeggios, like scales, can be built within the Octave Shape system. The first two major pentatonic shells we learned were Patterns I and III, and likewise, the first two major triad arpeggios you will learn are the Patterns I and III major triad arpeggios. We often abbreviate the word arpeggio and just say "arp", so get used to that. Here is a Pattern I major triad arpeggio:

Pattern I Major Triad Arpeggio

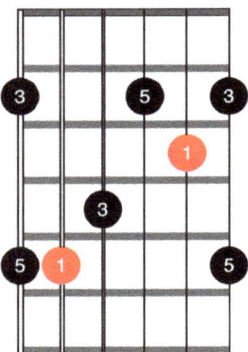

Use strict alternate picking, which presents some challenges with arpeggios. As you move across the neck, ascending or descending, some new strings are played with up strokes and some with down strokes. Be sure to watch your picking hand closely and don't allow yourself to break the alternate-picking pattern.

Here is a Pattern III major triad arpeggio:

Pattern III Major Triad Arpeggio

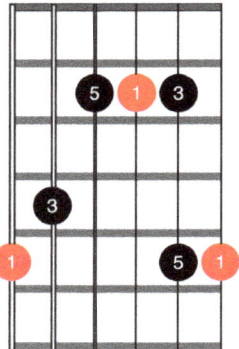

When playing arpeggios, use strict alternate picking, which presents some challenges with arpeggios. As before, make sure you watch your picking hand closely and don't let yourself to break the alternate-picking pattern.

Eventually the focus in the Improvisation Modules will shift to chord tones. So far you have just been thinking about playing notes from the scale when you solo, which is called "key-center soloing". Arpeggios will come into play in an important role as you move deeper into improvisation. Because arpeggios are by definition chord tones, you will rely on them heavily. Work hard on these so that when the study of chord-tone soloing begins, you have them under your fingers.

Chords

In the previous Units you learned three super shapes for major triads and three super shapes for minor triads. Each super shape can be divided into four three-string triad voicings. The most practical are string sets 1-2-3 and 2-3-4 because of the register where they lie.

There are practical reasons for learning three-string triad voicings. Many rhythm guitar parts call for three-string shapes. Also, having command of these shapes allows you to be very efficient with your fretting hand movement. With your knowledge of these three-string shapes, you can now work on some simple chord progressions. As before, your goal will be to be as efficient with movement as possible.

Here is a simple progression, this time using all minor triads.

Progression in G Minor

Using three-string triad shapes you will learn to play this six different and efficient ways.

Here is the first way:

- Start with string set 1-2-3 and play a Gmi triad from the first super shape. The root in the string set 1-2-3 voicing from the first super shape is voiced on the 1st string, and G is found on the 3rd fret of the 1st string.
- Next, find the closest way to play a string set 1-2-3 Cmi triad. That comes from the third super shape. The root in the string set 1-2-3 voicing from the third super shape is voiced on the 3rd string, and C is found on the 5th fret of the 3rd string.
- Next, find the closest possible way to play a string set 1-2-3 Dmi triad. That comes from the second super shape. The root in the string set 1-2-3 voicing from the second super shape is voiced on the 2nd string, and D is found on the 3rd fret of the 2nd string. There was very little hand movement in that example.

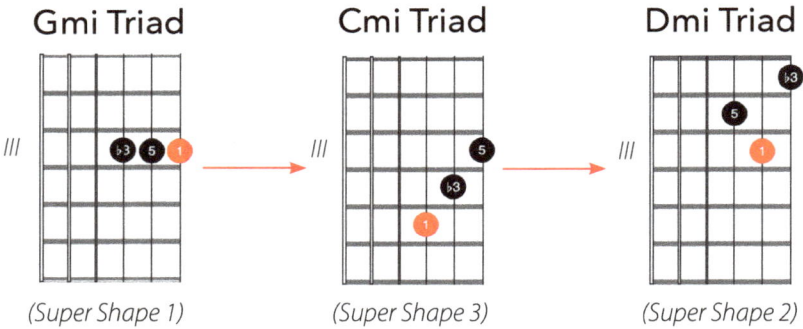

Here is the second way:

- Start with string set 1-2-3 and play a Gmi triad from the second super shape. The root in the string set 1-2-3 voicing from the second super shape is voiced on the 2nd string, and G is found on the 8th fret of the 2nd string.
- Next, find the closest possible way to play a string set 1-2-3 Cmi triad. That comes from the first super shape. The root in the string set 1-2-3 voicing from the first super shape is voiced on the 1st string, and C is found on the 8th fret of the 1st string.
- Next, find the closest possible way to play a string set 1-2-3 Dmi triad. That comes from the third super shape. The root in the string set 1-2-3 voicing from the third super shape is voiced on the 3rd string, and D is found on the 7th fret of the 3rd string.

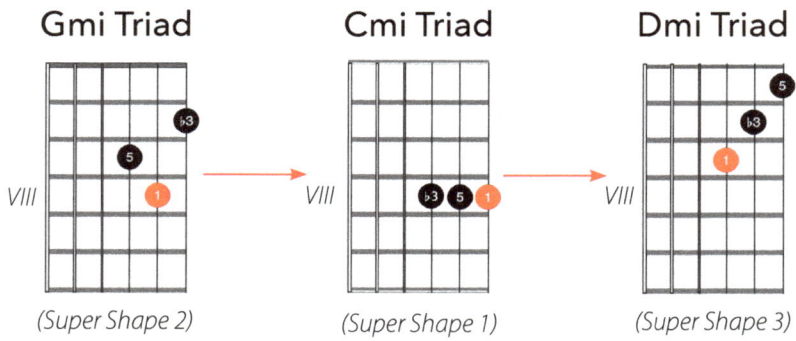

Here is the 3rd way:

- Start with string set 1-2-3 and play a Gmi triad from the third super shape. The root in the string set 1-2-3 voicing from the third super shape is voiced on the 3rd string, and G is found on the 12th fret of the 3rd string.

- Next, find the closest possible way to play a string set 1-2-3 Cmi triad. That comes from the second super shape. The root in the string set 1-2-3 voicing from the second super shape is voiced on the 2nd string, and C is found on the 13th fret of the 2nd string.

- Next, find the closest possible way to play a string set 1-2-3 Dmi triad. That comes from the first super shape. The root in the string set 1-2-3 voicing from the first super shape is voiced on the 1st string, and D is found on the 10th fret of the 1st string.

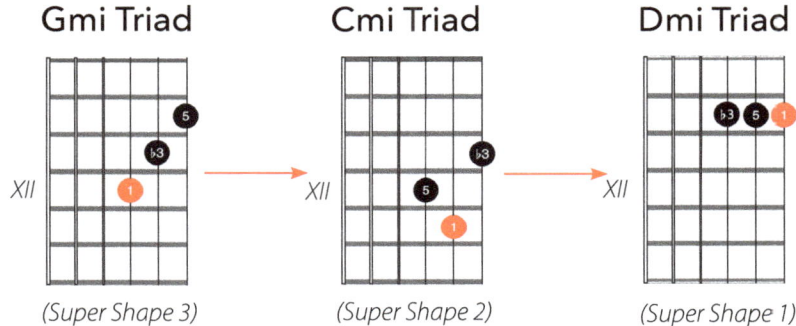

The three ways you just learned to play this mini-progression are voiced in a fairly high register and work well when the guitar needs to cut through a mix. Generally, these would be used in an arrangement where other instruments are filling out the middle register.

Now, let's take a look at three more ways to play this mini-chord progression, but this time on string set 2-3-4. These are played in the middle register. Generally, these would be used in an arrangement where the guitar needs to fill out the harmony, perhaps because there is no other chording instrument.

Here is the first way:

- Start with string set 2-3-4 and play a Gmi triad from the first super shape. The root in the string set 2-3-4 voicing from the first super shape is voiced on the 4th string, and G is found on the 5th fret of the 4th string.
- Next, find the closest way to play a string set 2-3-4 Cmi triad. That comes from the third super shape. The root in the string set 2-3-4 voicing from the third super shape is voiced on the 3rd string, and C is found on the 5th fret of the 3rd string.
- Next, find the closest way to play a string set 2-3-4 Dmi triad. That comes from the second super shape. The root in the string set 2-3-4 voicing from the second super shape is voiced on the 2nd string, and D is found on the 3rd fret of the 2nd string.

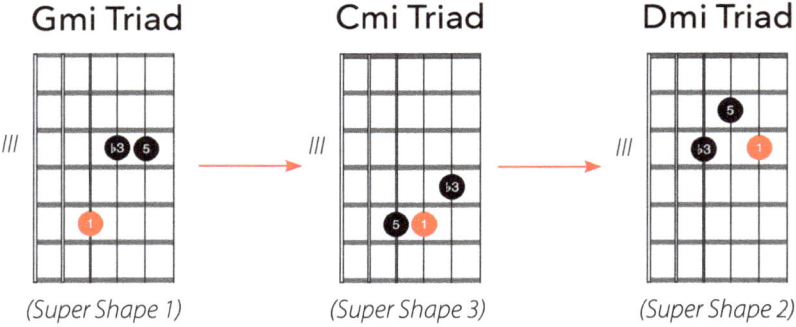

Here is the second way:

- Start with string set 2-3-4 and play a Gmi triad from the second super shape. The root in the string set 2-3-4 voicing from the second super shape is voiced on the 2nd string, and G is found on the 8th fret of the 2nd string.
- Next, find the closest possible way to play a string set 2-3-4 Cmi triad. That comes from the first super shape. The root in the string set 2-3-4 voicing from the first super shape is voiced on the 4th string, and C is found on the 10th fret of the 4th string.
- Next, find the closest possible way to play a string set 2-3-4 Dmi triad. That comes from the third super shape. The root in the string set 2-3-4 voicing from the third super shape is voiced on the 3rd string, and D is found on the 7th fret of the 3rd string.

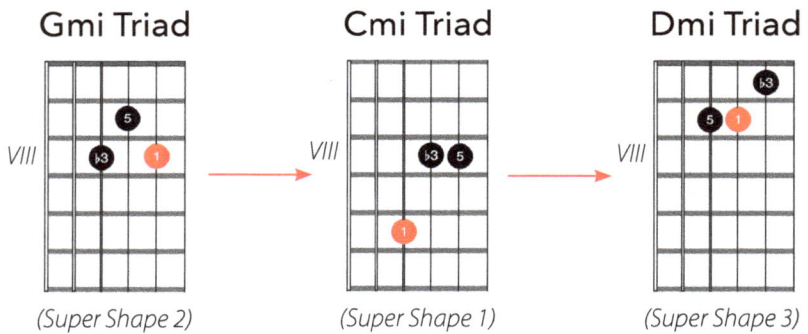

Here is the third way:

- Start with string set 2-3-4 and play a Gmi triad from the third super shape. The root in the string set 2-3-4 voicing from the third super shape is voiced on the 3rd string, and G is found on the 12th fret of the 3rd string.
- Next, find the closest possible way to play a string set 2-3-4 Cmi triad. That comes from the second super shape. The root in the string set 2-3-4 voicing from the second super shape is voiced on the 2nd string, and C is found on the 13th fret of the 2nd string.
- Next, find the closest possible way to play a string set 2-3-4 Dmi triad. That comes from the first super shape. The root in the string set 2-3-4 voicing from the first super shape is voiced on the 4th string, and D is found on the 12th fret of the 4th string.

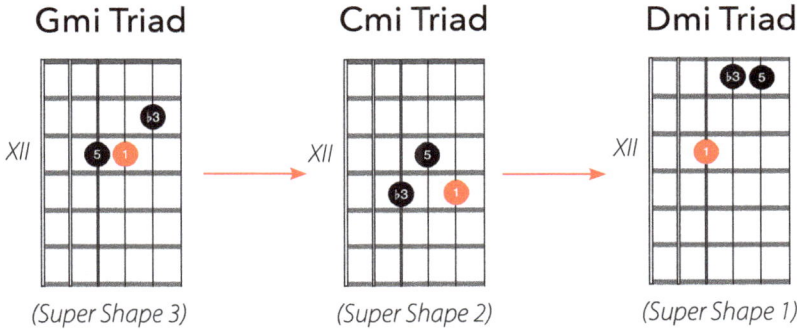

Interval Shapes on the Fretboard

So far you have learned interval shapes in the bottom four-string region of the neck. Turn your attention to the interval shapes for the top three strings. Some of these shapes in this region are different than the bottom four strings is because of the different interval between the 2nd and 3rd strings -- a major 3rd. All interval shapes that crosses the line between the 2nd and 3rd string will be different than what we've seen so far.

The guitar is tuned primarily in 4ths except between the 2nd and 3rd strings, which again, is a major 3rd. Standard tuning for the guitar is:

- 6th (E) to 5th (A) – Perfect 4th
- 5th (A) to 4th (D) – Perfect 4th
- 4th (D) to 3rd (G) – Perfect 4th
- 3rd (G) to 2nd (B) – Major 3rd
- 2nd (B) to 1st (E) – Perfect 4th

The major 3rd between the 2nd and 3rd strings in standard tuning facilitates playing chords on the top four strings. If the guitar was tuned uniformly in 4ths, the stretches required to play chords would be difficult and awkward. Barre chords would be virtually impossible to play. While having the distance between all stings be 4ths would make for convenient, repetitive and "tidy" shapes for scales and arpeggios, playing chords, especially on the upper strings, would be difficult. In addition, if the guitar was tuned in all 4ths, it would look like this: E, A, D, G, C, F. The low E and high F would be a minor 2nd apart which would be very challenging for voicing chords, especially barre chords.

Learn the major and minor 2nd and major and minor 3rd shapes on adjacent strings in the top three-string region of the fretboard.

Minor 2nd Interval

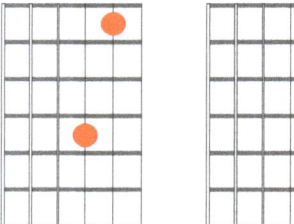

Major 2nd Interval

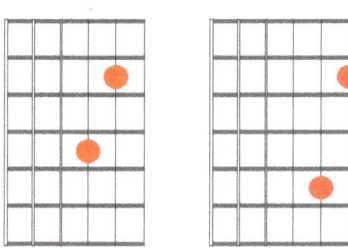

Minor 3rd Interval

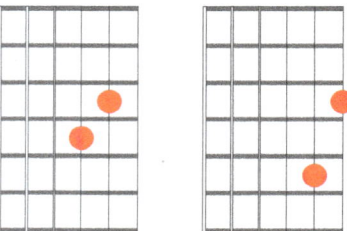

Major 3rd Interval

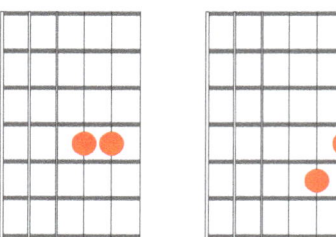

TECHNIQUE

In the last Module you learned how to apply alternate picking to 8th-note triplets. Now apply strict alternate picking to syncopated 8th-note triplet rhythms. Remember that when applying strict alternate picking to 8th-note triplets, the first 8th note is a down stroke, the second 8th note is an up stroke, and the third 8th note is a down stroke. Then on beat two, play the first 8th note with an up stroke, the second 8th note with a down stroke, and the third 8th note with an up stroke. Beat three will be like beat one: down-up-down. Beat four will be like beat two: up-down-up. This is a two-beat cycle that repeats itself.

As with 8th-note and 16th-note syncopation, regardless of whether there is a note or a rest, the assignment of down strokes and up strokes to each possible 8th-note location in the two-beat pattern stays the same. Like this:

8th-Note Triplet Picking Pattern

8th-Note Syncopated-Triplet Picking Pattern

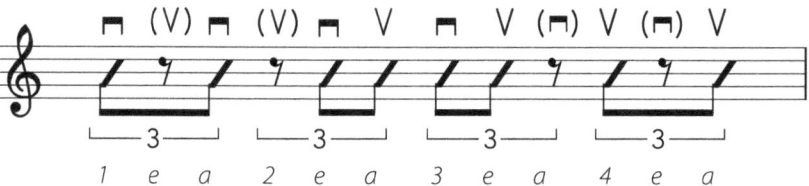

RHYTHM NOTATION

4/4 time is very common. In fact, 4/4 time is so common that it is often referred to as "common time" and the time signature is sometimes written as "C" on the staff instead of 4/4. Because of your familiarity with the 4/4 time signature, the introduction to the rules of spacing and grouping will be in 4/4 time.

Spacing and Grouping

Music should be written and organized as clearly and simply as possible. This makes it possible for the musician to focus more attention on the performance and less on deciphering what is written. Written music should "look the way it sounds". In order to accomplish this, there are two aspects of notation that deserve special attention: spacing and grouping.

Spacing

Spacing refers to how physical space on the staff is used to notate rhythm, melody, and harmony.

Grouping

Grouping refers to how smaller-value notes are organized together into groups for ease in reading.

Spacing

Spacing plays an important role in written music looking the way it sounds. Notes and their surrounding "personal space" should occupy the physical region of a measure proportionate to their value.

- A whole note or rest and the space around it should occupy the entire measure.

Whole Note

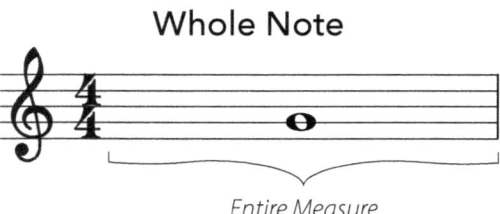

Entire Measure

- A half note or rest and the space around it should occupy half the measure.

Half Notes

Half of the Measure

- A quarter note or rest and the space around it should occupy a quarter of the measure.

Quarter Notes

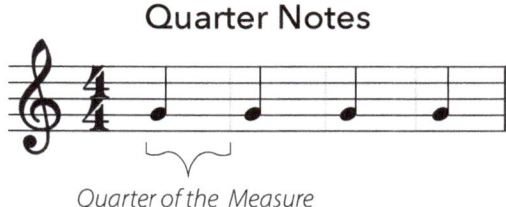

Quarter of the Measure

- An 8th note or rest and the space around it should occupy an eighth of the measure.

Eighth Notes

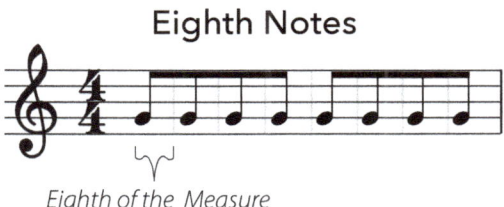

Eighth of the Measure

- A 16th note or rest and the space around it should occupy a sixteenth of the measure.

Sixteenth Notes

Sixteenth of the Measure

Grouping

Proper grouping organizes notes so that rhythms are easy to recognize and read. In 4/4 time, there are several rules, but there are exceptions, too. Learning to group notes clearly is one of the most challenging tasks for rhythm notation.

- When the smallest note or rest value in a measure is a quarter note, there is no rule about grouping.

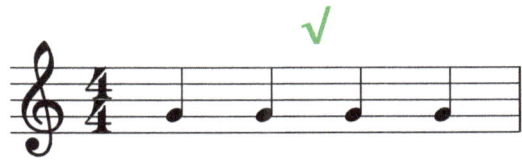

- Beams are used in place of flags when grouping notes smaller than quarter notes together.

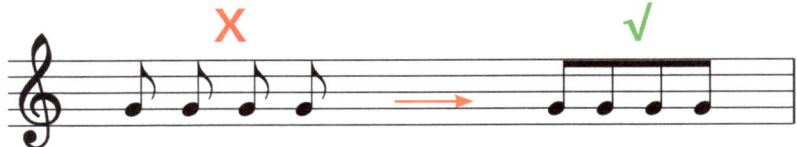

- When the smallest note or rest value in a measure is an 8th note, beat three must be marked with a note or rest. If a note is carried over from the beat or beats before, a tie is used to extend the note from the first half of the measure to the symbol on beat three. Beams cannot cross from beat two to beat three when the smallest note or rest value in a measure is an 8th note.

- When the smallest note or rest value in a measure is a 16th note, all four beats must be marked with a note or rest. If a note is carried over from the beat or beats before, a tie is used to extend the note from the previous beat to the symbol on the beat. Beams cannot cross from beat to beat when the smallest note or rest value in a measure is a 16th note.

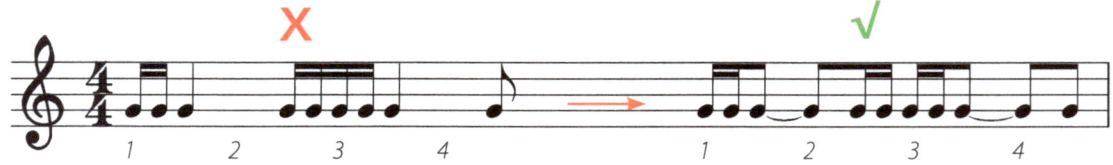

In each example above, the rhythm figure on the left would be performed the same way as the rhythm figure on the right. The difference is that the rhythm figure on the left are notated incorrectly, and the rhythm figure on the right use the correct notation. Study these rules and you will study them more in the next few Modules.

RHYTHM GUITAR

Rock Rhythm Guitar

This next series of Units explores the core essentials of Rock rhythm guitar. Rock rhythm guitar is as much about attitude and sound as it is about time, pocket, and voicings. Keep that in mind when playing these examples. "Rock" is a very broad term and the genre has evolved a long way from its roots in Blues -- and in many directions. Central to Rock rhythm guitar is the "power chord", which most guitarists discover soon after picking up a guitar for the first time. You may or may not already know a lot about power chords. Regardless, we will take the time to be thorough.

Power Chord Construction

A power chord is a dyad, meaning a two-note combination of notes. It has a root and a perfect 5th above it. Some don't even consider it a chord because the common definition of a chord is three or more notes played at the same time. The two most common power-chord voicings are derived from Patterns IV and II barre chords. The two lowest notes in each of those barre chords are the root and 5th. It is easy to double the root one octave higher. There are also power-chord voicings where either the root or 5th (or both) can be played in multiple octaves.

Pattern IV Power Chord
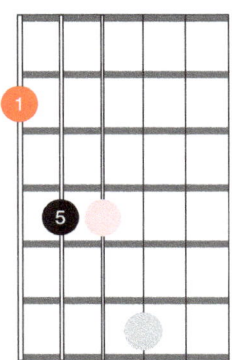

Pattern II Power Chord
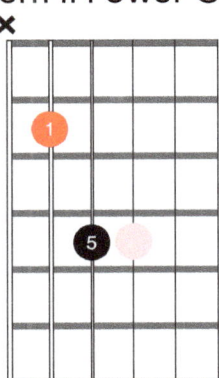

There is no 3rd in a power chord, so they don't have a major or minor quality. However, a major or minor quality is almost always implied by the context in which the chord is used. This will be discussed more a little later.

It is also possible to play power chords derived from Pattern V. In a Pattern V barre chord the root is on the 4th string and the 5th is on the 3rd string.

Name

Power chords get their name from their commanding sound. The open 5th, usually voiced fairly low, has a very strong sound. When played aggressively, the sound is solid like a rock—especially when combined with the root played by the bass guitar. Power chords are written as "5" chords, as in G5 or D5. This is not to be confused with the V chord, using a Roman numeral V, which labels a chord built on the 5th scale degree.

Pattern V Power Chord (5 Chord)

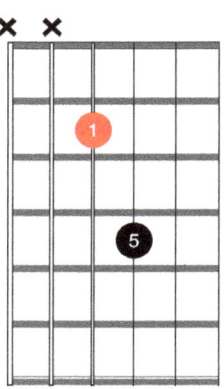

Pattern V Power Chord

Sound

Power chords can be played with a clean, crunch, or distorted sound. The open 5th and distortion work well together. Intervals like 2nds and 3rds played with a distorted sound on guitar, particularly in the lower register, create a pretty uncomfortable sound because of the clashing frequencies. But the 5th in a power chord sounds great.

For these examples, use a crunch tone, which means a sound that has a light degree of distortion and is not 100% clean. A little bit of distortion – a crunch – makes for a bigger note-footprint than a completely clean sound. Too much distortion and the sharp edge of attack gets shaved off and the "power" of the chord is weakened. Experiment with different degrees of distortion.

Here is a short example using power chords. You will find the audio track for this progression on the Fretboard Biology website. This example has an 8th-note subdivision and, because the tempo allows, use all down strokes, which ensures a consistent sound and attack. Play this first with all Pattern IV voicings, then mix Pattern IV and II voicings.

Rock Progression in G Minor

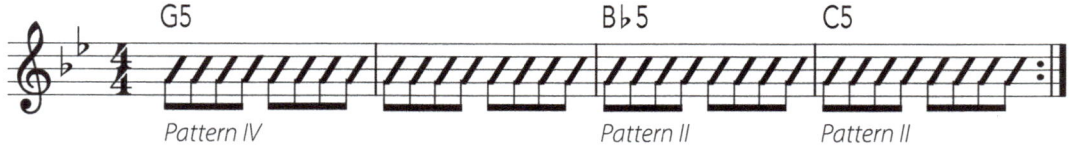

Level 2 Unit 6 • Rhythm Demo

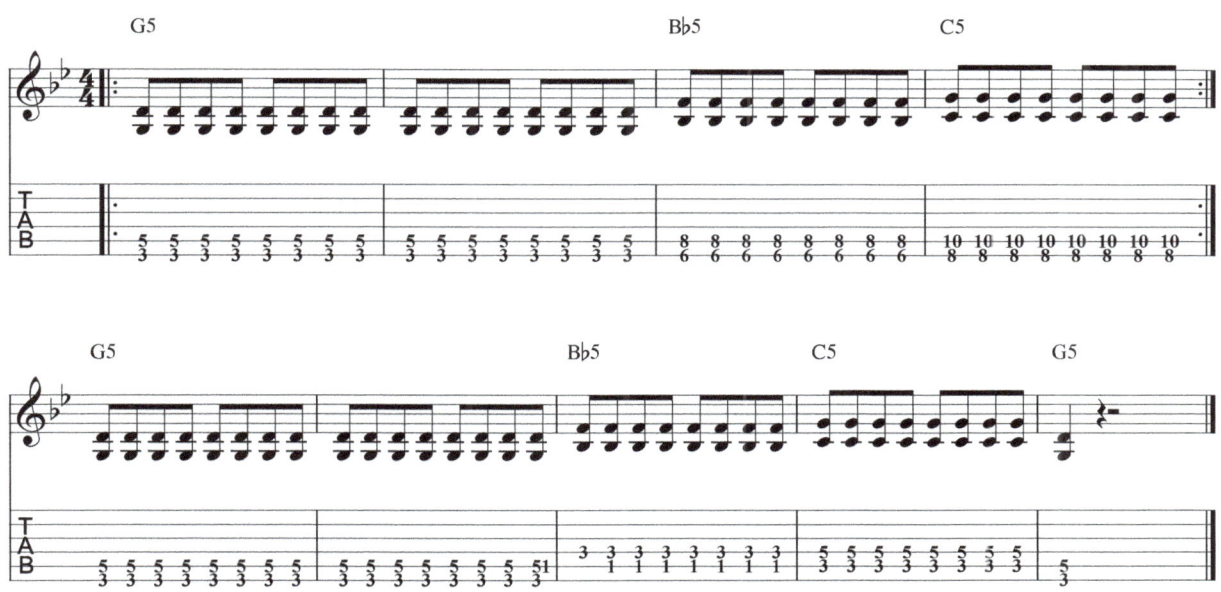

Doubling a with a Pattern V power chord in a higher register creates a very full sound. Power chords can be doubled by multiple guitars or played in different octaves for effect. The sound is impressive when spread out over different octaves on several guitars.

Implied Quality

Power chords don't have a major or minor quality because they don't contain a 3rd. But quality is usually implied by the context in which they are used. In the example we just played, the key of G minor is implied by the roots of the chords. While the key of G major has the notes G and C, it does not have B♭. The key of G minor, however, has the notes G, B♭, and C. So while G5 chord has no quality, the key of G minor is implied by the root movement from G to B♭ to C.

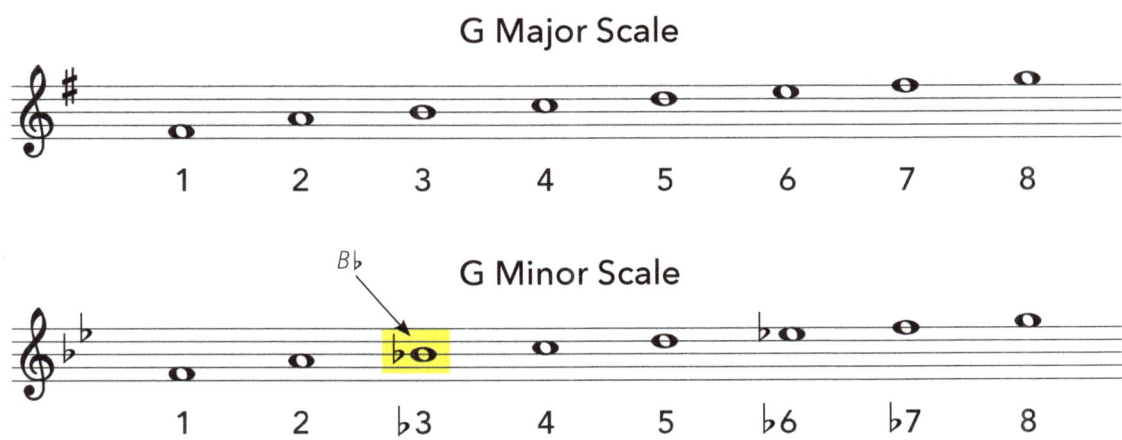

Years ago before the "5" was adopted as a power chord symbol, arrangers would write a chord with a quality and then note "Power Chords" above the staff. The instructions informed the guitarist to voice the chord with root and 5th only. There was an advantage to this way of writing—the guitarist could see what quality was being implied by the melody or being played by some other instrument. Here is an example:

ROCK SONG TITLE

This system is still in use and is my personal preference because of how it informs the guitarist about the implied quality. But the "5" power chord naming system seems to be here to stay.

IMPROVISATION

In the Technique Module for this Unit, alternate picking for 8th-note triplet subdivision with syncopation is introduced.

Here is another progression using an 8th-note triplet groove in C major. It is a repeating two-bar phrase. Stay with the 8th-note triplet alternate-picking pattern you have learned, but include some syncopation.

Progression in C Major

Practice playing with the track two different ways:

- First, find a pattern of C major pentatonic or the C major scale you are comfortable with. Focus on your picking hand and play 8th-note triplet lines to until you are comfortable with the 8th-note triplet subdivision. Add some syncopation, staying true to the alternate-picking pick-direction rules.

- Second, create a 16-bar solo which is eight times through the two-bar phrase. Either a clean or overdrive sound will work fine. Record it and listen back, checking for good time and feel and for how well you told a story.

C Major Pentatonic Scales

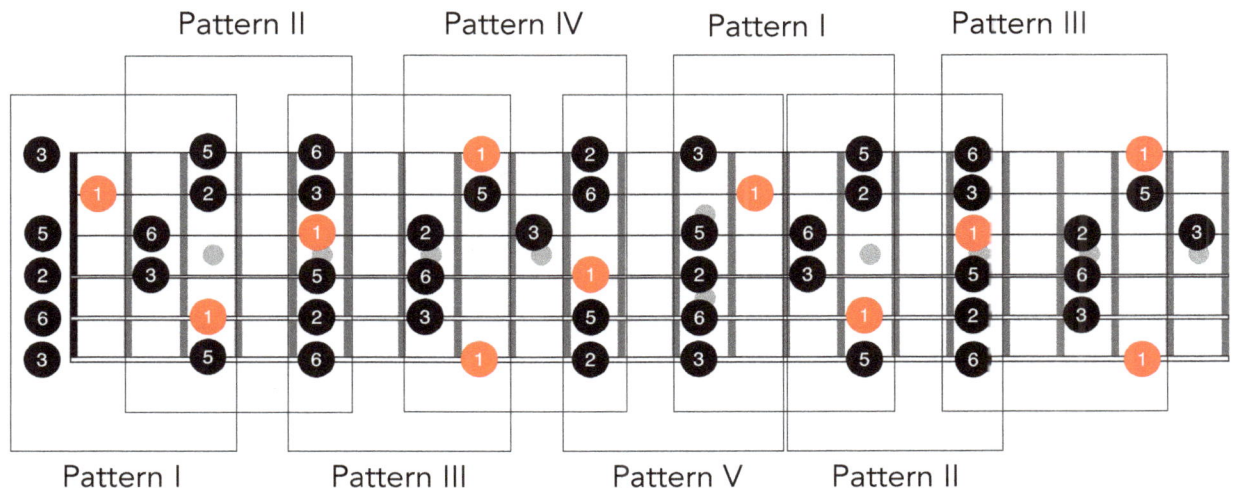

Level 2 Unit 6 • Example Solo

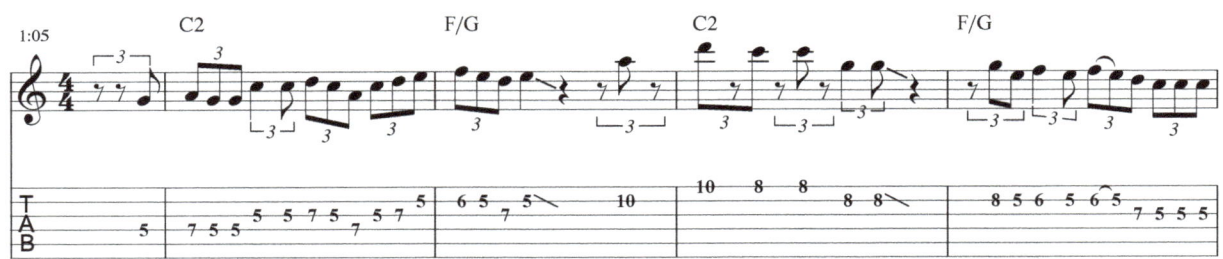
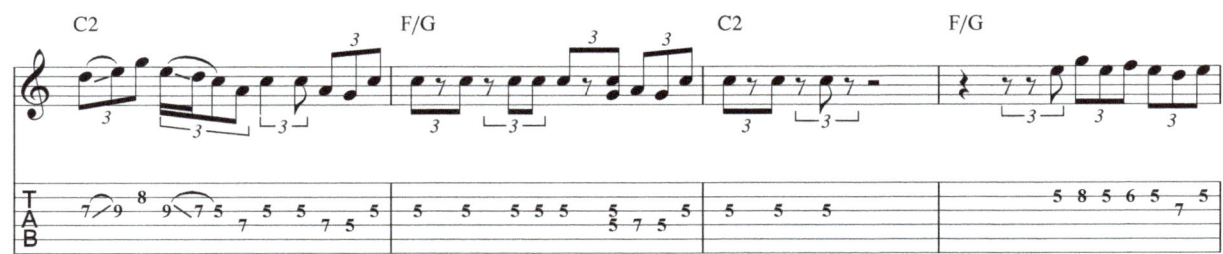

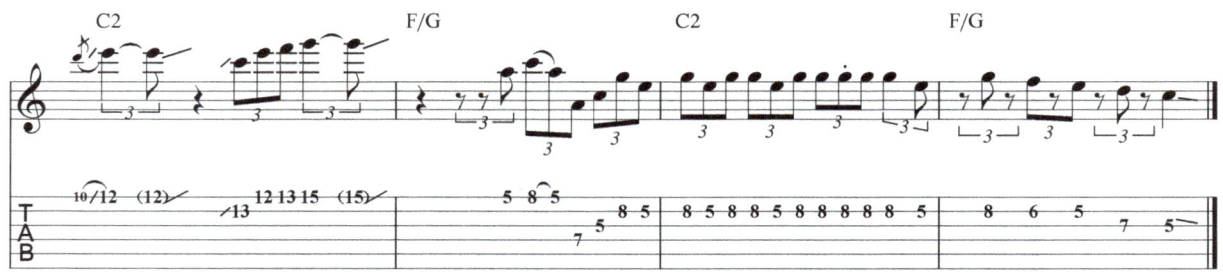

PRACTICE

Theory

- ❏ Go to the tabs below the Theory video on the website and compete the quiz.
- ❏ Understand how to harmonize the major scale with triads.

Fretboard Logic

- ❏ Learn the Pattern V minor pentatonic scale and the Pattern V natural minor scale, and add them to your practice routine.
- ❏ Understand the concept of arpeggios and learn the Patterns I and Pattern III major triad arpeggios.
- ❏ Continue learning to use the super shapes and the triads within each of them.
- ❏ Memorize the 2nd and 3rd interval shapes on adjacent top three strings. Use the exercise in the tabs below the video to practice your recognition of intervals on the fretboard.
- ❏ Look at how the new information from this Unit relates to the everything else in the Octave Shape Family Tree.

Technique

- ❏ Practice playing with a syncopated 8th-note triplet pattern using strict alternate picking.

Rhythm Notation

- ❏ Learn proper note spacing and grouping.

Rhythm Guitar

- ❏ Learn the basics of power chords.

Improvisation

- ❏ Create a 16-bar solo using whichever patterns of the C major scales you prefer. As always, record yourself and listen back.

UNIT 7

Learning Modules

> **Theory** - Chord Families and Analyzing Chord Progressions in Major Keys

> **Fretboard Logic** - How Pentatonic Shells Fit Together on the Fretboard, Patterns II and IV Minor Triad Arpeggios, Voice Leading, Intervals: 4ths and 5ths on Adjacent Top Three Strings

> **Technique** - Alternate Picking with 16th-Note Triplets

> **Rhythm Notation** - Note Grouping with 8th Notes

> **Rhythm Guitar** - Classic Rock, Open-A Power Chord Vocabulary

> **Improvisation** - Soloing with 16th-Note Triplets

> **Practice** - Continue Practice Routine Development

THEORY

In the last unit you learned about the harmonized major scale which is required to analyze chord progressions.

The process of analyzing chord progressions is called harmonic analysis. Harmonic analysis helps you understand how chords work together in progressions and informs you about what notes to use when you solo, play chords, or write and arrange music. In this Unit, as you learn about harmonic analysis, you will learn to look at the chords of a song and determine the key and the number of each chord (Ima, IImi, IIImi etc.).

The major scale and the chords we get from harmonizing it are called "the major diatonic system", meaning everything is "of the scale". Later, we will learn the minor diatonic system. We will begin here by learning harmonic analysis in major keys.

Chord Families

Organizing chords of a key into "chord families" is an important part learning the diatonic system. Each family has an emotional effect on the listener. Chords in the major diatonic system belong to one of three families:

- Tonic Family: This is the family of the I chord. Chords in this family give a feeling of home or rest when the listener hears them in the context of a song.

- Subdominant Family: This is the family of the IV chord. Chords in this family give a feeling of moving away from home – that is, away from the tonic family – when the listener hears them in the context of a song.

- Dominant Family: This is the family of the V chord. Chords in this family give a feeling of moving toward home – in other words, resolving to home – when the listener hears them in the context of a song.

Each chord family has a different emotional effect on the listener. This emotional effect is called the "chord function."

Chord Function

You could say that the chords in each of these families actually perform an emotional function. In fact, the word "function" is often used when referring to the Roman numeral designation of a chord. We will talk more about that in a minute. But again, the function of a chord refers to the emotional effect of a chord:

- The function of a chord in the tonic family is to give a feeling of rest or home.

- The function of a chord in the subdominant family is to give a feeling of moving away from home.

- The function of a chord in the dominant family is to pull the listener back home.

You have felt the effect of chord families as long as you have listened to music, but didn't consciously know it was happening. It's interesting how the functions of these three families mimic our daily life. We get up in the morning at home (tonic family), we go away to work or school (subdominant family), we head back home later in the day (dominant family) and we are home at night (tonic).

Let's look deeper into the families:

- The Tonic Family is the family of the I chord. Both the III and VI chords are also considered members of the tonic family as well. The Tonic Family includes: I, III, and VI.
- The Subdominant Family is the family of the IV chord. The II chord is also a subdominant chord. The Subdominant Family includes: IV and II.
- The Dominant Family is the family of the V chord. The VII chord is a dominant as well. The Dominant Family includes: V and VII.

Chord Families in Major

FAMILY	MEMBERS	EMOTIONAL EFFECT
Tonic	I, III, VI	At home, resolved
Subdominant	IV, II	Moving away from tonic
Dominant	V, VII	Moving toward tonic

Analyzing Chord Progressions

Analyzing chord progressions is harmonic analysis and it is important to become proficient at it. It's common to be on a gig or at a rehearsal and see crude chord charts that have no key signature, so there is no immediate indicator of the key. I've been in situations with songwriters or in the studio where the chord chart is scribbled on a piece of scrap paper with no key signature. It is pretty common.

There are several ways to determine the key and, as a result, the function of each chord in a progression if there is no key signature. Don't assume that the first chord played in a progression is the tonic chord (I chord). It is more likely that the final chord of a progression is the tonic chord. It is not always the case, but it is more common than not.

The first method of harmonic analysis you will learn is slow, but thorough. To analyze any chord progression, you need to know the harmonized scale.

In this Module we will work with progressions in major keys. In the following major key progression, determine all of the keys to which each chord could belong:

- The A chord could be the I chord in the key of A, the IV chord in the key of E, or the V chord in the key of D.
- The D chord could be the I chord in the key of D, the IV chord in the key of A, or the V chord in the key of G.
- The E chord could the I chord in the key of E, the IV chord in the key of B, or the V chord in the key of A.

The only key to which all chords belong is A. Therefore, this progression is in the key of A. Next look at the function of each chord by identifying which chord family each chord belongs to:

- The A is the I chord, so it is a member of the Tonic Family.
- The D is the IV chord, so it is a member of the Subdominant Family.
- The E is the V chord, so it is a member of the Dominant Family.

Here is another major key progression. Determine the keys to which each chord could belong:

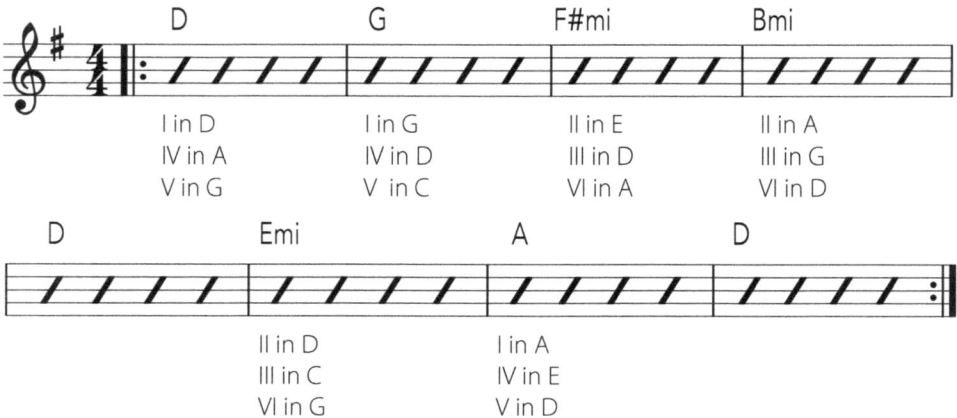

- The D chord could be the I chord in D, the IV chord in A, or the V chord in G.
- The G chord could be the I chord in G, the IV chord in D, or the V chord in C.
- The F#mi chord could be the II chord in E, the III chord in D, or the VI chord in A.
- The Bmi chord could be the II chord in A, the III chord in G, or the VI chord in D.
- The Emi chord could be the II chord in D, the III chord in C, or the VI chord in G.
- The A chord could be the I chord in A, the IV chord in E, or the V chord in D.

The only key to which all chords belong is D. Therefore, this progression is in the key of D. Next look at the function of each chord by identifying which chord family each chord belongs to:

- The D (I), F#mi (III), and Bmi (VI) are all part of the Tonic Family.
- The G (IV) is a member of the Subdominant Family.
- The A (V) is a member of the Dominant Family.

Shortcuts to Finding the Key

There are other clues in both of these progressions that can help you arrive at the same analysis. The last chord offers a clue, as it is often the tonic chord, but that is not 100% reliable.

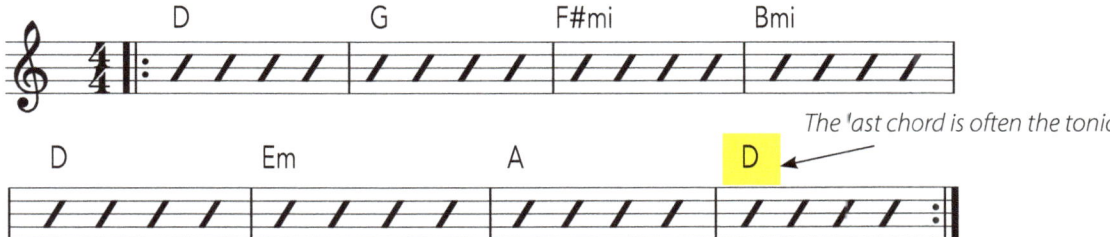

The last chord is often the tonic

Another option is to look for two major chords or minor chords that are one step apart, because in the harmonized major scale, there is only one place where two major chords are one step apart: IVma and Vma, and one place where two minor chords are one step apart: IImi and IIImi. In the case of the progression in D, the roots of Emi and F#mi are a whole step apart. There is only one place in the harmonized major scale where two minor triads are positioned one whole step apart: IImi and IIImi.

Two minor chords a whole step apart

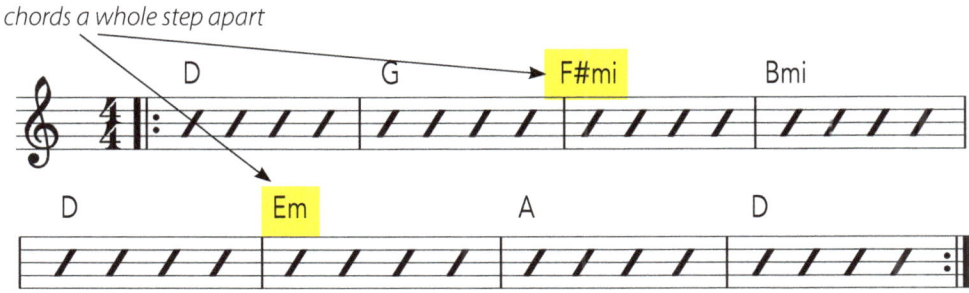

The roots of the G and A are a whole step apart, too. There is only one place in the harmonized major scale where two major triads are positioned one whole step apart: IVma and Vma. These clues hint that the progression is in the key of D.

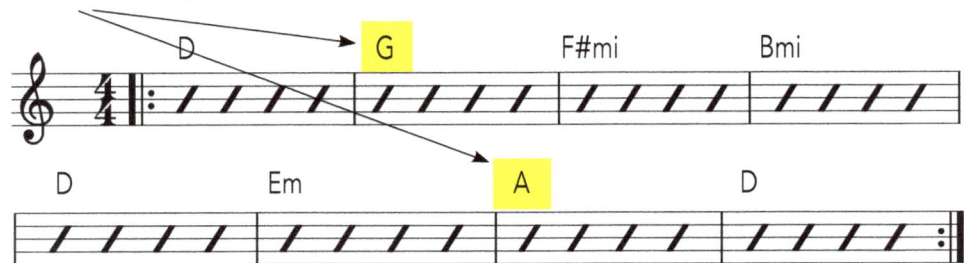

Harmonic analysis is the beginning of understanding what is going on inside a song. Understanding the harmony will open your mind to options you won't have otherwise.

Practice analyzing the songs you already know. Find songs or parts of songs and see if you can determine each chord's number – that is, its function – which tells you the chord family to which it belongs.

FRETBOARD LOGIC

Scales

In this Module we are going to zoom out and see the big picture of the fretboard. It's important to have this 30,000-foot perspective.

Here are all of the notes of the C major pentatonic scale with all of the Cs (the tonics) highlighted on the fretboard. In this graphic there are no individual Octave Shapes or pentatonic shells highlighted. The octave shapes overlap and connect with each other to form one continuous pattern of notes on the fretboard.

C Major Pentatonic Scales

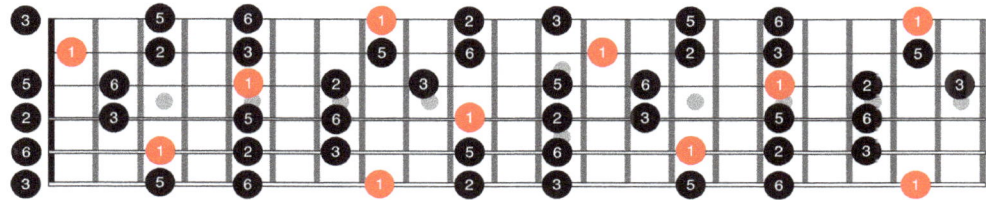

In the following diagrams, each individual shell is highlighted to show how they connect with each other.

Pattern I C Major Pentatonic Scale

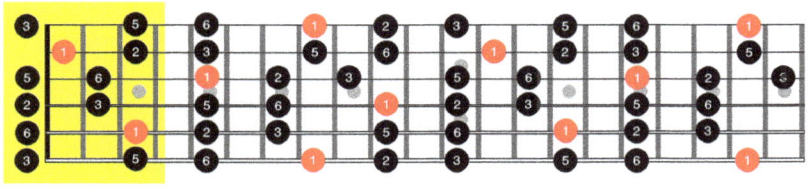

Pattern I

Pattern II C Major Pentatonic Scale

Pattern II

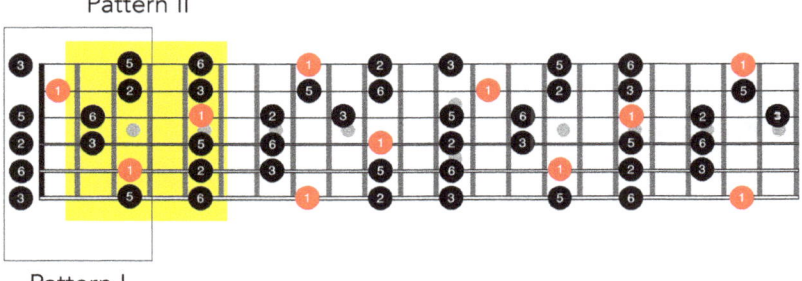

Pattern I

Pattern III C Major Pentatonic Scale

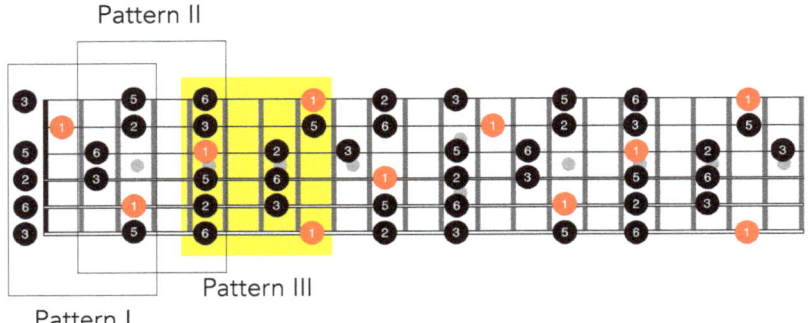

Pattern IV C Major Pentatonic Scale

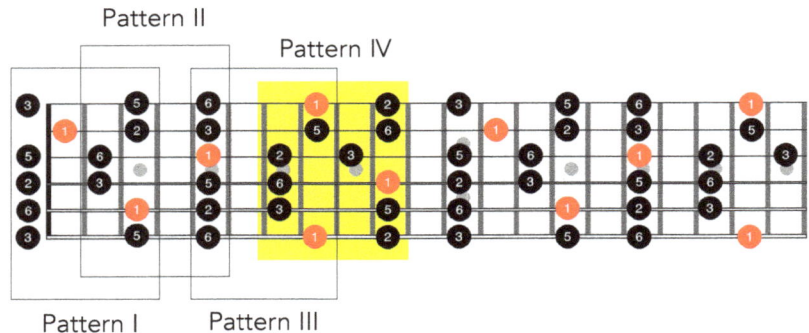

Pattern V C Major Pentatonic Scale

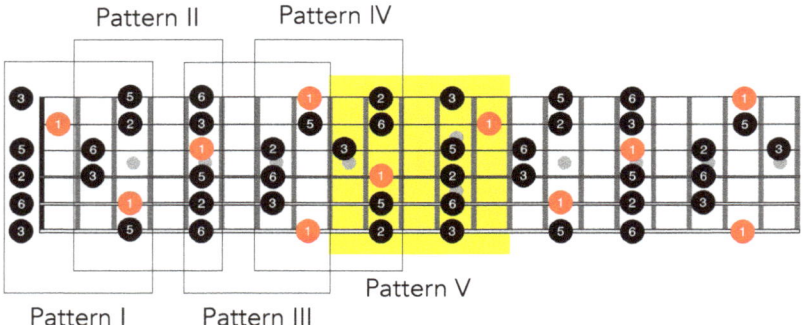

The octave shape patterns provide a convenient way to organize all of the possible notes of the pentatonic scale within five sections of the neck. Our discussion up to this point has focused on playing within each individual shell, but don't restrict yourself to playing inside just one all of the time. Your personal exploration of the fretboard should include learning how to move from one shell to the next – one higher and one lower – to take full advantage of the range of the guitar when soloing.

Each string can be a point of transition between the two shapes. In order to transition from one shell to the adjacent shell (above or below) you need to see the shell you want to move to in advance. Try the transition exercises to learn to transition between all of your pentatonic shells.

Ascending Transition Exercise

To practice transitioning ascending, pick a shell and start on the lowest tonic and play the scale ascending:

- For the first way to transition, play ascending to the next string higher from where you started. At that point, move up into the next shell higher and continue ascending in the second shell.
- For the second way to transition, play ascending to the second string higher from where you started. At that point move up into the next shell higher and continue ascending in the second shell.
- For the next way to transition, play ascending to the third string higher from where you started. At that point move up into the next shell higher and continue ascending in the second shell.
- For the next way to transition, play ascending to the fourth string higher from where you started. At that point move up into the next shell higher and continue ascending in the second shell.
- For the next way to transition, play ascending to the fifth string higher from where you started. At that point move up into the next shell above and continue ascending in the second shell.

Descending Transition Exercise

To practice transitioning descending, start on the highest note of your starting shell and play the scale descending:

- For the first way to transition, play descending to the next string lower from where you start. At that point move down into the next shell lower and continue descending in the second shell.
- For the second way to transition, play descending to the second string lower from where you started. At that point move down into the next shell lower and continue descending in the second shell.
- For the next way to transition, play descending to the third string lower from where you started. At that point move down into the next shell lower and continue descending in the second shell.
- For the next way to transition, play descending to the fourth string lower from where you started. At that point move down into the next shell lower and continue descending in the second shell.
- For the next way to transition, play descending to the fifth string lower from where you started. At that point move down into the next shell lower and continue descending in the second shell.

You can start this exercise with any of the pentatonic shells. Therefore there are five places to do this exercise. It will show how all the shells fit together. This will help complete your understanding of the notes available in a key. You can make up other exercises as well, like working your way up the scale using just one string.

Another good way to explore how the patterns fit together is to work out with pairs of strings like strings one and two, or strings two and three, or strings three and four, and so on. All these exercises are more fun when played with a backing track.

The five Octave Shape system is only one of the ways to see and organize the fretboard. You can work out other ways to view the neck in a more horizontal way by thinking about transitioning to the next shell higher or lower every other string or randomly. However, the five pentatonic shells work great for learning the fretboard in a segmented way. The pentatonic shells also work great for deriving the seven-note diatonic scales.

A Minor Pentatonic Scales

Here are all of the notes possible for the A minor pentatonic scale with all of the A's highlighted. None of the individual Octave Shapes or pentatonic shells highlighted.

A Minor Pentatonic Scales

And here are the exact same notes, but in this graphic each minor pentatonic shell is outlined. This makes clear again how this segmented approach organizes all of the possible notes within five patterns on the fretboard.

A Minor Pentatonic Scales

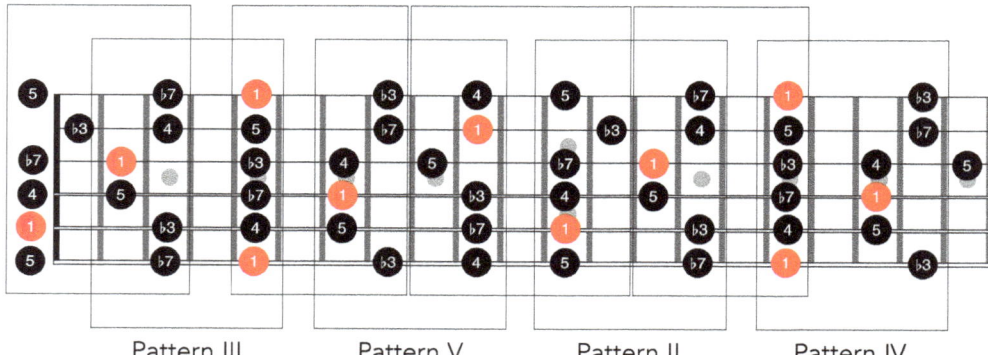

As with the major pentatonic shells, don't feel restricted to playing inside one minor pentatonic shell at a time. You should explore the fretboard using the minor pentatonic shells and learn how to move from one shell to the next one higher and the next one lower. Adapt the same practice tips you learned for the major pentatonic shells presented earlier in this Module. All these exercises are more fun when played with a backing track.

Arpeggios

In the last Module you learned that an arpeggio is a chord broken into a melodic sequence of notes. Instead of playing the notes of a chord simultaneously in a "block" format, the individual components (the chord tones) are played one at a time.

You learned the Patterns I and III major triad arpeggios. Major triad arpeggios will serve as the foundation for major 7th, dominant 7th, and other arpeggios in coming Modules. Arpeggios are important because they can outline the chord as part of a melody or in a solo.

In this Module you will learn two minor triad arpeggios: Patterns II and IV. From these two triad arpeggios you will eventually learn minor 7th, minor major 7th arpeggios, and other arpeggios in future Modules.

Here are the Patterns II and IV minor triad arpeggio. When practicing these, make sure to use strict alternate picking.

Pattern II Minor Triad Arpeggio

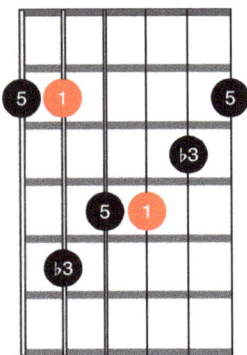

Pattern IV Minor Triad Arpeggio

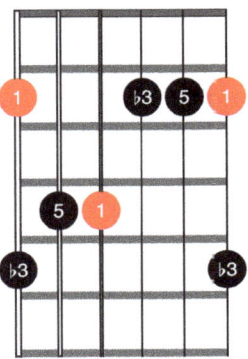

Later in the Level 2 Improvisation Modules the focus will shift to soloing with chord tones as an addition to the key-center solo approach. Arpeggios will come in to play in a very important way as you move through the program. Arpeggios are by definition chord tones, and you will rely heavily on them. Learn them so you have them under your fingers when the focus shifts to chord-tone soloing.

Chords

In the last two Units you used your knowledge of the three super shapes for major triads and the three super shapes for minor triads to play short progressions. By using three-string triad shapes, you were able to keep your physical movement from chord to chord to a minimum.

Smooth Voice Leading

Another positive result from being efficient in your movement is called "smooth voice leading". Voice leading is a term that refers to the movement of each individual voice of a chord to the next chord. With smooth voice leading, the distance is minimal.

Here is a progression that we looked at previously: G-C-D.

Progression in G Major

The first way you played this was using the 1-2-3 string set moving between voicings from the three major super shapes.

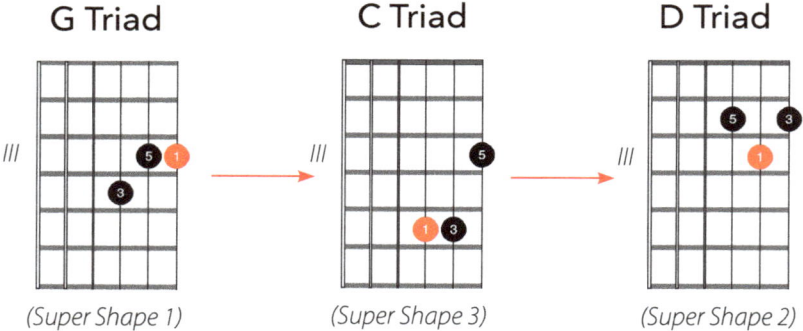

Look at this a slightly different way. Imagine each string as a "voice"—a part that a vocalist might sing. Look at how the voice on each string moves from chord to chord. Let's use the same set of triads to illustrate the concept.

On the 1st string of the G triad play G at the 3rd fret. On the 1st string for the next chord, the C triad, play the same note, G, at the 3rd fret. In other words, that voice doesn't move at all, and that is good. On the 1st string for the next chord, the D triad, the voice only moves a half step down to F#. The voice on the 1st string in these three chords goes G-G-F#. That is smooth voice leading. The 1st string voice moves a very short distance.

Voice Leading on the 1st String

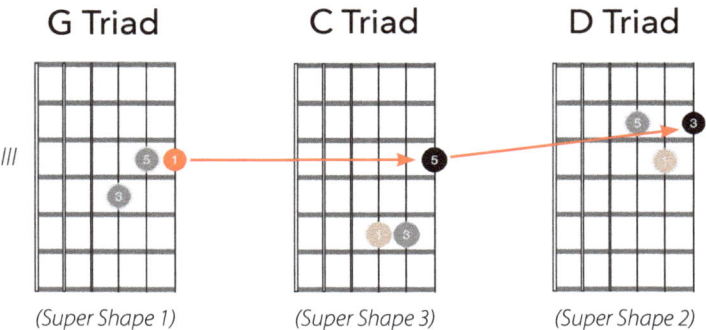

On the 2nd string of the G triad play D at the 3rd fret. On the 2nd string for the next chord, the C triad, move up a 2 frets to E at the 5th fret. This voice moves up a whole step. On the 2nd string for the next chord, the D triad, move back down a whole step to D at the 3rd fret. The voice on the 2nd string in these three chords moves D-E-D. That is smooth voice leading. The voice on the 2nd string moves a very short distance.

Voice Leading on the 2nd String

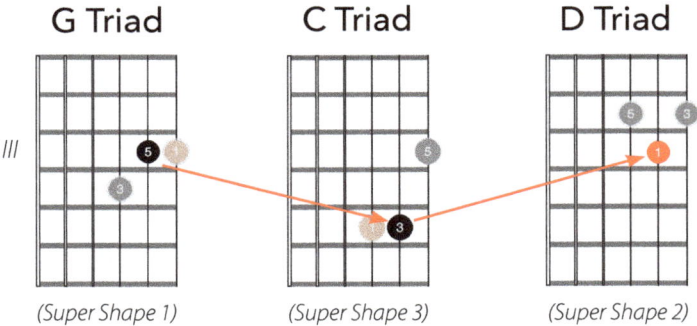

On the 3rd string for the G triad play B at the 4th fret. On the 3rd string for the next chord, the C triad, move up a half step to C at the 5th fret. That voice moves up a half step. On the 3rd string for the next chord, the D triad, move back down a minor 3rd to A at the 2nd fret. The voice on the 3rd string in these three chords moves B-C-A. That' is smooth voice leading - but not as smooth as the 1st ad 2nd strings. The voice on the 3rd string moves a very short distance.

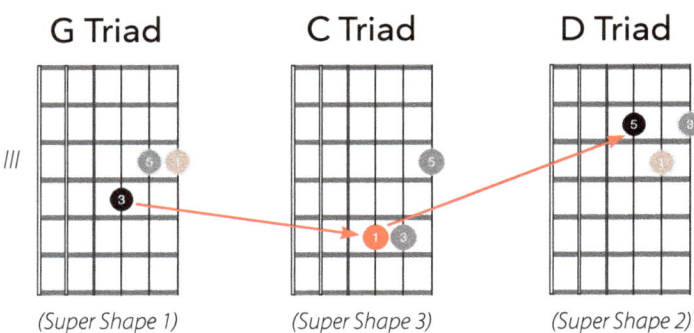

Keyboard players are naturally adept at smooth voice leading because that is the way they learn chords. Guitarists are generally self-taught and learn big block barre chords that slide up and down the neck. This simple explanation of voice leading can make a big difference in how you think about using voicings. When making decisions about what chord voicings to use in a chord progression, consider looking for shapes that are physically close to each other on the fretboard and check out the voice leading. There will be more on this later in the program.

Interval Shapes on the Fretboard

Continue your study of interval shapes on the fretboard with the perfect 4th, augmented 4th, perfect 5th, and diminished 5th shapes on adjacent strings in the top three-string region of the fretboard. Remember that the interval between the 2nd and 3rd strings is a major 3rd, making the interval shapes between them different from the shapes between all of the other strings.

Perfect 4th Interval

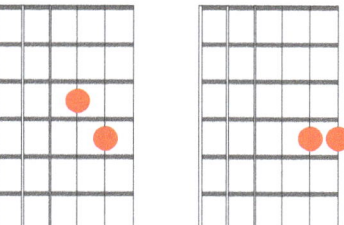

Augmented 4th Interval

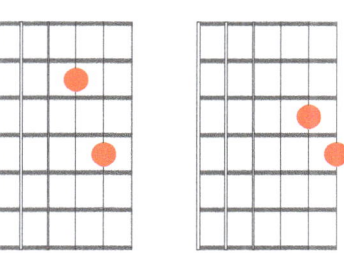

Diminished 5th Interval

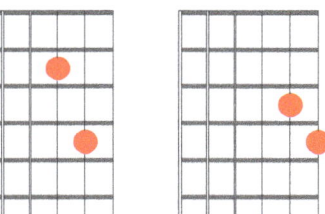

Perfect 5th Interval

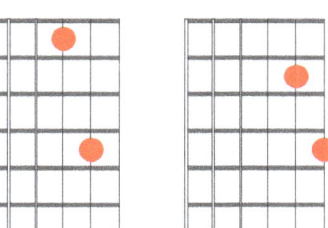

Augmented 5th Interval

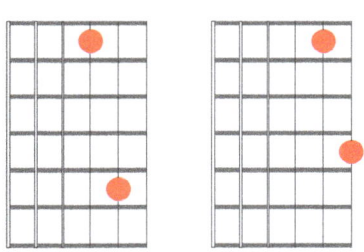

TECHNIQUE

You have learned alternate picking for 8th notes, 8th-note triplets, and 16th notes. In this Module you will apply alternate picking to 16th-note triplets. Just to review, a quarter note divided into two parts results in two 8th notes. An 8th note divided into two parts is two 16th notes. An 8th note divided into three parts results in three 16th-note triplets.

16th-note triplets are notated with a "3" above (or below) the notes. Remember, there is a wide variety of ways triplets are written: The 3 is sometimes under and sometimes above a bracket or curved line and sometimes the bracket or curved line is broken in the middle to make a place for the 3. Expect to see many different styles of triplet notation, but there will always be the number 3.

There are six 16th-note triplets per quarter note (or beat) in 4/4 time: Three on the first half of the beat and three on the second half. When applying strict alternate picking to 16th-note triplets, the first 16th note is a down stroke, the second 16th note is an up stroke and the third 16th note is a down stroke. Now you are ready to start the second half of the beat. Your last attack on the third 16th note was a down stoke so play the first 16th note of the second half with an up stroke, the second 16th note with a down stroke, and the third 16th note with an up stroke.

Occasionally when playing rhythm guitar, I'll reverse the alternate-picking pattern

16th-Note Triplet Picking Pattern

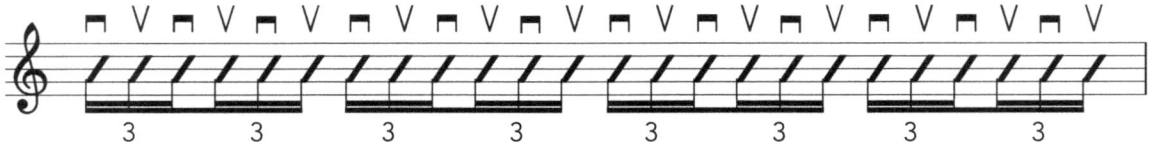

because it allows me to make a strong accent on the "and" with a down stroke. When doing this, I play the first 16th note with an up stroke, the second 16th note with a down stroke, and the third 16th note with an up stroke. Then, for the second half of the beat, the first 16th note will be a down stroke, the second 16th note will be an up stroke, and the third 16th note will be a down stroke.

RHYTHM NOTATION

In the last Module you learned that written music should "look the way it sounds" – both melodically and rhythmically – and for notating rhythm there are two key aspects to focus on: spacing and grouping. In this Module you'll learn how to approach clear notation with regard to these two aspects. These examples use the familiar 4/4 time signature to introduce the rules for spacing and grouping.

If music is written and organized as clearly, musicians can focus more attention on the performance and less on deciphering the notation.

In the last Module you learned these important points:

- When the smallest note or rest value in a measure is a quarter note, there is no rule about grouping but spacing is important.
- Beams are used in place of flags when grouping notes smaller than a quarter note together.
- When the smallest note or rest value in a measure is an 8th note, beat three must be shown with a note or rest. If a note is carried over from the beat or beats before, a tie is used to extend the note from the first half of the measure to the symbol on beat three.
- Beams cannot cross from beat two to beat three when the smallest note or rest value in a measure is an 8th note.

Here is an example in 4/4 time and the rhythms are written poorly. All of the notes add up to four beats but the grouping and spacing are wrong and beat three is not shown clearly. Remember the rule: If the smallest note (or rest) value in a measure is an 8th note, beat three must be shown with either a note or rest, even if there is a note or rest being sustained from earlier in the measure.

In this case the two 8th notes should be beamed together because they both belong

to beat one. The half note occupies two beats, which means it is sustained across the line between beats two and three—the middle of the measure. Because beat three needs to be shown with a symbol (either a note or rest), the half note must be broken into two quarter notes. Then they are tied together to achieve the same duration of a half note.

The reader now has a reference point on beat three in the middle of the measure. This is important when reading music and trying to stay locked with the time, whether that's marked by tapping the foot on all four beats, listening to a click, or watching a conductor. To complete the measure, the quarter note stands alone in the space for beat four.

Here is another example in 4/4 time. There are six 8th notes and a quarter note. A first glance it seems like all the 8th notes could be beamed together but that would result in a beam from beat two to beat three, crossing the middle of the measure. You just learned that beat three must be shown when an 8th note or rest is present in a measure. To ensure that beat three is shown, beams can never cross the line from beat two to beat three.

For more demonstration of writing measures with 8th-note rhythms correctly, go to the exercise tab below the Level 2 Unit 7 Rhythm Notation video on the FredboardBiology.com website and do as many of these as possible.

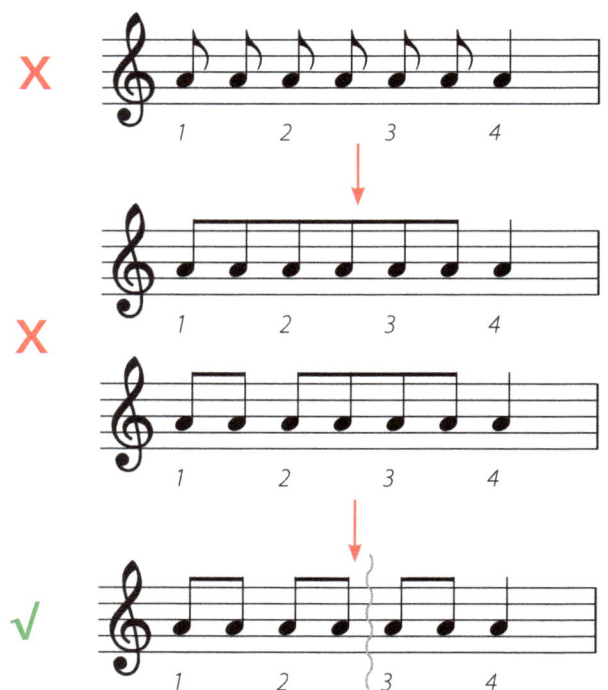

RHYTHM GUITAR

Rock rhythm guitar does not have to be complicated. There are intricate parts in some mainstream Classic Rock, but our goal here is to understand the foundations from which you can build all kinds of parts. Remember that Rock rhythm guitar is primarily about attitude and sound. Because much of the Classic Rock repertoire is written on guitar, "guitar friendly" keys like E, A, and D are common. These keys use the fullness of the open strings in E, A, and D chords. The open-A chord is iconic in Rock. It sounds great with the whole range of tones, from clean to full distortion. And because it's in the middle register, its a great fit between the bass guitar and any instrument played in a higher register or vocals.

Here is an example that uses a classic power-chord voicing using the open A on the 5th string and E on the 4th string, 2nd fret. It is mixed with a classic-sounding Bluesy riff on the 5th and 6th strings. The 8th-note groove should be played with all down strokes. Pull C on the 5th string and G on the 6th string a little sharp with your 2nd finger for some added attitude.

Progression in A Major

Add to that example with a second section. This mixes more power chords and a short riff.

Progression in A Major

This part draws from several Classic Rock rhythm songs. The open-A power chord and the notes around it can be manipulated a lot of different ways. When in the key of A, mimicking this part will come in handy.

Level 2 Unit 7 • Rhythm Demo

IMPROVISATION

In the Technique Module for this Unit, alternate picking for a 16th-note triplet subdivision is introduced. Here is a 16th-note triplet groove in A minor. It is a repeating four-bar phrase. Use the 16th-note triplet alternate-picking pattern you have learned. This groove is sometimes called a "16th-note shuffle".

Progression in A Minor

Practice playing with the track two different ways:

- First, find a pattern of A minor pentatonic or the A Blues scale you like.
- Focusing on your picking hand, play 16th-note triplet lines to get familiar with the 16th-note triplet subdivision and add some syncopation staying true to the alternate-picking pick-direction rules.
- Second, create a 32-bar solo. That is eight times through the four-bar phrase. Either a clean or overdrive sound will work fine. Record it and listen back check for good time and feel and for how well you told a story.

A Minor Pentatonic Scales

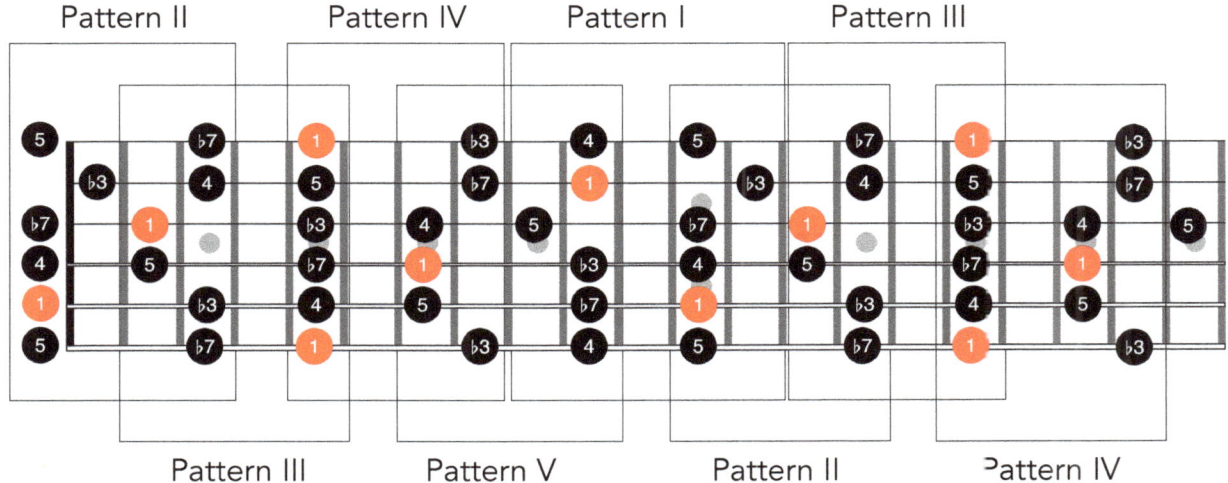

Level 2 Unit 7 • Example Solo

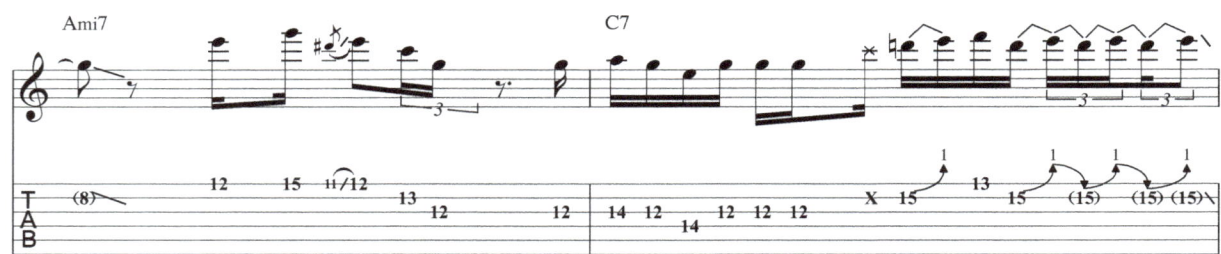
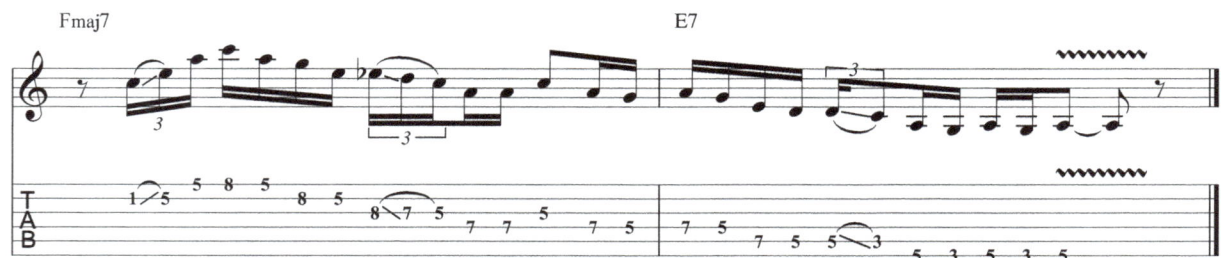

PRACTICE

Theory

- ❏ Go to the tabs below the Theory video on the website and complete the quiz.
- ❏ Understand the emotional effect of the three chord families: tonic, dominant, and subdominant.
- ❏ Practice analyzing chord progressions in major keys.

Fretboard Logic

- ❏ Understand how the pentatonic shells fit together on the fretboard.
- ❏ Understand the concept of arpeggios and learn the Pattern II and Pattern IV minor triad arpeggios.
- ❏ Continue learning to use super shapes and the triads within each of them.
- ❏ Learn and practice smooth voice leading in all progressions you play.
- ❏ Memorize the 4th and 5th interval shapes on adjacent top three strings. Use the exercise in the tabs below the video to practice your recognition of intervals on the fretboard.
- ❏ Look at how the new information from this Unit relates to the everything else in the Octave Shape Family Tree.

Technique

- ❏ Practice playing with a syncopated 16th-note triplet pattern using strict alternate picking.

Rhythm Notation

- ❏ Learn proper grouping in measures containing 8th notes.

Rhythm Guitar

- ❏ Learn common riffs using the open-A power chord.

Improvisation

- ❏ Create a 16-bar solo using your choice of patterns of the A minor scales. As always, record yourself and listen back.

UNIT 8

Learning Modules

> **Theory** - Harmonizing the Minor Scale, Analyzing Chord Progressions in Minor Keys

> **Fretboard Logic** - How the Major and Minor Natural Scales Fit Together on the Fretboard, Patterns II, IV, and V Major Triad Arpeggios, Voice Leading, Intervals: 6ths on Non-Adjacent Top Four Strings

> **Technique** - Alternate Picking with Syncopated 16th-Note Triplets

> **Rhythm Notation** - Note Grouping with 16th-Note Measures

> **Rhythm Guitar** - Classic Rock, 1st Inversion Power Chords

> **Improvisation** - Soloing with 8th-Note Shuffle Groove

> **Practice** - Continue Practice Routine Development

THEORY

In an earlier Unit you learned to harmonize the major scale. In this Unit you will learn to harmonize the natural minor scale. To understand the harmonic structure of a song in a minor key, it is essential to understand the harmonized minor scale. This provides the knowledge required to arrange, create solid chord parts, solo, and improvise.

The Harmonized Minor Scale

To harmonize a scale, build chords on each scale degree. As with the major scale, in the natural minor scale a chord built on the first scale degree is called the I chord. To harmonize it, find the diatonic notes from the scale that are a 3rd higher and a 5th higher; this forms a triad and triad's quality is determined by the combination of qualities of the two intervals.

A chord built on the 2nd scale degree is called the II chord, and so on, with each note in the natural minor scale: I, II, ♭III, IV, V, ♭VI, and ♭VII. The resulting seven chords are called the harmonized natural minor scale. As you learned earlier, chords are numbered with Roman numerals. When numbering chords, also write an abbreviation for the quality. Use "ma" for a major triad, "mi" for a minor triad, "+" for an augmented triad, and " ° " for a diminished triad.

The notes used to build each chord are diatonic notes, meaning "of the scale". Follow the same procedure used to harmonize the major scale when harmonizing the natural minor scale.

First, examine the C natural minor scale. The scale degrees are numbered one through seven: 1, 2, ♭3, 4, 5, ♭6, and ♭7. Notice ♭3, ♭6, and ♭7; these scale degrees differ from the major scale.

C Minor Scale

The I Chord

Start with the 1st scale degree, C.

Find the note a 3rd above C, and it has to be from the key, which is C minor. The note is E♭, the 3rd of the triad. Next, find the note that is a 5th above C, and it has to be from the C minor scale, too. That note is G. This the 5th of the triad.

Analyze the intervals and then compare them to the triad interval formulas. E♭ is a minor 3rd above C and G is a perfect 5th above C. The triad with a minor 3rd and a perfect 5th is a minor triad.

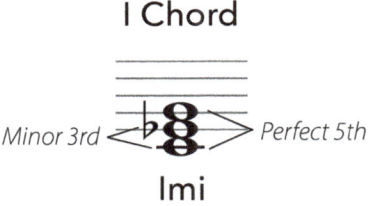

Conclusion: The I chord is minor. Label it Imi.

The II Chord

Build the II chord. Start with the 2nd scale degree, D.

The II Chord

Find the note a 3rd above D from the key of C minor. The note is F, the 3rd of the triad. Next, find the note that's a 5th above D from the scale. That note is A♭. This the 5th of the triad.

The II Chord

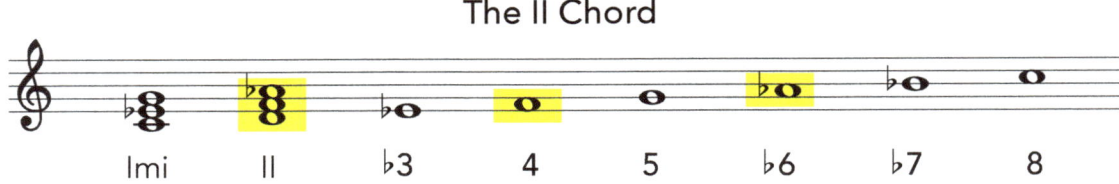

Analyze the intervals and then compare them to the triad interval formulas. F is a minor 3rd above D and A is a diminished 5th above D. The triad with a minor 3rd and a diminished 5th is a diminished triad.

II Chord

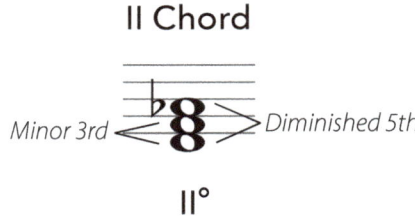

II°

Conclusion: The II chord is diminished. Label it II°.

The ♭III Chord

Build the ♭III chord. It is ♭III because it is built on the flatted (lowered) 3rd scale degree. Start with the flat 3rd scale degree of the C minor scale, which is E♭.

Find the note a 3rd above E♭ from the key of C minor. That note is G, the 3rd of the triad. Next, find the note a 5th above E♭ from the key of C minor. The note is B♭ and it is the 5th of the triad.

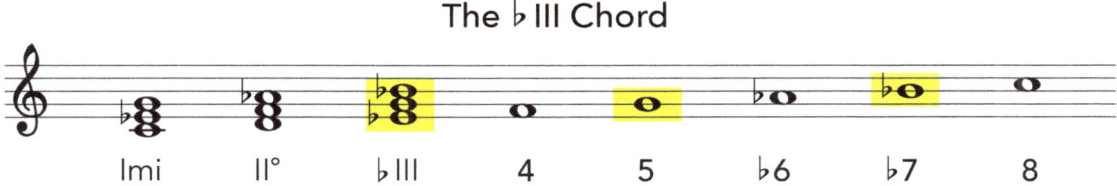

Analyze the intervals and then compare them to the triad interval formulas. G is a major 3rd above E and B♭ is a perfect 5th above E. The triad with a major 3rd and a perfect 5th is a major triad.

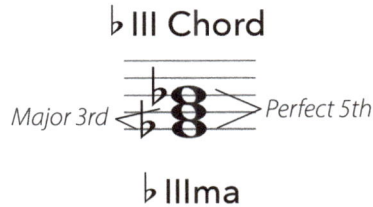

Conclusion: The ♭III chord is major. Label it ♭IIIma.

The IV Chord

Build the IV chord. Start with the 4th scale degree, F.

The IV Chord

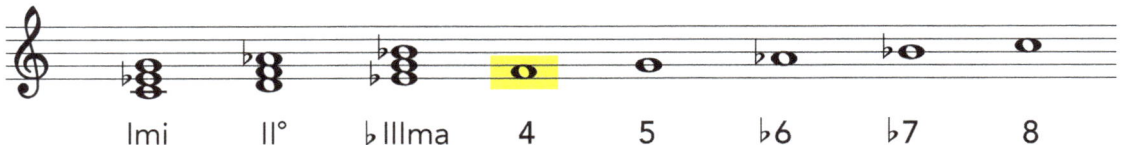

Find the note a 3rd above F from the key of C minor. The note is A♭, the 3rd of the triad. Next, find the note a 5th above F from the C minor scale. That note is C, the 5th of the triad.

The IV Chord

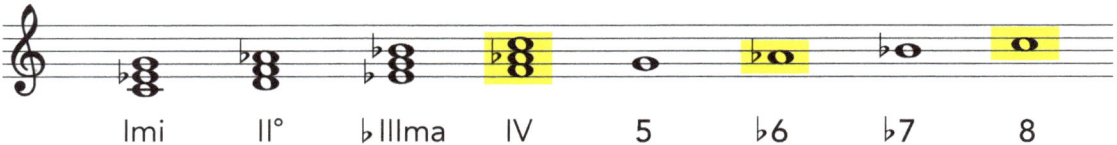

Analyze the intervals and then compare them to the triad interval formulas. A♭ is a minor 3rd above F and C is a perfect 5th above F. The triad with a minor 3rd and a perfect 5th is a minor triad.

IV Chord

IVmi

Conclusion: The IV chord is minor. Label it IVmi.

The V Chord

Build the V chord. Start with the 5th scale degree, G.

The V Chord

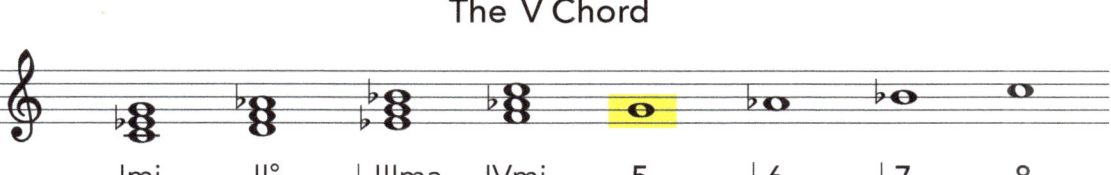

Find the note that a 3rd above G from the key, C minor, B♭. This the 3rd of the triad. Next, find the note a 5th above G from the C minor scale. That note is D, the 5th of the triad.

The V Chord

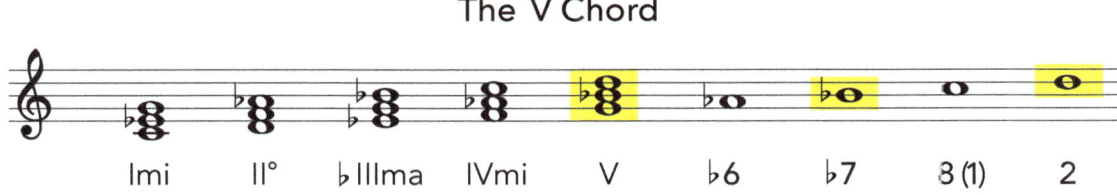

Analyze the intervals and then compare them to the triad interval formulas. B♭ is a minor 3rd above G and D is a perfect 5th above G. The triad with a minor 3rd and a perfect 5th is a minor triad.

V Chord

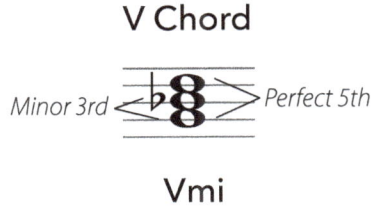

Vmi

Conclusion: The V chord is minor. Label it Vmi.

Note that often a major triad is used as the V chord in a minor key. This is a result of a brief entrance into the harmonic minor scale for the duration of the V chord only. This will be discussed in great detail later.

The ♭VI Chord

Build the ♭VI chord. Start with the flatted 6th scale degree, which is A♭.

Find the note a 3rd above A♭ from the key of C minor. The note is C, the 3rd of the triad. Next, find the note a 5th above A♭ from the C minor scale. That note is E♭, the 5th of the triad.

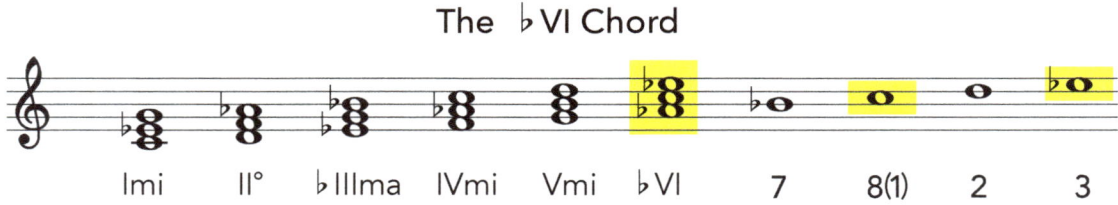

Analyze the intervals and then compare them to the triad interval formulas. C is a major 3rd above A♭ and E♭ is a perfect 5th above A♭. The triad with a major 3rd and a perfect 5th is a major triad.

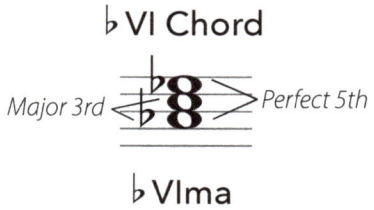

Conclusion: The ♭VI chord is major. Label it ♭VIma.

The ♭VII Chord

Finally, build the ♭VII chord. Start with the flatted 7th scale degree, which is B♭.

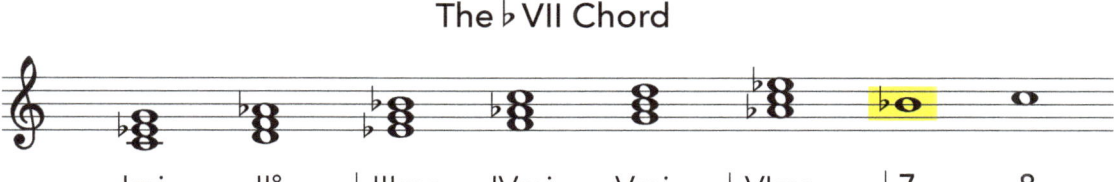

Find the note a 3rd above B♭ from the key of C minor. The note is D, the 3rd of the triad. Next, find the note a 5th above B♭ from the C minor scale. The note is F. This the 5th of the triad.

Analyze the intervals and then compare them to the triad interval formulas. D is a major 3rd above B♭ and F is a perfect 5th above B♭. The triad with a major 3rd and a perfect 5th is a major triad.

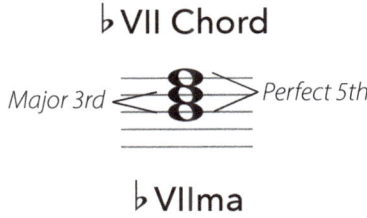

Conclusion? The ♭VII chord is major. Label it ♭VIIma.

The Harmonized C Minor Scale

Here is the harmonized C minor scale:

The Harmonized C Minor Scale

Imi   II°   ♭IIIma   IVmi   Vmi   ♭VIma   ♭VIIma   Imi

- The I chord is minor
- II is diminished
- ♭III is major
- IV is minor
- V is minor
- ♭VI is major
- ♭VII is major

These chords are diatonic to the key of C natural minor. If you repeat this process on any other Natural Minor scale tonic, the result will be the same. The I chord will always be minor, the II chord will always be diminished, the ♭III chord will always be major, the IV chord will always be minor, the V chord will always be minor, the ♭VI chord will always be major, and the ♭VII chord will always be major.

Memorize this. There is no way around it. But here is a little trick that might help. In a minor key:

- I, IV, and V are all minor triads
- II is diminished
- The rest are major: ♭III, ♭VI, and ♭VII

Keep in mind, there are situations in minor keys where progressions use a V major instead of V minor. That topic will be discussed in great detail later.

Harmonic Analysis

Now that you know the harmonized Natural Minor scale, harmonic analysis for chord progressions in minor keys is now possible. This important skill is used for understanding what notes to play when improvising, playing chords, or arranging in minor keys. For this reason, you need to know the chords in all minor keys. In other words, you should be able to answer questions like: What is the IV chord in Gmi? Or what is the ♭VI chord in Fmi? And similar questions for all chords in any key.

Because key signatures determine the notes of every key and because the qualities of the chords built on each scale degree is the same in all minor keys, any chord (I through ♭VIIma) in any minor key can be identified easily.

To prepare for harmonic analysis, quiz yourself on what chords are diatonic in every minor key. Your knowledge of the chord qualities of the harmonized minor scale combined with your knowledge of all minor scales (because of your understanding of key signatures), helps you answer questions such as:

- What is the II chord in Dmi?
- What is the V chord in Emi?
- What is the ♭VII chord in Bmi?
- What is IV chord in Fmi?
- What is the ♭III chord in Gmi?
- What is the ♭VI chord in C#mi?

Chord Function

The collection of notes in the minor scale and the chords that result from harmonizing it are called "the minor diatonic system" and you need to know it for harmonic analysis in minor keys. As you learned in the last Unit, chords in diatonic systems belong to one of three families:

- Tonic
- Subdominant
- Dominant

Here are the chord families in the minor diatonic system. This should look very similar to the chord families in major, with a slight difference:

- The tonic family is the family of the I chord. The ♭IIIma chord is a member of the tonic family as well. (Note that the ♭VIma chord isn't part of the tonic family as it is in the major diatonic system.)
- The subdominant family is the family of the IV chord. The IIdim and ♭VIma chords are subdominant chords, too. (Note that the ♭VIma chord is included, unlike in the major diatonic system.)

- The dominant family is the family of the V chord. The ♭VIIma chord is part of the dominant family, too.

Chord Families in Minor

FAMILY	MEMBERS	EMOTIONAL EFFECT
Tonic	I, ♭III	At home, resolved
Subdominant	IV, II, ♭VI	Moving away from tonic
Dominant	V, ♭VII	Moving toward tonic

Earlier you learned that a chord's number is often referred to as its function, because function refers to the emotional effect a chord has on the listener when heard in the context of the key. With that in mind:

- The function of Imi or ♭IIIma – both members of the tonic family – is to establish a feeling of home or rest.
- The function of IVmi, II°, or ♭VIma – all members of the subdominant family – is to give the listener a feeling of moving away from home.
- The function of Vmi or ♭VIIma – both members of the dominant family – is to pull the listener back toward home.

If a chord is identified as Imi or ♭IIIma chord, it means more than just a chord built on the 1st or flat 3rd scale degree. It means it is a chord that evokes a feeling of rest or home. Similarly, a chord identified as IVmi, II°, or ♭VIma means more than just a chord built on the 4th, 2nd, or flat 6th scale degree. It means it is a chord that gives the listener a feeling of moving away from home. If a chord is identified as Vmi or ♭VIIma chord, it means more than just a chord built on the 5th or flat 7th scale degree. It means it is a chord that gives the listener a feeling of moving toward home. The number means more than just the scale degree of the root; it is also a description of the emotional effect.

Analyzing Chord Progressions

The function indicates the "family" each chord belongs to and therefore its emotional effect, allowing you to substitute a chord from within the family for the original chord written, called reharmonization. You will study this in a later Module. Another benefit of knowing about chord families is to use the arpeggio of another chord within the same family as a melodic device.

It is common to see crude chord charts that have no key signature. Even when you no key signature is written, you need a way to determine the key and there are several ways to accomplish this. As a result, you will also know the function of each chord in a progression.

Don't assume the first chord of a progression is the tonic chord. It is more likely that the final chord of a progression is -- but that is not always the case.

Use the same methodical way to analyze chord progressions in minor keys as you used with major keys. This is slow but thorough.

In the following minor key progression, determine all of the keys to which each chord could belong. In this progression, that is A minor.

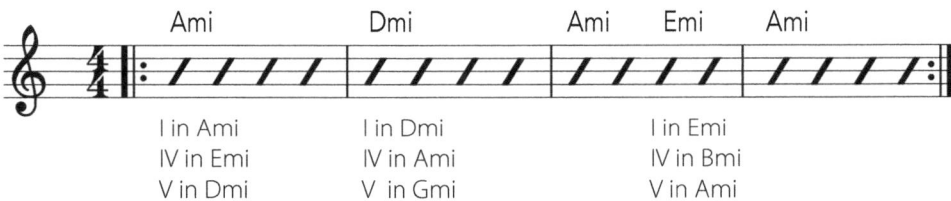

Ami	Dmi	Ami Emi	Ami
I in Ami	I in Dmi	I in Emi	
IV in Emi	IV in Ami	IV in Bmi	
V in Dmi	V in Gmi	V in Ami	

Look at another. In this minor key progression, determine all of the keys to which each chord could belong. That is D minor. There are other clues in both of these progressions.

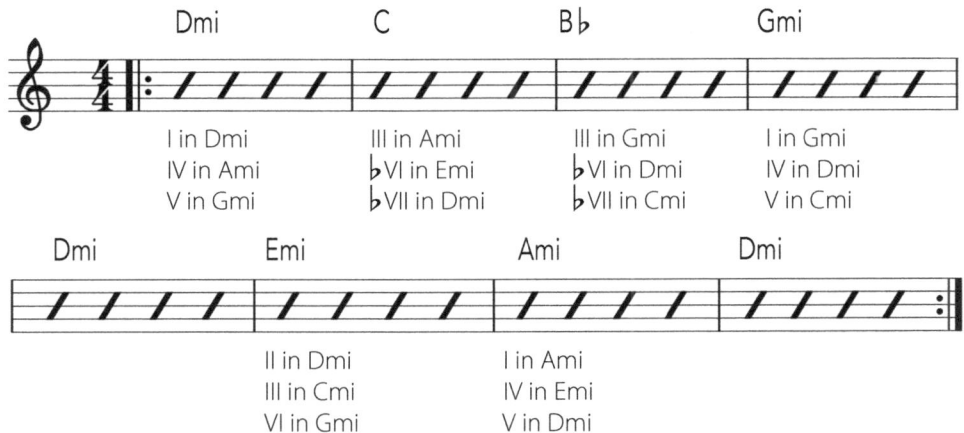

Dmi	C	B♭	Gmi
I in Dmi	III in Ami	III in Gmi	I in Gmi
IV in Ami	♭VI in Emi	♭VI in Dmi	IV in Dmi
V in Gmi	♭VII in Dmi	♭VII in Cmi	V in Cmi

Dmi	Emi	Ami	Dmi
	II in Dmi	I in Ami	
	III in Cmi	IV in Emi	
	VI in Gmi	V in Dmi	

The last chord offers a clue, as it is often the tonic chord, but that is not 100% reliable.

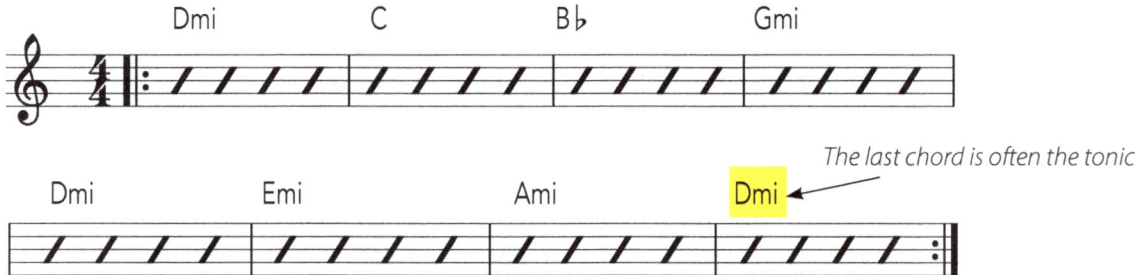

The last chord is often the tonic.

The roots of Gmi and Ami are a whole step apart. There is only one place in the harmonized minor scale where the roots of two minor triads are a whole step apart: IVmi and Vmi. And notice the roots of B♭ and C are a whole step apart. There is only one place in the harmonized minor scale where the roots of two major triads are positioned a whole step apart: ♭VIma and ♭VIIma. Therefore, this progression has to be in the key of Dmi.

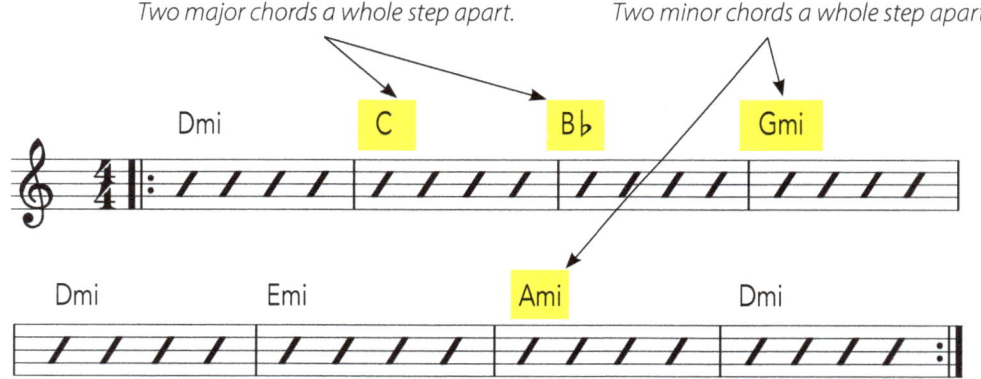

You have reached an important milestone in harmony and theory. You have learned basic harmonic analysis in both major and minor keys. As you do with harmonic analysis for songs in major keys, practice analyzing songs you already know that are in minor keys. Find songs or parts of songs and see if you can figure out each chord's number—its function—which tells you to which chord family each one belongs.

You now know both the harmonized major and minor scales which provides a strong foundation on which to build.

FRETBOARD LOGIC

Scales

The last Unit illustrated the big picture for both major and minor pentatonic scales on the fretboard. The bird's eye perspective is important for understanding how all the patterns fit together. In this Unit the same idea is presented, but this time with the major and natural minor scales.

Here are all of the notes of the C major scale on the fretboard. All of the C's are highlighted. Notice there are no individual patterns highlighted. This is to show how they fit together to form one continuous pattern of notes on the fretboard.

C Major Scales

Next each of the major scale patterns are highlighted to show how they fit with each other.

Pattern I C Major Scale

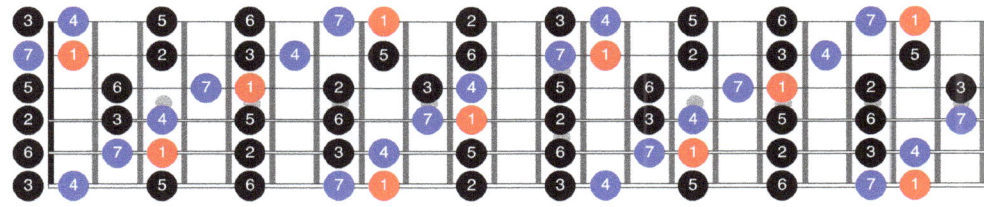

Pattern I

Pattern II C Major Scale

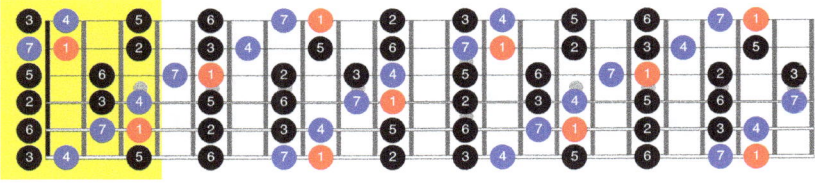

Pattern I

Pattern III C Major Scale

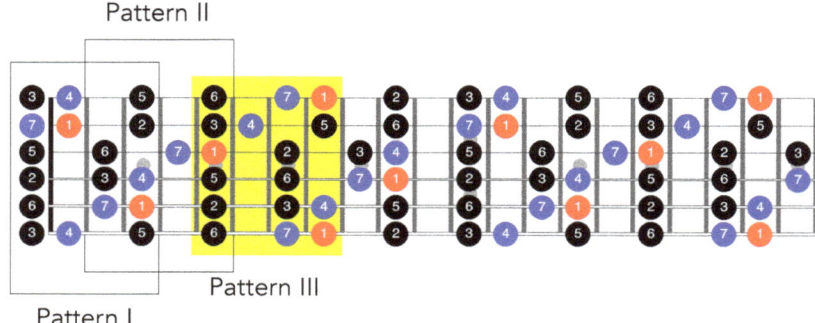

Pattern IV C Major Scale

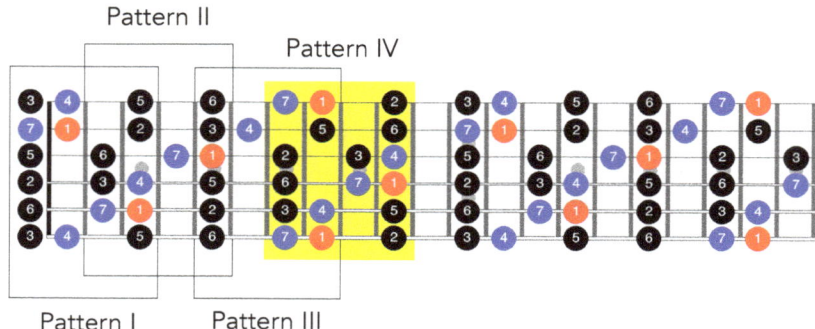

Pattern V C Major Scale

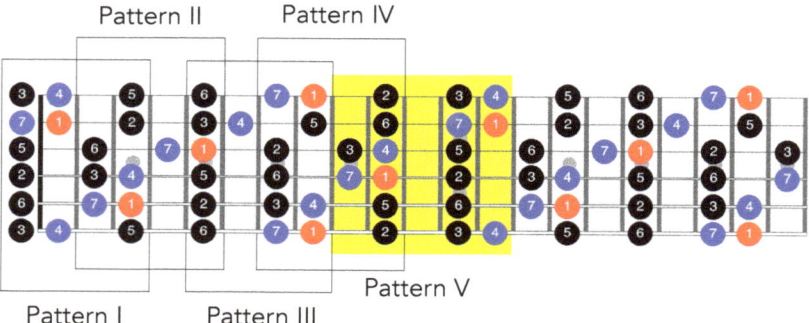

As with the pentatonic shells, these individual scale patterns organize all of the possible notes in a given key within five segments of the fretboard. You should not feel restricted to playing inside one Octave Shape during a solo. Your personal exploration of the fretboard should involve learning how to move from any scale pattern to the next one higher and the next one lower. For example, starting with the C Pattern III major scale in 5th position, experiment moving to the next pattern higher, Pattern IV. Then, start with the C Pattern III major scale in 5th position and experiment moving to the next shell lower, Pattern II.

Each string can be a point of transition between the two shapes. In order to transition from one shell to the adjacent shell (higher or lower) it is important to see the shell you want to move to in advance.

Ascending Transition Exercise

Try this exercise between all of your major scale patterns:

To practice transitioning ascending, start on the lowest tonic of the pattern you choose to start with and play the scale ascending.

- For the first transition, play ascending to the next string higher from where you started. At that point move up into the next pattern higher and continue ascending in the second pattern.
- For the second transition, play ascending to the second string higher from where you started. At that point move up into the next pattern above and continue ascending in the second pattern.
- For the next transition, play ascending to the third string higher from where you started. At that point move up into the next pattern above and continue ascending in the second pattern.
- For the next transition, play ascending to the fourth string higher from where you started. At that point move up into the next pattern above and continue ascending in the second pattern.
- For the next transition, play ascending to the fifth string higher from where you start. At that point move up into the next pattern above and continue ascending in the second pattern.

Descending Transition Exercise

To practice transitioning descending, start on the highest note of the pattern you choose to start with and play the scale descending.

- For the first transition, play descending to the next string lower from where you started. At that point move down into the next pattern below and continue descending in the second pattern.
- For the second transition, play descending to the second string lower from where you started. At that point move down into the next pattern below and continue descending in the second pattern.
- For the next transition, play descending to the third string lower from where you started. At that point move down into the next pattern below and continue descending in the second pattern.
- For the next transition, play descending to the fourth string lower from where you started. At that point move down into the next pattern below and continue descending in the second pattern.

- For the next transition, play descending to the fifth string lower from where you started. At that point move down into the next pattern below and continue descending in the second pattern.

You can repeat this exercise starting with any of the major scale pattern so there are five places to do this. This is just a suggested exercise to help you see the bigger picture of how all the patterns fit together. This will help complete your understanding of the notes in a key. You can make up other exercises as well, like working your way up the scale with one string.

Another good way to explore how the patterns all fit together is to work out with pairs of strings like strings one and two, strings two and three, strings three and four, and so on. All these exercises are more fun when played with a backing track. Go to the library of backing tracks, find a major key progression and have fun.

The five Octave Shape system is only one way to organize the fretboard. It can be organized in a more horizontal way by thinking about transitioning to the next shell higher or lower every other string or randomly. The point is that the five major scale patterns work great for learning the fretboard in a segmented way. Explore and experiment with transitions that work for you.

A Natural Minor Scales

Here are all of the notes possible for A natural minor with every A highlighted. There are no individual Octave Shapes or minor scale patterns shown.

A Natural Minor Scales

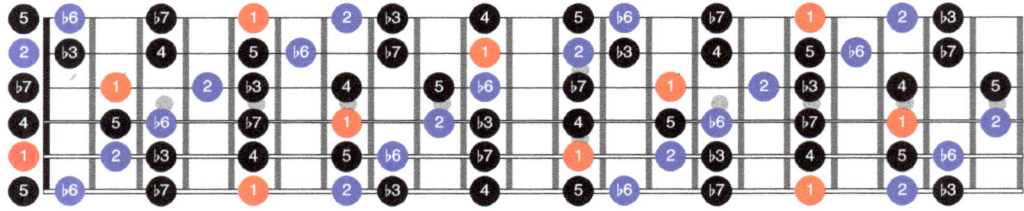

Here are the exact same notes, but in this graphic each minor scale pattern is highlighted. This makes clear again how this vertical approach organizes all of the possible notes within five manageable segments of the neck.

A Natural Minor Scales

As before, do not feel restricted to playing inside one natural minor scale pattern when you solo. You should explore the fretboard with the natural minor scale pattern moving to the pattern above and the pattern below. Adapt the same practice tips presented earlier in this Module. And again, all these exercises are more fun when played with a backing track. Go to the library of backing tracks, find a minor key progression and have fun.

Arpeggios

In this Module you will learn the three remaining major arpeggios: Patterns II, IV, and V. From these triad arpeggios, major 7th and dominant 7th arpeggios can be built.

Here is a Pattern II major triad arpeggio. Add this to your practice routine and be sure to use strict alternate picking.

Pattern II Major Triad Arpeggio

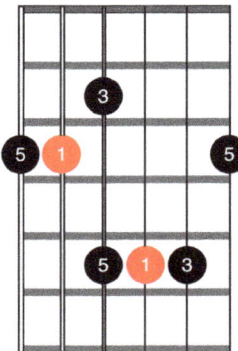

Here is a Pattern IV major triad arpeggio. Add this to your practice routine and be sure to use strict alternate picking..

Pattern IV Major Triad Arpeggio

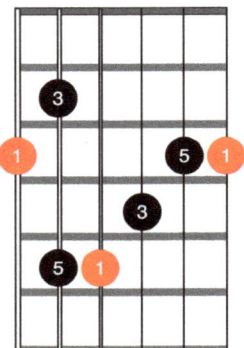

Here is a Pattern V major triad arpeggio. Add this to your practice routine and be sure to use strict alternate picking.

Pattern V Major Triad Arpeggio

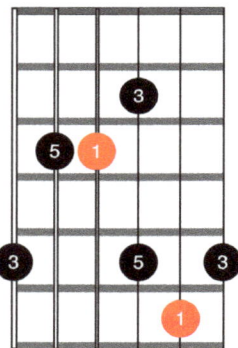

Eventually the focus in the Improvisation Modules will be shift to soloing with chord tones (in addition to key-center soloing) and arpeggios will be the primary tool.

Chords

In the last Unit you learned about smooth voice leading. In this Module, work with a longer chord progression that mixes major and minor chords and create a rhythm guitar part using three-string triad shapes.

Here is the new progression:

Progression in G Minor

The choice of what triads to use is yours but the suggested exercise is to do what we did in Units 5 and 6. Work through the progression six different ways:

1. Use string set 1-2-3, starting with a triad from the first super shape and then playing all subsequent chords as close as possible.

2. Use string set 1-2-3, starting with a triad from the second super shape and then playing all subsequent chords as close as possible.

3. Use string set 1-2-3, starting with a triad from the third super shape and then playing all subsequent chords as close as possible.

4. Use string set 2-3-4, starting with a triad from the first super shape and then playing all subsequent chords as close as possible.

5. Use string set 2-3-4, starting with a triad from the second super shape and then playing all subsequent chords as close as possible.

6. Use string set 2-3-4, starting with a triad from the third super shape and then playing all subsequent chords as close as possible.

Practice these progressions using three-string shapes from the super shapes using smooth voice leading. The goal is for this to feel.

Interval Shapes on the Fretboard

The major and minor 6th intervals in this module cross the line between the 2nd and 3rd strings. They are on non-adjacent strings in the top-four string region of the fretboard. You will recall the interval between the second and third strings is a major 3rd, making the interval shapes between them different from the shapes between the other strings.

Look at 6th intervals between the 4th and 2nd strings. Starting with a minor 6th interval, a minor 6th is one fret lower on the 2nd string, and a major 6th is on the same fret on the 2nd string.

Look at 6th intervals between the 3rd and 1st strings. The shapes are the same as between the 4th and 2nd strings. Starting with a minor 6th interval, a minor 6th is one fret lower on the 1st string, and a major 6th is on the same fret on the 1st string.

There are many great guitar parts that use these shapes. This will be discussed in Improvisation Modules later in the course.

Minor 6th Interval

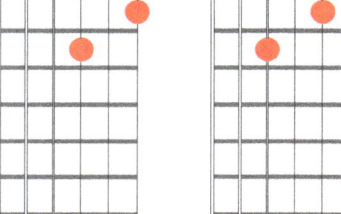

Major 6th Interval

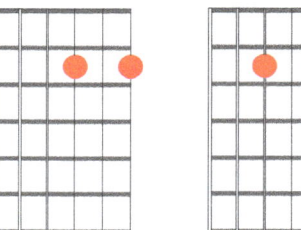

TECHNIQUE

In the last Module you learned how to apply alternate picking to 16th-note triplets. Now you will apply strict alternate picking to syncopated 16th-note triplet rhythms. When applying strict alternate picking to 16th-note triplets, the first 16th note will be a down stroke, the second 16th note will be an up stroke, and the third 16th note will be a down stroke. On the second half of the beat, play the first 16th note with an up stroke, the second 16th note with a down stroke, and the third 16th note with an up stroke.

As with 8th- and 16th-note syncopation, as well as with 8th-note triplet syncopation, regardless of whether there is a note or a rest, the assignment of down strokes and up strokes to each possible 16th-note location in the pattern stays the same. Like this:

16th-Note Syncopated-Triplet Picking Pattern

You have now learned alternate picking and syncopation for the common subdivisions of rhythm. This should serve as a guide for how you play lines and rhythm guitar moving forward. My opinion, as with most things related to technique, is to use alternate picking in a strict way when practicing but do not think about it too much when performing.

RHYTHM NOTATION

Written music should look the way it sounds. In the last Module you put the concept to work: You looked at examples for proper grouping and spacing where the quarter note was the smallest subdivision and also when the 8th note was the smallest subdivision.

In this Module you will learn how to approach proper grouping and spacing when the 16th note is the smallest subdivision. Because of your familiarity with the 4/4 time signature, these examples will be in 4/4.

A couple of Modules ago you learned that when the smallest note or rest value in a measure is a 16th note, each beat must be marked with a note or rest. If a note is carried over from the beat or beats before, a tie is used to extend the note from the first beat to the symbol on the next beat. Beams cannot cross from beat to beat when the smallest note or rest value in a measure is a 16th note.

Here are some poorly-written rhythms that need to be organized so they are clear. Here is how that works.

Example 1

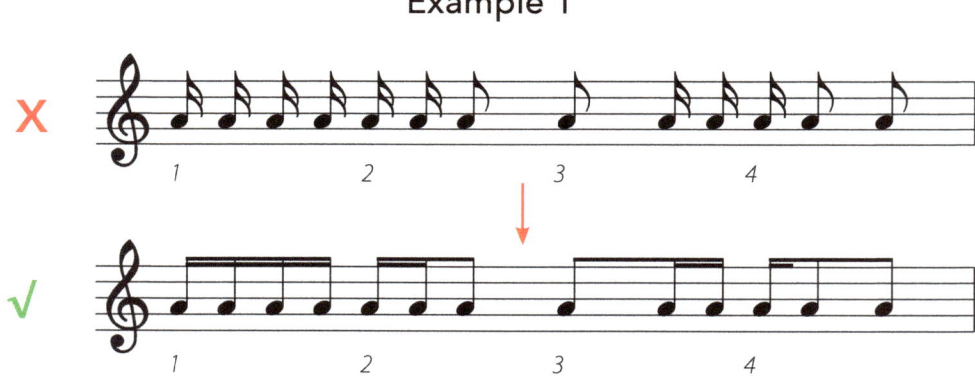

In the example above, all of the beats (1, 2, 3, and 4) are visible, so the main task is to group and space these correctly. A double beam is placed across the four 16th notes in beat one, the 16th and 8th notes are beamed correctly in beats two, three and four. This example shows how to group notes correctly.

Example 2

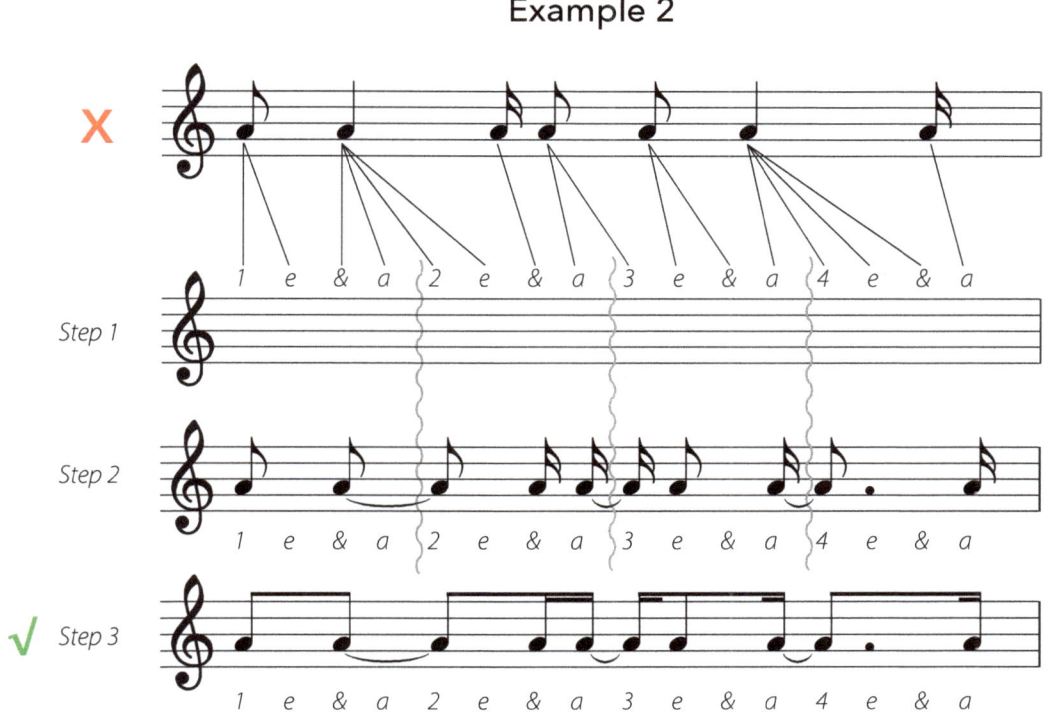

Example 2 is a bit more complicated because some of the beats are not visible. We will use a process similar to the one we did with 8th notes.

In step one, write out each of the subdivisions for each beat. Because the smallest note in this example is a 16th note, subdivide each quarter note into four parts (16th notes) and label them "1 e & a", "2 e & a", and so on. Assign each note in the poorly written example to the location in each beat where it belongs by drawing lines that connect the notes to the "1 e & a", "2 e & a" locations. The first 8th note is be assigned to the beat "1" and the "e" of beat 1. The next quarter note is be assigned to the "&" and "a" of beat one, and the "2" and "e" of beat two, and so one.

In step two, write in the notes showing based on their assignment to locations within the measure --- "1 e & a", "2 e & a", and so on. Use ties where necessary to represent the duration of the notes.

In step three, complete the rewrite. Use beams to group notes together and ties if necessary to show the duration of the notes. All four beats should be visible.

The result is a properly notated measure that is much easier to read. This is another skill that requires repetition. Go to the exercise tab and do as many of these as possible until you feel very confident in your ability to notate rhythms properly.

RHYTHM GUITAR

There is an important voicing that should be part of every guitarist's Rock rhythm guitar vocabulary. It is derived from a triad but the notes are voiced differently than you have learned so far. This voicing is called an "inversion".

Inversions

Inversions will be explained in great detail in a Theory Module later in Fretboard Biology, but here is a brief explanation for now. You learned to build triads by voicing them, lowest to highest, root, 3rd, and a 5th. A chord with the root as the lowest note is said to be in "root position". This is not to be confused with the use of the word position as a location on the fretboard.

For example, here is a B chord in root position:

The B Chord (root position)

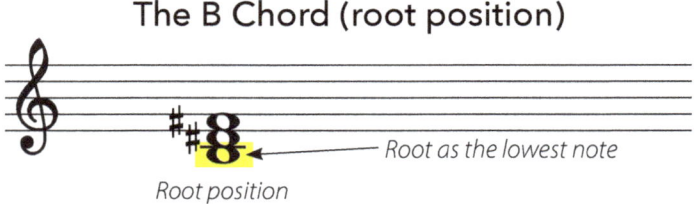

There are occasions where the 3rd or 5th is voiced as the lowest note. If the 3rd is voiced as the lowest note, the chord is voiced in 1st inversion. Here is a B chord in root position and beside it is a B chord in 1st inversion:

The B Chord (1st inversion)

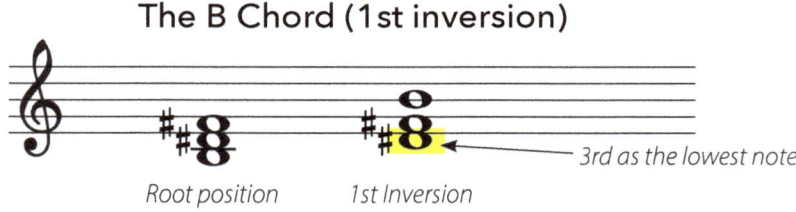

If the 5th is voiced as the lowest note, the chord is voiced in 2nd inversion. Here is a B chord in root position, in 1st inversion, and then in 2nd inversion:

The B Chord (2nd inversion)

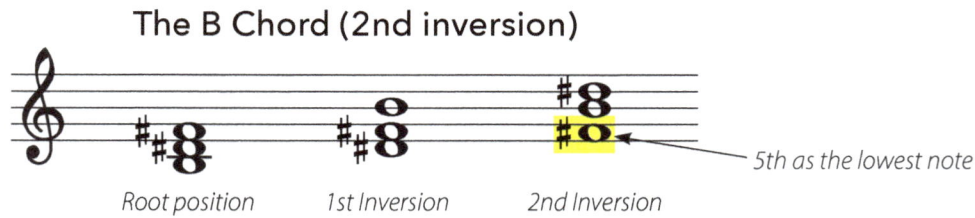

Inversions are often used to create smooth and stepwise bass lines, with the bass guitar, or with a guitar or keyboard part.

Look at this power-chord progression:

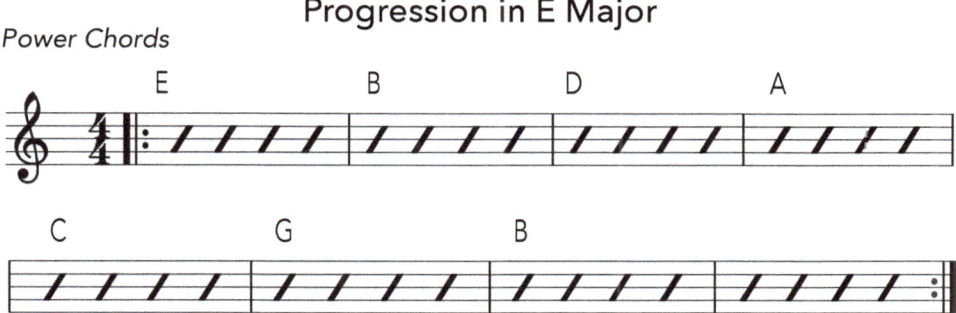

Progression in E Major

There is a common way to play a power-chord progression using inversions. It will use a sort of "quasi"-power chord. Look at each chord individually. Here is the E5 power chord based on a Pattern II Octave Shape:

E5 Power Chord

Pattern II Power Chord

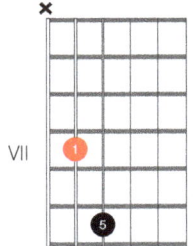

Here is the B5 power chord based on a Pattern IV Octave Shape:

B5 Power Chord

Pattern IV Power Chord

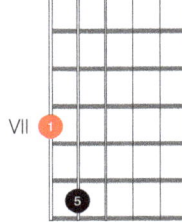

Take another look at the B chord in root position and in 1st inversion. Notice the note voiced at the bottom of the chord – also called the "bass" – is D#?

The B Chord (1st inversion)

1st Inversion — 3rd in the bass

Play the root above it and leave out the 5th.

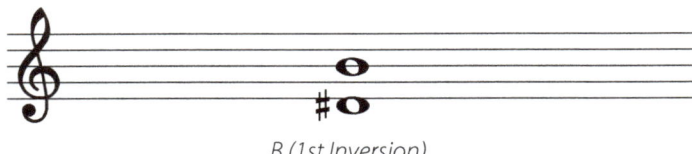

B (1st Inversion)

Starting from the E5 on the first chord the bass note moves from E to D#, a half step, instead of from E down to B, a more angular perfect 4th.

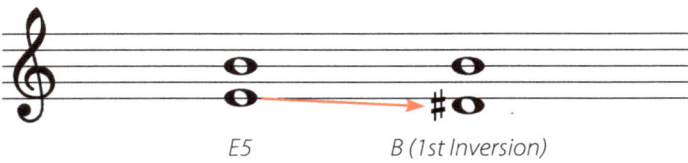

E5   B (1st Inversion)

If you play only two notes, as you do with power chords, the 1st inversion B looks like this:

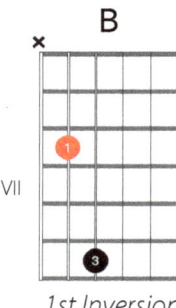

1st Inversion

The move from E5 to 1st inversion B looks like this:

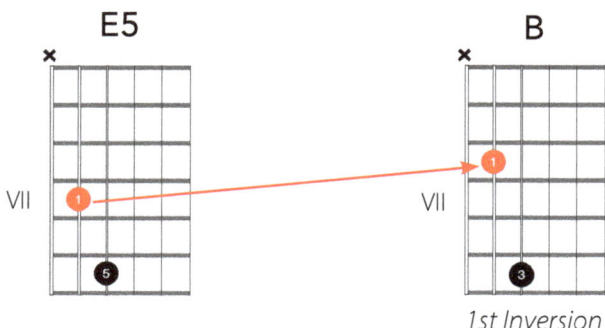

1st Inversion

The next chord is D5, a half step below the D#. The bass line started on E and is moving down in half steps.

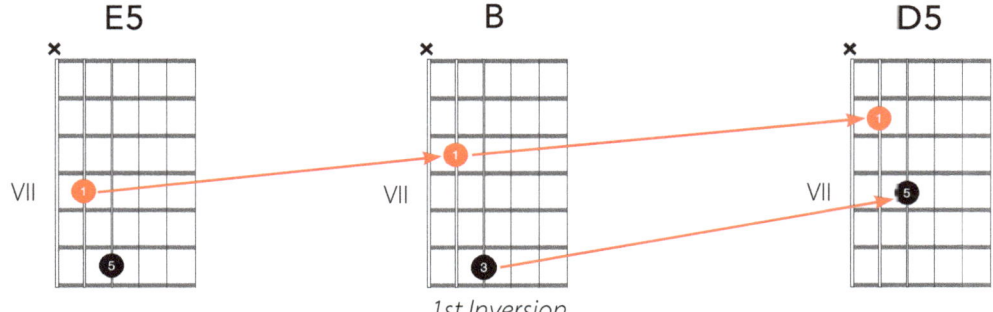

Next, after the D5 power chord is the A5 power chord based on a Pattern IV Octave Shape.

A5 Power Chord
Pattern IV Power Chord

Dissect the A chord in root position:

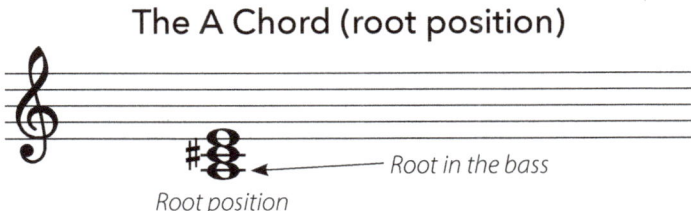

Voice the 3rd in the bass, making it a 1st inversion chord. The note in the bass is now C#. Play the root, A, above it and omit the 5th.

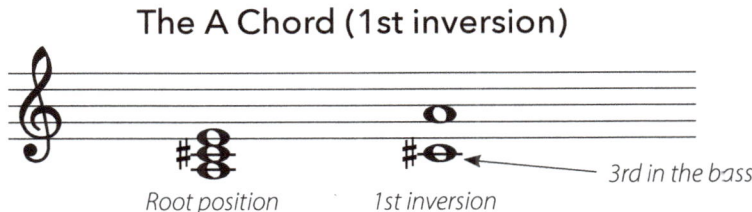

Moving from D, the bass note moves from D to C#, a half step, instead of from D down to A, which is a perfect 4th, which is angular.

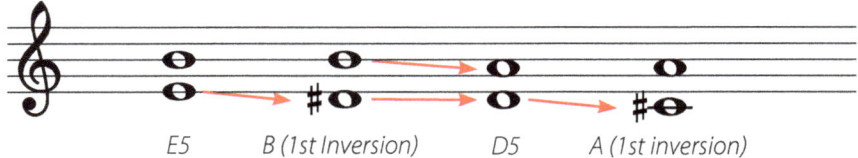

If you just play two notes as you do with power chords, it looks like this:

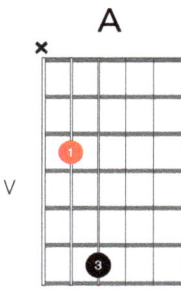

The next chord is C5, a half step below the C#. Like the E5 and D5, it is based on the Pattern II Octave Shape with the root on the 3rd fret of the 5th string. Follow the sequence of chords. The bass line started on E and is moving down in half steps: E-D#-D-C#-C.

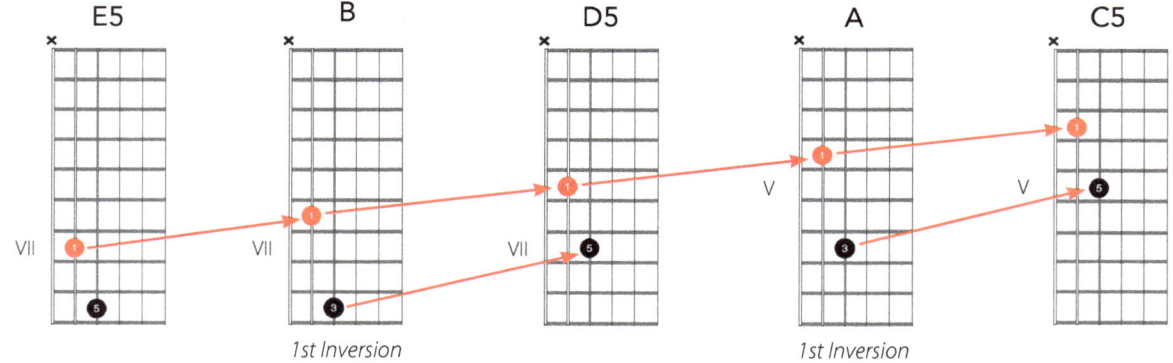

There are two more steps in this progression: the G chord in first inversion, and finally the B chord. The inversion process for is the same for the G chord as it was for the B and A chords, so there is no need to go through all of the steps, but here is the result.

If you play the 3rd in the bass of a G triad, the note in the bass is B. And like with the others, play the root, G, above, and omit the 5th, D.

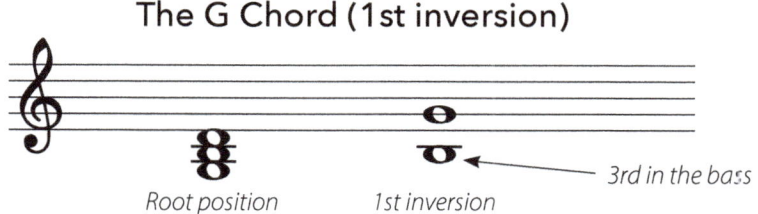

Starting from the C5, the bass note moves from C to B, a half step, instead of from C down to G, a perfect 4th which is more angular. Playing only two notes as you did in the other examples, the sequence looks like this:

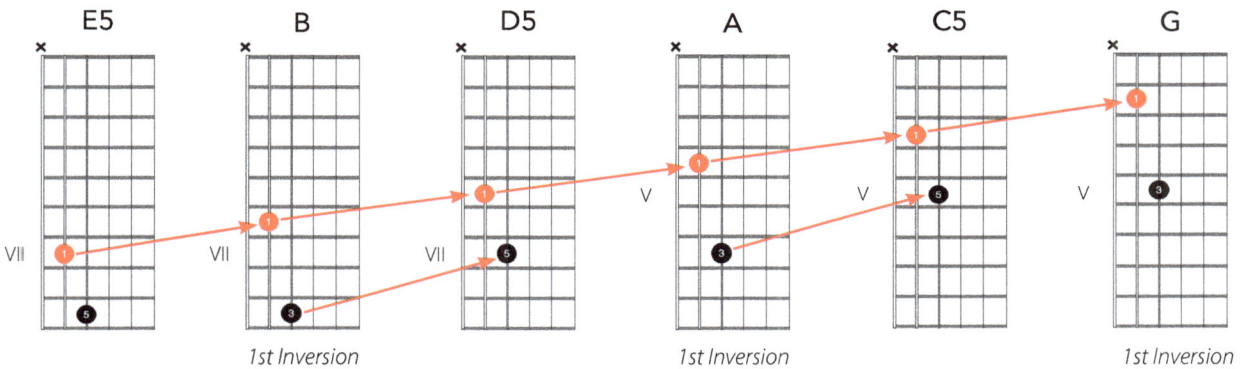

The next and final chord is B, a half step below the C. The bass line started on E and moves down in half steps: E-D#-D-C#-C-B.

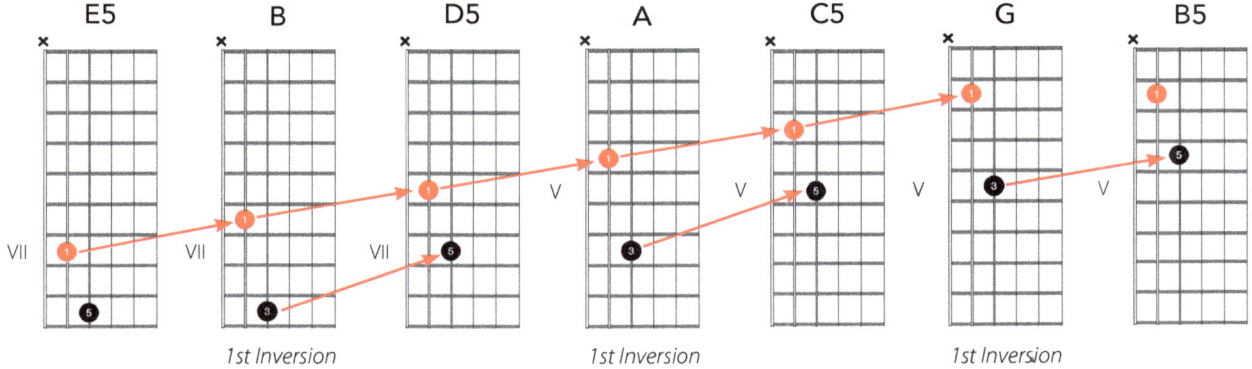

Compare the two ways this can be played. First, with each chord in root position. Second, with the smoother bass lines moving in half steps using inversions.

Chord Progression Bass Line (root position)

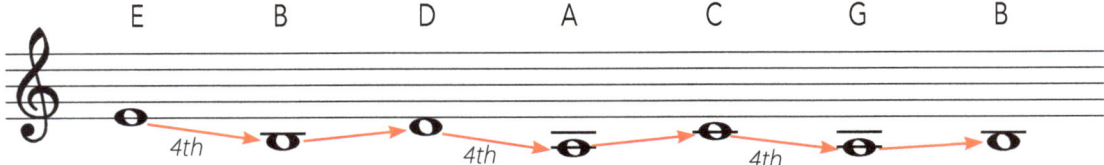

Notice that in the chord progression used here, the bass line between every other chord before we used inversions moved down in perfect 4ths: E down to B is a 4th. D down to A is a 4th. C down to G is a 4th. This makes for an angular bass line

By using 1st inversion on the second chord of each of the pairs it is possible to create a smooth bass line.

Chord Progression Bass LIne (using inversions)

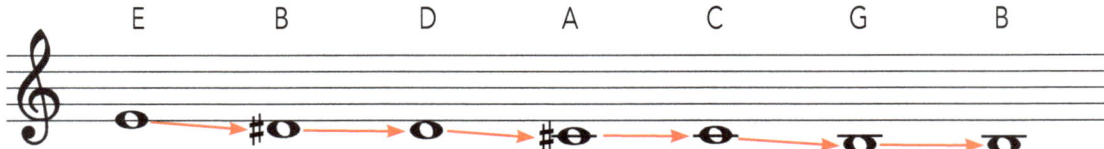

Learn all the interval shapes presented in all of the Logic Modules. This is just one example of why the interval shapes are important.

Level 2 Unit 8 • Rhythm Demo

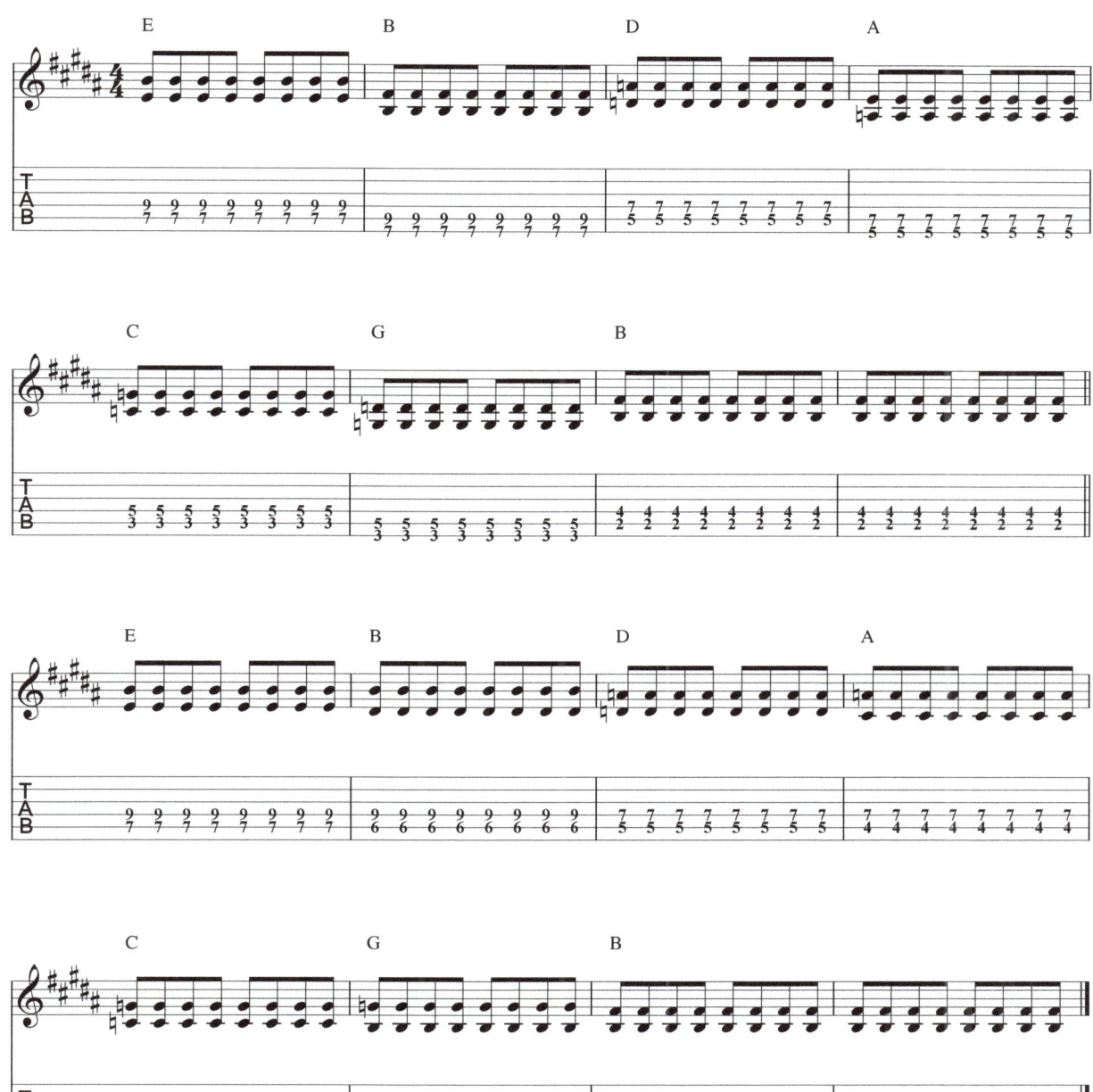

IMPROVISATION

In this module you will learn how to use alternate picking with a shuffle groove. You learned how a shuffle groove can be explained with 8th-note triplets in the Level 1 Rhythm Guitar Blues Modules Review that now.

Shuffle Groove

To mathematically understand the shuffle feel, start with a measure of 8th-note triplets. In the Unit 5 Rhythm Notation Module you learned that a tie extends the duration of the note on the left side of the tie by the value of the note on the right side of the tie.

So here, tie the first and second 8th notes of each 8th-note triplet group together. The result looks like a quarter note and 8th note under a triplet bracket.

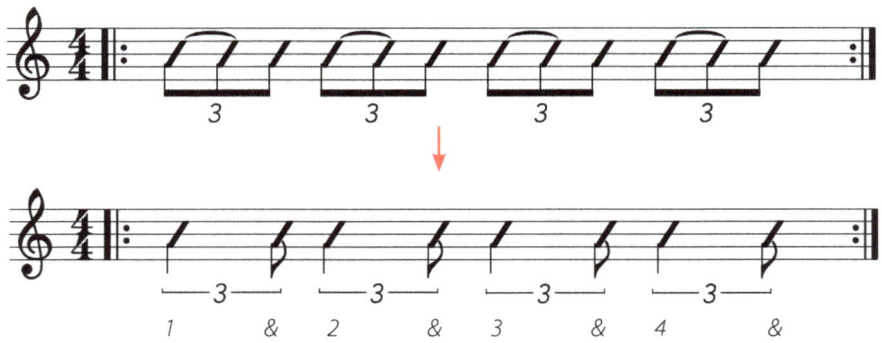

The shuffle rhythm is felt as the first and third attacks of each 8th-note triplet group. This rhythm is often written as straight 8th notes but interpreted as a quarter-and-8th under the triplet bracket and in these cases, the word "shuffle" is usually written under the song title near the key and time signatures. This directs you to interpret "straight 8ths" as "shuffled 8ths." This would appear in the music like this:

Song Title

If you stayed true to the 8th-note triplet alternate-picking rules, you play two down strokes followed by two up strokes. But with a shuffle, play the attack on the beat with a down stroke and treat the second attack, which is literally on the third 8th note of the triplet subdivision, as an "and". In other words, play it with an up stroke, which allows you to play alternate picking through entire passages of these "shuffled" 8th notes. That "and" is often called the "swung and".

Shuffle Picking Pattern

Here is a two-bar progression with a shuffle feel in A.

Progression in A Major

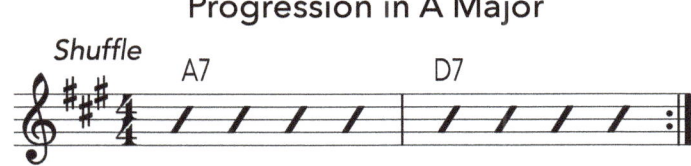

You can use either A minor pentatonic or A major pentatonic scale. Both these sounds will work as a source of notes for this exercise. Both the Blues scale, which is a minor sound, and the major pentatonic, which is a major sound, will sound good in this.

A Minor Pentatonic Scales

Practice playing with the track in two different ways:

- First, focus on your picking hand and play 8th note shuffle lines just getting comfortable with how you fit into the groove.
- Second, create a 16-bar solo—that is eight times through this two-bar phrase. Use a crunch Blues sound. Record it and listen back to check for good time and feel and for how well you told a story.

Level 2 Unit 8 • Example Solo

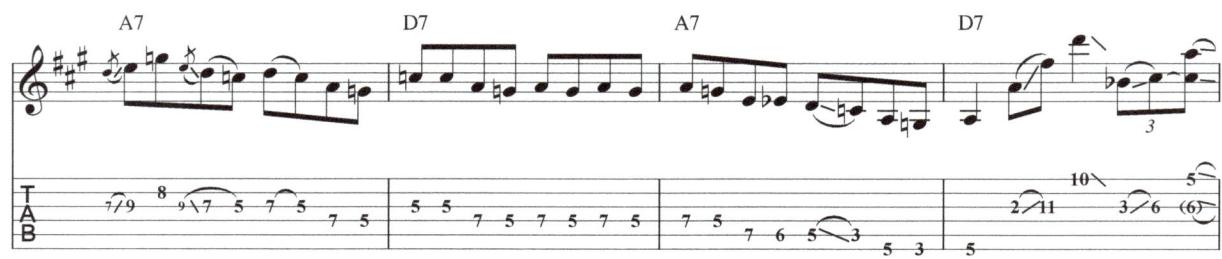

PRACTICE

Theory

- ❏ Go to the tabs below the Theory video on the website and complete the quiz.
- ❏ Practice analyzing chord progressions in minor keys.

Fretboard Logic

- ❏ Understand how the major and natural minor scale patterns fit together on the fretboard.
- ❏ Learn the Pattern II, Pattern IV, and Pattern V major triad arpeggios.
- ❏ Study the use of voice leading when moving from chord to chord.
- ❏ Memorize the 6th interval shapes on non-adjacent top four strings. Use the exercise in the tabs below the video to practice your recognition of intervals on the fretboard.
- ❏ Examine how the new information from this Unit relates to the everything else in the Octave Shape Family Tree.

Technique

- ❏ Practice playing with a syncopated 16th-note pattern using strict alternate picking.

Rhythm Notation

- ❏ Learn proper note grouping in measures containing 16th-notes.

Rhythm Guitar

- ❏ Learn the use of 1st-inversion power chords in Classic Rock.

Improvisation

- ❏ Create a 16-bar solo with an 8th-note shuffle feel using your choice of the A blues scales. As always, record yourself and listen back.

UNIT 9

Learning Modules

> **Theory** - Constructing the Blues Scale

> **Fretboard Logic** - Patterns II and IV Blues Scale, Patterns I, III, and V Minor Triad Arpeggios, Practical Major Triad Shapes in each Octave Shape, Intervals: 7ths on Non-Adjacent Top Four Strings

> **Technique** - Alternate Picking with Various Articulation Devices

> **Rhythm Notation** - Common Meters other than 4/4 Time

> **Rhythm Guitar** - Classic Rock Using Pattern III Triad Shapes

> **Improvisation** - Soloing with Chord Tones

> **Practice** - Continue Practice Routine Development

THEORY

In the last few Theory Modules you have learned about the major and minor diatonic systems. This Unit changes direction and you learn to construct another scale: the Blues scale. Nearly everything in American Pop music can be traced back to the Blues: Jazz, Rock, R&B, Funk, and a good bit of Country. All of those styles have threads connecting them with the Blues.

It is important to note that experienced Blues players use more notes than those in the Blues scale. But the Blues scale is a good starting point for learning the style.

The Blues Scale

This introduction to the Blues scale is brief, but there will be much more about Blues in later Units. Learning the Blues scale is very simple and only requires adding one note to the minor pentatonic scale.

Here is the A minor pentatonic scale.

A Minor Pentatonic Scale

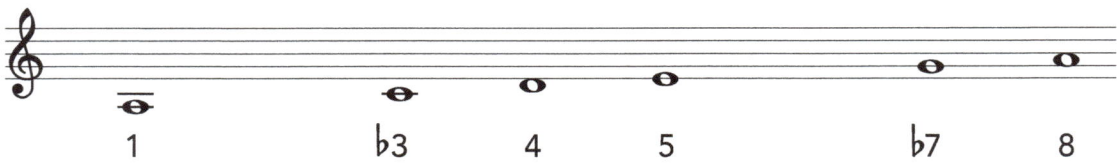

To create the Blues scale, add one note, the ♭5 between the 4th and the 5th.

A Blues Scale

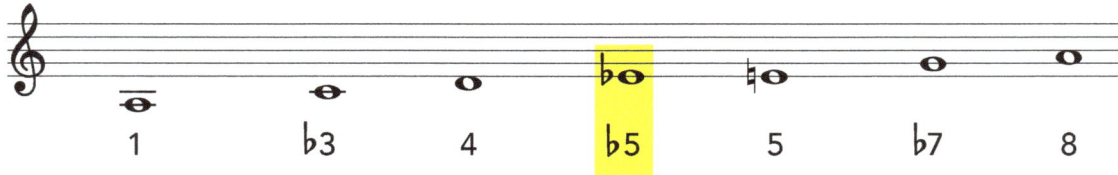

Adding the ♭5th between the 4th and 5th creates a three-note group of successive notes, each a half step apart: D (the 4th), E♭ (the ♭5), and E natural (the 5th).

This is called a chromatic section (or passage) of the scale. "Chromatic" is a term used for several kinds of things that happen in music. For example, the chromatic scale is a scale that uses every possible note from tonic to octave, and therefore the one single interval between all the scale degrees is a half step.

A Blues Scale

1   ♭3   4   ♭5   5   ♭7   8

Chromatic passage (under 4, ♭5, 5)

If someone refers to a "chromatic passage" in a song, they are speaking about two, three, or more successive notes in a line that ascend and/or descend in half steps.

The three-note group, scale degrees 4, ♭5, and 5, of the Blues scale are referred to as a chromatic group of notes. There will be much more on playing Blues later on in this course.

FRETBOARD LOGIC

Scales

In this Unit you will learn two patterns of the Blues scale. As you learned in Theory Module, experienced Blues guitarists use more than just the Blues scale as a source of notes in their solos, but it is a very good place to start.

The Blues scale is easy to build from a minor pentatonic shell. You need only to add a flatted 5th to create a Blues scale. Look at the Pattern IV A minor pentatonic shell in 5th position. Add a flat 5 in two places in the scale (in blue).

Pattern IV Blues Scale

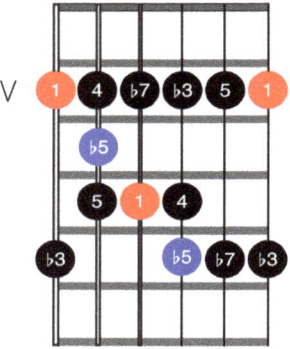

Look at the Pattern II D minor pentatonic shell in 5th position. Add a flat 5 in two places in the scale (in blue). Add these scale patterns to your practice routine.

Pattern II Blues Scale

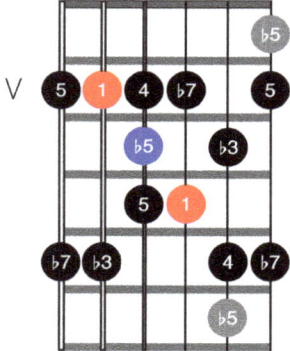

Arpeggios

Let's learn the three remaining minor triad arpeggios: Patterns I, III, and V. From these triad arpeggios, minor 7th arpeggios and minor major 7th arpeggios can be built. Add these arpeggios to your practice routine and be sure to use strict alternate picking.

Here is a Pattern I minor triad arpeggio.

Pattern I Minor Triad Arpeggio

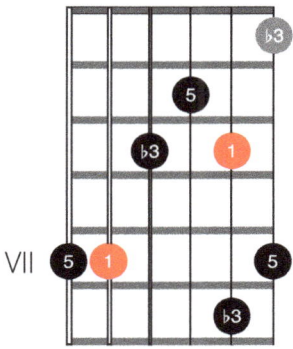

Here is a Pattern III minor triad arpeggio.

Pattern III Minor Triad Arpeggio

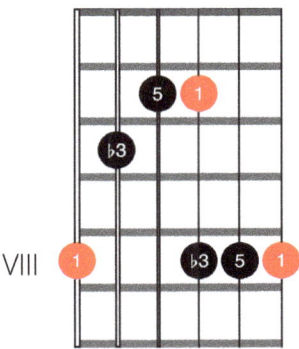

Here is a Pattern V minor triad arpeggio.

Pattern V Minor Triad Arpeggio

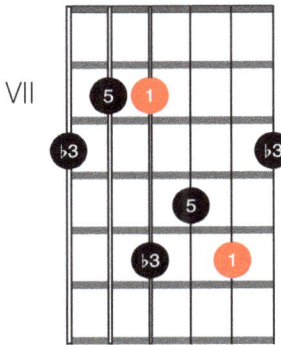

You now have five major triad arpeggios and five minor triad arpeggios in your practice routine. Play them slowly and accurately. Arpeggios are chord tones. For chord-tone soloing, a topic coming up in Improvisation, it is more important that we know where the chord tones are rather than to be able to run up and down the arpeggios really fast. Chord-tone soloing is much more about targeting the chord tones.

Chords

In this Module you will learn the practical major triad chord voicings found inside each of the five Octave Shapes. This will be accomplished with a few easy steps.

Octave Shape I Major Triad Chord Voicings

Start with Octave Shape I.

Step 1: See the Octave Shape.

Step 2: See the entire major scale built within the Octave Shape.

Step 3: Both the major scale and a major triad have a major 3rd and a perfect 5th above the tonic of the scale (which is the root of the triad you will build) Highlight those three notes everywhere possible in the pattern to show all notes available for a triad built on 1. Notice that these are the same notes of the pattern I arpeggio.

Step 4: Identify the 3-string voicings, 4-string voicings, or maybe even 5-string voicings that are the most practical to play. These are also the most-commonly used.

Octave Shape I Triad Chord Voicings

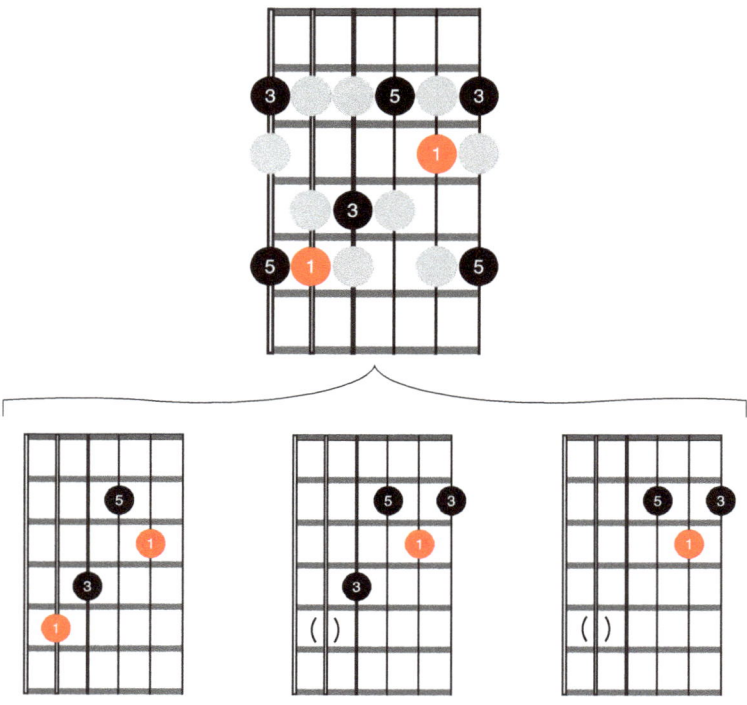

Octave Shape II Major Triad Chord Voicings

Here is another example, this time with Octave Shape II.

Step 1: See the Octave Shape.

Step 2: See the entire major scale built within the Octave Shape.

Step 3: Highlight all of the roots, 3rds, and 5ths to show every note available to play a triad. Again, notice that these are the same notes of the Pattern II arpeggio.

Step 4: Identify the 3-string voicings, 4-string voicings, or maybe even 5-string voicings that are the most practical to play. These are also the most-commonly used.

Octave Shape II Triad Chord Voicings

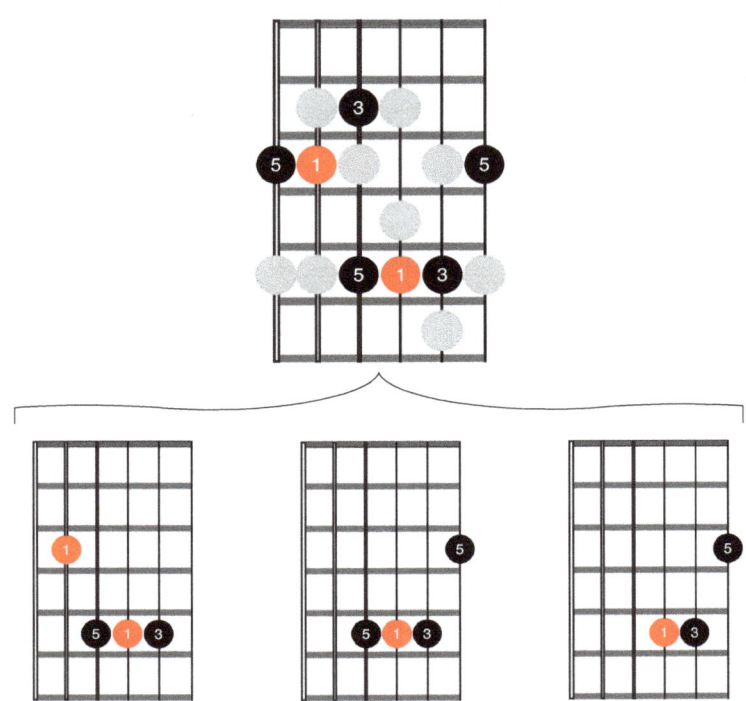

Octave Shape III Major Triad Chord Voicings

Here is another example, using Octave Shape III with C on the 6th string.

Step 1: See the Octave Shape.

Step 2: See the entire major scale built within the Octave Shape.

Step 3: Highlight all of the roots, 3rds, and 5ths to show every note available to play a triad. Notice that these are the same notes of the Pattern III arpeggio.

Step 4: Identify the 3-string voicings, 4-string voicings, or maybe even 5-string voicings that are the most practical to play. These are also the most-commonly used.

Octave Shape III Triad Chord Voicings

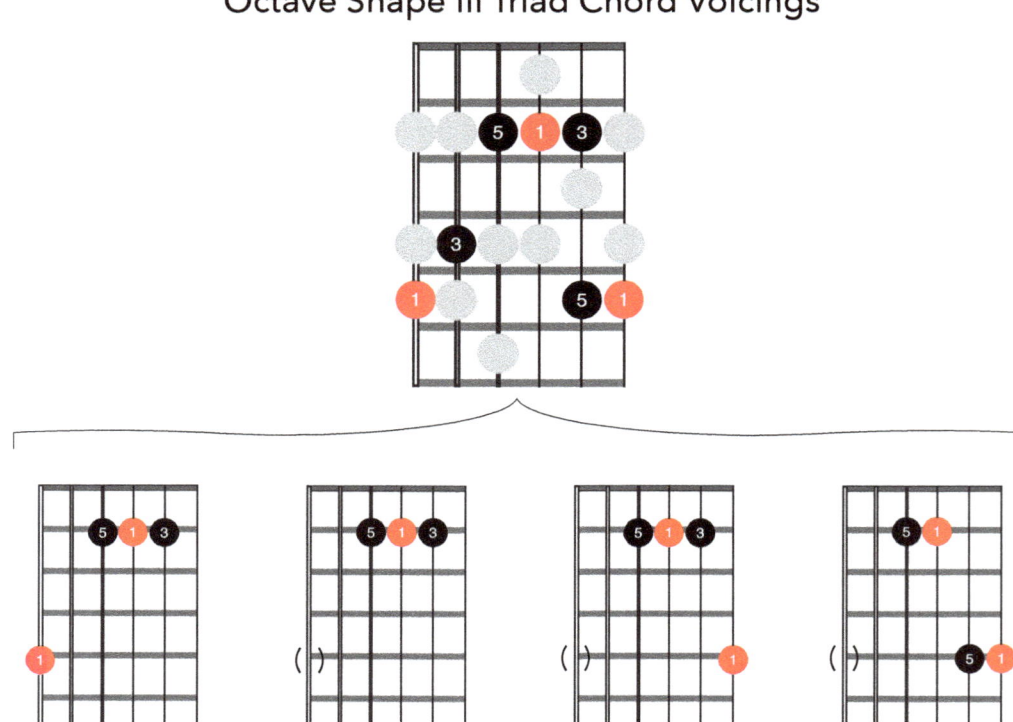

Octave Shape IV Major Triad Chord Voicings

Here is another example using Octave Shape IV.

Step 1: See the Octave Shape.

Step 2: See the entire major scale built within the Octave Shape.

Step 3: Highlight all of the roots, 3rds, and 5ths to show every note available to play a triad. Notice that these are the same notes of the Pattern IV arpeggio.

Step 4: Identify the 3-string voicings, 4-string voicings, or maybe even 5-string voicings that are the most practical to play. These are also the most-commonly used.

Octave Shape IV Triad Chord Voicings

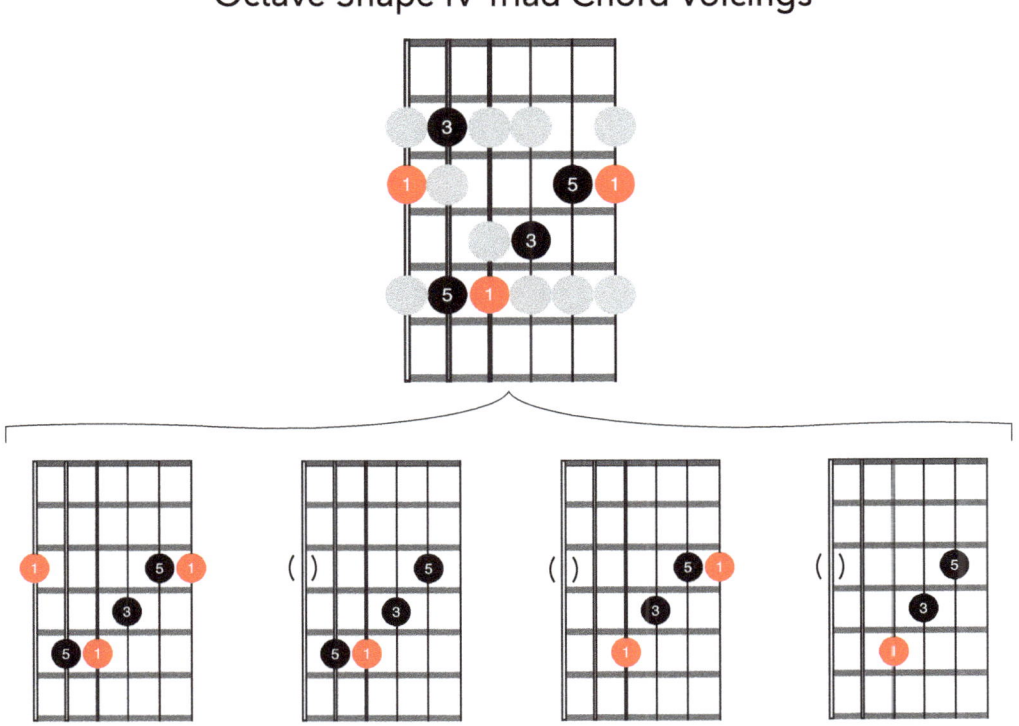

Octave Shape V Major Triad Chord Voicings

Look at one more example with Octave Shape V.

Step 1: See the Octave Shape.

Step 2: See the entire major scale built within the Octave Shape.

Step 3: Highlight all of the roots, 3rds, and 5ths to show every note available to play a triad. Notice that these are the same notes of the Pattern V arpeggio.

Step 4: Identify the most practical voicings to play.

Octave Shape V Triad Chord Voicings

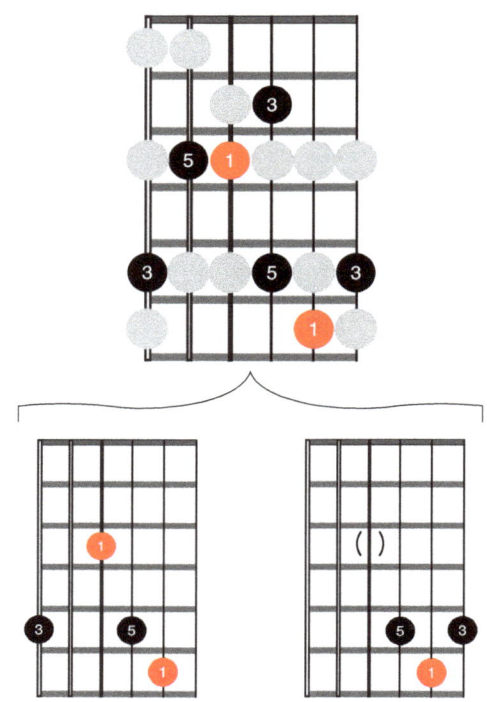

Interval Shapes on the Fretboard

In this Unit learn major and minor 7th intervals on non-adjacent strings in the top-four string region of the fretboard. The top four strings are isolated here because the shapes that cross the 2nd and 3rd strings are different than other places on the fretboard.

Look at 7th intervals between the 4th and 2nd strings. Starting with a minor 7th interval, play an A at the 7th fret of the 4th string. A minor 7th is one fret higher on the 2nd string. A major 7th is two frets higher on the 2nd string.

Look at 7th intervals between the 3rd and 1st strings. The shapes are the same as between the 4th and 2nd strings. Starting with a minor 7th interval, play D at the 7th fret of the 3rd string. A minor 7th is one fret higher on the 1st string. A major 7th will be two frets higher on the 1st string.

Minor 7th Interval

Major 7th Interval

You have now learned most of the simple interval shapes on the guitar; "simple" meaning an octave or smaller. Keep refreshing your knowledge of these.

TECHNIQUE

There is a topic related to alternate picking that is often overlooked and that is how alternate picking is applied when playing lines that incorporate articulation devices like hammer-ons, bends, release bends, and slides. The pick does not strike the string with these devices, but the general pick direction rules are the same.

8th-Note Picking with Articulation Devices

For 8th-note rhythms, when playing a line that incorporates any of these devices, the assignment of a down stroke to the beat and an up stroke to an "and" is the same, regardless of whether there is a pick attack or whether the note is articulated differently. This means that even though you may be using one of these articulation devices, the next note that is played with the pick should follow the pick-direction rules: If it is on the beat it should be a down stroke and if it is on the "and" it should be an up stroke.

It is natural to make the pick direction motion in your picking hand even if you are not striking the string. It helps you stay in time for the next time you use the pick in the same figure.

16th-Note Picking with Articulation Devices

When playing a syncopated 16th-note rhythm, the assignment of down strokes to beats and "and" and up strokes to the "e" and "uh" is the same, regardless of whether there is a pick attack or whether the note is articulated with one of the devices listed before. This means that even though you may be using one of these articulation devices, the next note that is played with the pick should follow the pick-direction rules: If it is on the beat or on the "and" it should be a down stroke and if it is on the "e" or "a" it should be an up stroke. The same idea goes for 8th- and 16th-note triplet figures.

RHYTHM NOTATION

You have learned ways to achieve proper spacing and grouping when the smallest notes in a measure are quarter notes, 8th notes, and 16th notes. The examples used the 4/4 time signature because how common it is. Music written in other meters generally uses the same logic, which is to notate music as clearly as possible for the reader.

3/4 Time

In 3/4 time it is best to make each beat visible when an 8th note is the smallest subdivision. The same goes for when a 16th note is the smallest subdivision.

6/8 Time

In 6/8 time, the norm is to show two groups of three 8th notes.

12/8 Time

In 12/8 the norm is to show four groups of three 8th notes.

2/2 Time

In 2/2 the norm is to show each half beat, which is a quarter note.

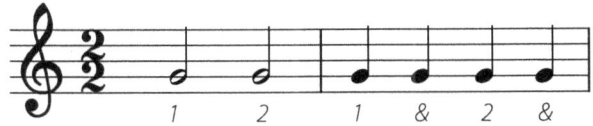

In odd meters, grouping is usually dictated by where the accents are in the particular measure.

5/8 Time

For example, 5/8 might be 3 + 2 or 2 + 3.

7/8 Time

In 7/8 the grouping might be 3 + 4, 4 + 3, 2 + 3 + 2.

This same logic holds true for any other "odd meter" measure.

RHYTHM GUITAR

The rock rhythm guitar parts so far have used power-chord techniques. Now the focus will shift to Rock rhythm guitar parts based on three-string triad shapes. There are simple voicings that can be played with standard tuning that are part of many guitarists' vocabulary; these are often associated with Keith Richards and the Rolling Stones.

These shapes can be seen as part of the "Super Shape" system you learned in the Fretboard Logic Modules. For this module, look at the Super Shape that includes the Pattern III Octave Shape. This shape, of course, can be moved to any root.

Super Shape I

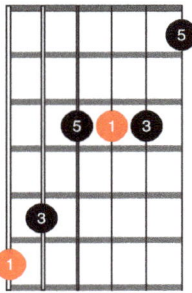

Focus on four notes from this shape:

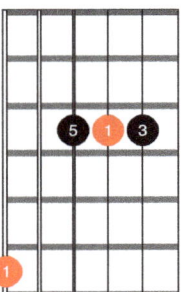

Play the root with your 4th finger on the 6th string. Next, barre across the 4th, 3rd, and 2nd strings with your 1st finger. The 5th is played on the 4th string. The root is repeated on the 3rd string. The 3rd is played on the 2nd string. Mute the 1st string with the flesh of your 1st finger. Mute the 5th string with the flesh of your 4th finger and/or the tip of your 1st finger.

This voicing may put some strain on the back of your hand. If that happens, don't force it. If it hurts, I suggest leaving out the root on the 6th string to start.

If you examine this closely you see this entire major triad shape lives inside of Pattern III. But notice that the three notes played on the 4th, 3rd, and 2nd strings are also part of the Pattern II Octave Shape, and it is only a matter of where you play the lowest root; the 5th string or the 6th string.

Super Shape I

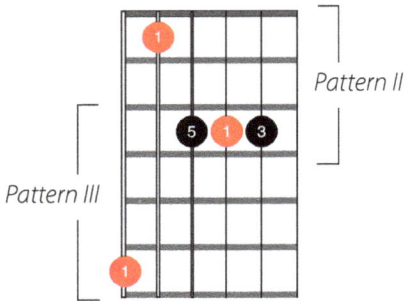

There are several classic rhythm guitar moves within this Pattern III shape. Remember to mute the 1st string with the flesh of your 1st finger and to mute the 5th string with the flesh of your 4th finger and/or the tip of your 1st finger.

Classic Move 1

The first classic move is to play a suspended 4th (or sus4 as it is commonly called) by replacing the 3rd on the 2nd string with the 4th played with your 2nd finger.

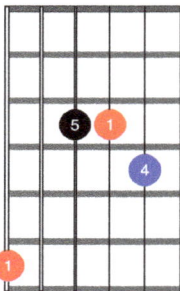

Move back and forth between the triad and this sus4 shape.

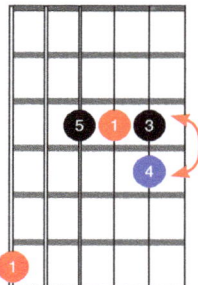

Fretboard Biology

Classic Move 2

The next classic move is to play a 6 like you learned in the Blues Rhythm Guitar Modules by replacing the 5th on the 4th string with the 6th using your 3rd finger.

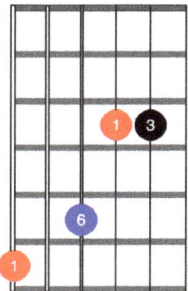

Move back and forth between the triad and 6 shape.

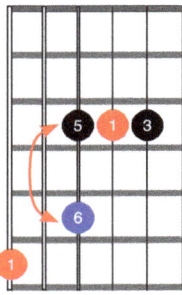

Classic Move 3

This next example has a real Keith Richards-like sound, but it can be heard in countless rhythm guitar parts by many guitarists. It is also a common embellishment for keyboardists. You can play a sus6/4, where the 4th replaces the 3rd and the 6th replaces the 5th. Replace the 3rd on the 2nd string with a 4th played with your 2nd finger and 5th on the 4th string with the 6th using your 3rd finger.

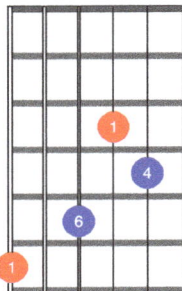

Move back and forth between the triad and this sus6/4 shape.

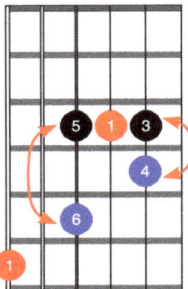

Classic Move 4

This next example also has a Keith Richards-signature sound but this, too, can be heard in countless rhythm guitar parts by many guitarists and is another common embellishment for keyboardists. You can play a sus2/4, where the 4th replaces the 3rd and the 2nd replaces the root. Replace the 3rd on the 2nd string with a 4th played with your 2nd finger and root on the 3rd string with the 2nd using your 3rd finger.

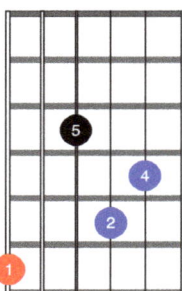

Move back and forth between the triad and this sus2/4 shape.

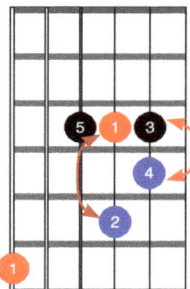

Classic Move 5

The next example can't be played with the 4th finger playing the root because that finger is needed for another string. Theoretically this could be called a sus6/2/4. I have never heard that term used in any theory text, but I've hard guitar players say that. The 4th replaces the 3rd, the 2nd replaces the root and the 6th replaces the 5th. Replace the 3rd on the 2nd string with a 4th played with your 2nd finger. Replace the root on the 3rd string with the 2nd with your 4th finger. Replace the 5th on the 4th string with the 6th using your 3rd finger.

Here is what it looks like:

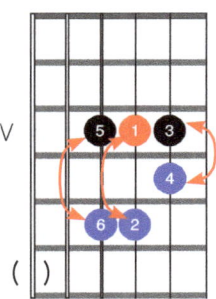

Notice this looks like a Pattern II minor barre chord. And played in the Pattern III C Octave Shape in 5th position, it looks like a D minor. This would commonly be written as "Dmi/C", which is a slash chord. Slash chords will be explained in greater detail in a later Theory Unit. The important to know for now is that with slash chord notation, the triad on the left (Dmi) is played with the note on the right (C) voiced in the bass.

Putting What We've Learned to Work

Example 1

This example mimics a classic Rolling Stones chord style. The 8th-note groove should be played with all down strokes. The chord voicings demonstrate the use of suspended 6/4 chords. Experiment with different levels of gain on your amp. Too much gain will make the notes indistinguishable. Practice with the backing track.

Progression in C

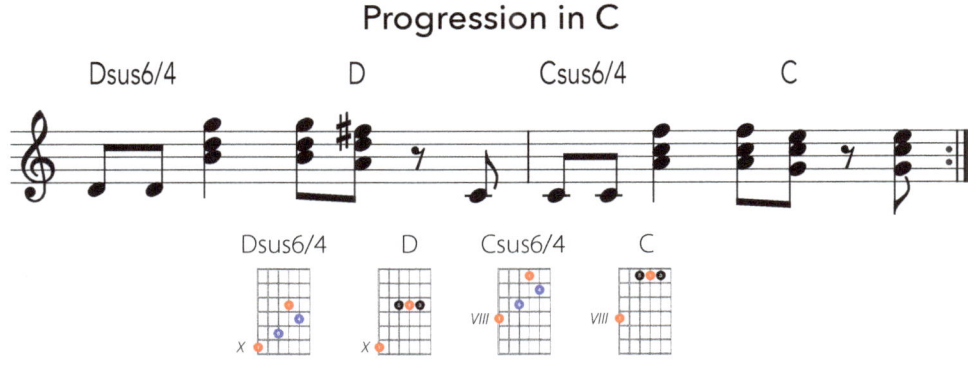

Level 2 Unit 8 • Rhythm Example 1

Example 2

This next example starts with the previous example and adds a second section, which demonstrates the use of suspended 4/2 chords. Practice with the backing track.

Progression in C

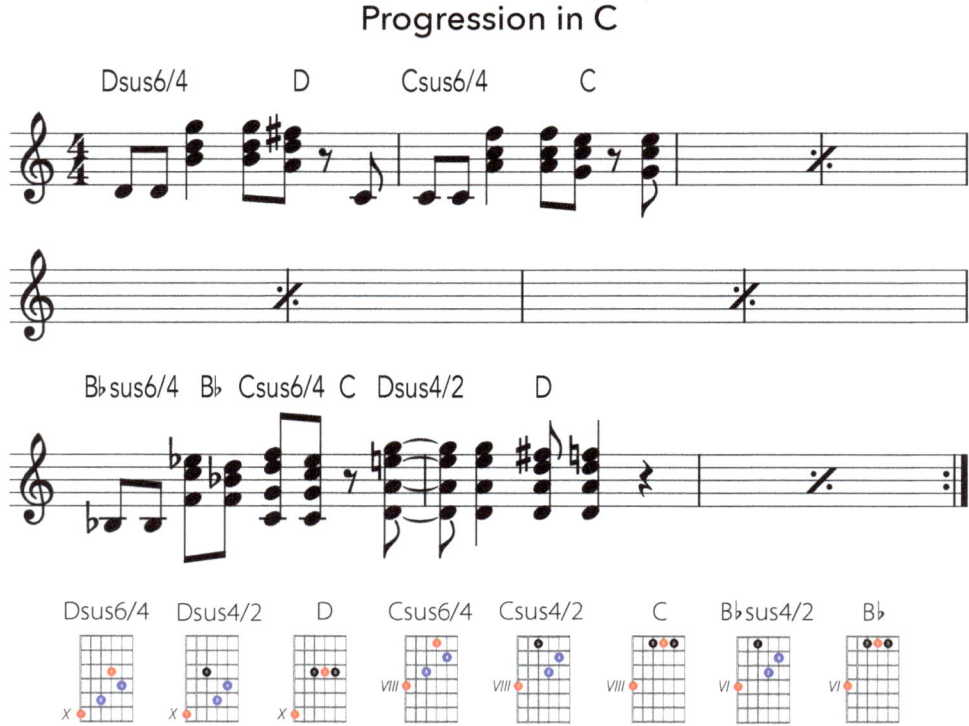

Level 2 Unit 8 • Rhythm Example 2

Have fun with these voicings but be sure to take care of your fretting hand. If you feel too much strain while stretching with your 4th finger to play the root on the 6th string, stop. To start using your 4th finger, try these voicings in a higher part of the fretboard where the frets are closer together and the stretch is not as extreme. Slowly build up your strength and gradually move down the neck to where the frets are farther apart.

IMPROVISATION

When musicians talk about chords to a song they often refer to them as "the chord changes" or even just "the changes".

Up to this point you have been using the key-center approach when you solo. With this approach, the scale of the key is the source of melodic material. There are drawbacks to this method, however. Key-center solos can sound vague and meandering. A good way to demonstrate this to yourself is to record an improvised key-center solo over a backing track. First, play it back with both the backing track and your guitar solo audible. It will probably sound okay. Next, play the track again with the backing track muted. Just listen to the solo track alone. Can you hear the chords reflected in your solo lines? In most cases with inexperienced improvisers, the answer will be no. In fact, if you had not already heard the chords being played behind your solo, what you will hear during playback of the solo track alone might just sound like a bunch of wandering, random notes from the scale.

Chord-Tone Soloing

This Unit introduces "chord-tone soloing". This approach incorporates the notes of the chords that are being played under the solo. This is an incredibly simple concept to understand but quite a challenging thing to master. If you are playing chord tones, you are "playing the changes".

Consider this: If you are soloing over a progression in A minor that moves back and forth between an A minor chord and D minor chord, the A minor pentatonic or A minor scale will sound adequate but there will be a sense of vagueness in your note choices; a sense that your line is not tailored to the chords.

With chord-tone soloing, at least some of the your note choices will be the notes that belong to the chord the band is playing at that instant. For example, if the progression is A minor to the D minor as mentioned above, over the A minor chord the soloist may focus on or include an A (the root), a C (the ♭3), and an E (the 5th). Over the D minor chord the soloist may focus on or include a D (the root), an F (the ♭3), and an A (the 5th).

In other words, the melodic line of your solo can outline the chords. There are many guitarists who aren't taught this and never figure it out on their own. Other guitarists come to it know through trial and error but this program will make a concerted effort to provide an organized and gradual approach to learning chord-tone soloing through the next several Levels. You have been learning about arpeggios and the reason should be clear: The arpeggio is the musical device used to integrate chord tones into solos. Think about the relationship between arpeggios and chord tones: If chord tones are the notes of a chord and an arpeggio is the notes of a chord played melodically, then arpeggios are simply chord tones.

Instead of primarily using scales as a source of notes, using arpeggios will make a solo sound like it "fits" the chord changes. At first, it is best to practice this with a simple two-chord progression. In this simple progression, both chords belong to the key of A minor. A minor is the I chord and D minor is the IV chord. You know that from your study of the harmonized minor scale.

A Minor Progression

To hear the difference between key-center soloing and chord-tone soling, try this two different ways:

- First, improvise with the track only using the Pattern IV A minor and/or A minor pentatonic scale over both chords. This is acceptable, but as I said at the beginning, probably less than satisfying.

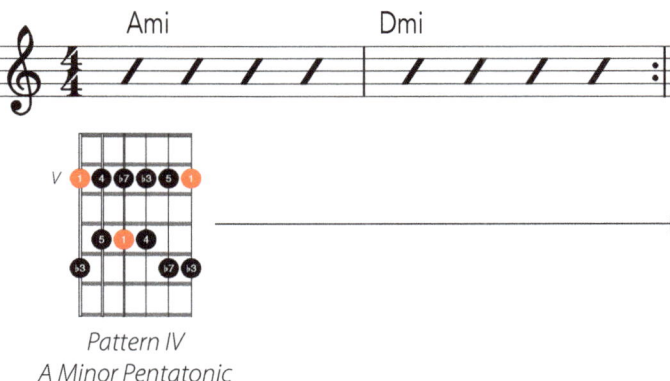

Pattern IV
A Minor Pentatonic

- Next, take the two arpeggios (Patterns IV and II minor triads) presented here and focus on playing with the track using some of the notes of the Pattern IV A minor triad arpeggio over the A minor and the Pattern II D minor triad arpeggio over the D minor, both in 5th position.

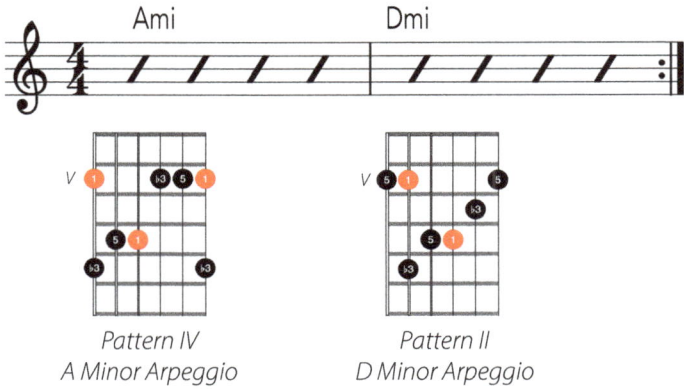

Pattern IV   *Pattern II*
A Minor Arpeggio   *D Minor Arpeggio*

All the notes of the A minor chord (A, C, and E) and all the notes of the D minor chord (D, F, and A) are part of the A minor scale. The point is to be specific and targeting the chord tones—the notes that belong to the chords the band is playing.

This may be a whole new way for you to think about soloing. To begin, it may seem difficult. Don't stress about it. You can start gradually. Just play a chord tone on the first beat of each chord. This will start you thinking and hearing chord-tone soloing and your solos will start to sound like you are, as we say, "playing the changes". As you become more confident in your knowledge of the shapes, incorporate more and more chord tones.

And a word of advice: Go slowly and play very few notes. This approach is very different from playing a key-center solo where you can just wander through the scale without making too many note choice decisions.

Practice this a lot. It is a whole new challenge. Learning to use the chord-tone approach in creating solos is an essential step in becoming a successful improviser. The concept is simple; the task is challenging but worth the effort. Dedicate yourself to the task. We will work on this for many upcoming Modules.

Level 2 Unit 9 • Example Solo

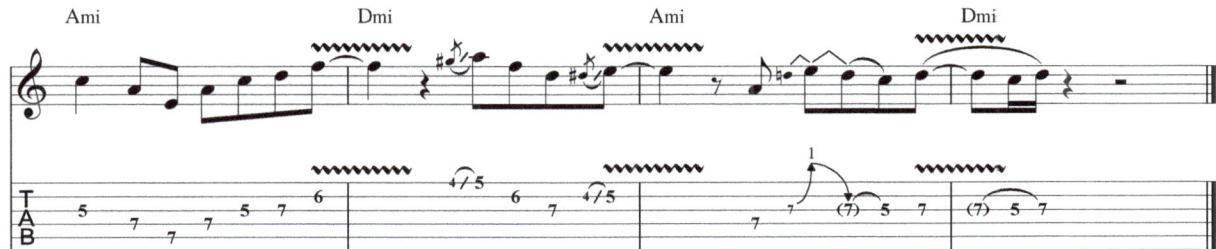

PRACTICE

Theory

- ❑ Go to the tabs below the Theory video on the website and complete the quiz.
- ❑ Learn how to construct the Blues Scale.

Fretboard Logic

- ❑ Learn the Pattern II and Pattern IV Blues scales.
- ❑ Learn the Pattern I, Pattern III, and Pattern V minor triad arpeggios.
- ❑ Learn the practical major triad chord shapes within each Octave Shape.
- ❑ Memorize the major and minor 7th interval shapes on non-adjacent top four strings. Use the exercise in the tabs below the video to practice your recognition of intervals on the fretboard.
- ❑ Look at how the new information from this Unit relates to the everything else in the Octave Shape Family Tree.

Technique

- ❑ Practice alternate picking when using various articulation devices.

Rhythm Notation

- ❑ Learn common meters other than 4/4 time.

Rhythm Guitar

- ❑ Learn Classic Rock moves using Pattern III triad shapes.

Improvisation

- ❑ Create a 16-bar solo using chord tones.

UNIT 10

Learning Modules

> **Theory** - Level 2 Summary

> **Fretboard Logic** - Patterns I, III, and V Blues Scale, Suspended 4th Arpeggios, Practical Minor Triad Shapes in Each Octave Shape, Intervals: Octaves on Non-Adjacent Strings

> **Technique** - Notating Pick Direction

> **Rhythm Notation** - Clarity in Notation

> **Rhythm Guitar** - Classic Rock, Triad Shapes on String Set 2-3-4

> **Improvisation** - Soloing with Chord Tones

> **Practice** - Continue Practice Routine Development

THEORY

You are at the end of Level 2 and have traveled a great distance in your study of Theory. You now have the ability to analyze a diatonic chord progression and identify its key and the function of each chord.

Why is this important? Understanding the key and chords of a progression helps you choose notes when you solo, comp, write, and arrange. The more you learn about harmony, the easier it is to learn options that you would not know otherwise.

- If you learn about harmony, you will know the chord tones of the chords over which you are soloing, You can target those notes as the framework for your lines. You can substitute the notes of chords within the same family.
- If you learn about harmony, you will know the scales that fit over those "hard chords" and you know why they work.
- If you know harmony, you can build all the other chords derived from triads we have learned – like 7th, 9th, 11th, and 13th chords – as well as inversions and many other chord types.
- If you learn about harmony, you can figure out new or better voicings than you could otherwise.
- If you learn about harmony, you can reharmonize the chord progression for a song you are arranging or writing using ideas you would not have otherwise.
- If you learn about harmony, you can write down your music and give it to the other musicians to speed up their learning and save time and frustration at band rehearsals.

Communication is another important benefit. If you are part a group of musicians who all understand theory, communication is easy. Each musician's ability to learn and memorize or read music is improved, which makes rehearsals more efficient. And if unexpected problems come up during the gig – as they always do – the schooled musician has the ability to react in the right way, often saving the day.

Being a complete musician is like a three-legged stool: The first leg is your talent, the second leg is hard work, the third leg is literacy—your knowledge of harmony and theory.

These four simple statements explain how you have reached this point in Theory:

- In order to analyze chord progressions you needed to know harmonized scales because the harmonized scale told you the number. In other words, it told you the function of each chord within a key.
- In order to harmonize scales you needed to know how to build triads because triad formulas told you which triads are built on each scale degree.

- In order to build triads, you needed to know how to build intervals because the combination of interval types defined the triad formulas.
- In order to build intervals, you needed to know the key signatures because the key signature told you what notes are available within a key.

This is the knowledge you need to understand the inner workings of a song. In Level 3 Theory you will learn about 7th chords and the harmonized major and natural minor scales with 7th chords. Keep going. Work hard.

FRETBOARD LOGIC

Scales

In this Unit you will learn the remaining three patterns of the Blues scale. Look at the Pattern I E minor pentatonic shell in 5th position. Add the ♭5 in three places in the scale.

Pattern I Blues Scale

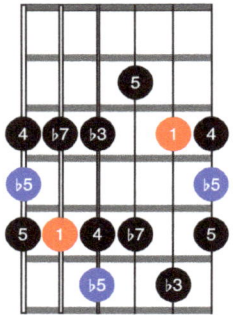

Look at the Pattern III C minor pentatonic shell in 5th position. Add the ♭5 in two places in the scale.

Pattern III Blues Scale

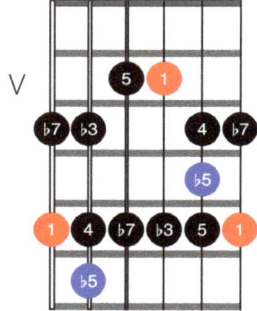

Look at the Pattern V A minor pentatonic shell in 7th position. Add the ♭5 in three places in the scale.

Pattern V Blues Scale

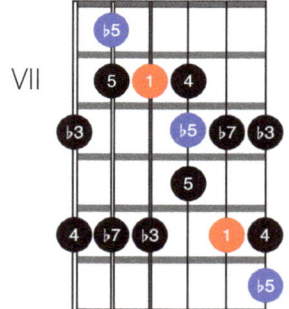

The two previous Units focused on the big picture of the fretboard. Take a minute to do that with the Blues scale. Here are all of the notes of the A Blues scale on the fretboard with all "As" – the tonics – highlighted. The individual Octave Shapes or Blues patterns are not highlighted. This graphic shoes how they connect with each other to form one continuous pattern of notes on the fretboard.

A Blues Scales

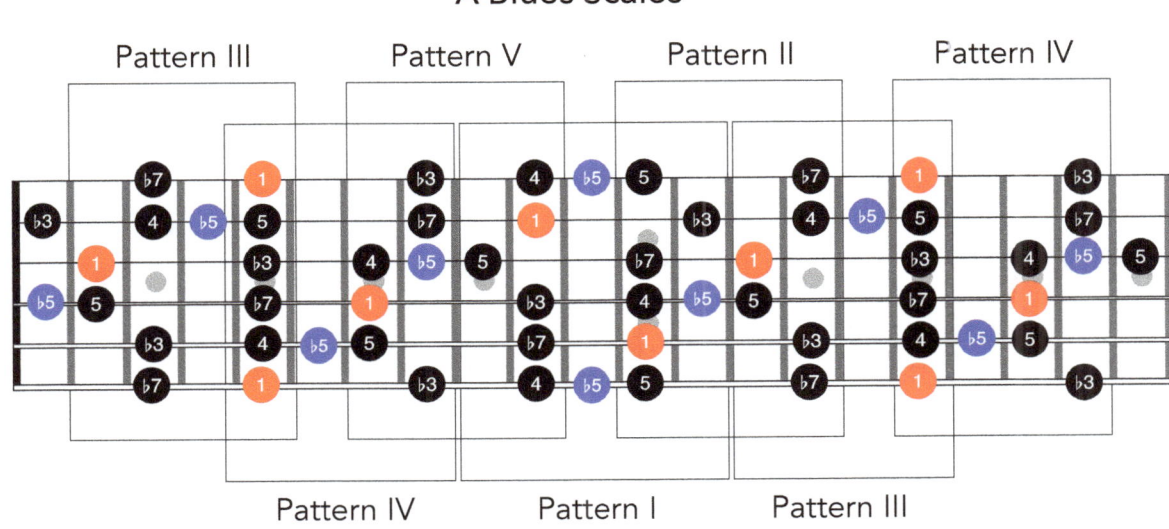

Next, each of the shells are highlighted to show the individual patterns and how they connect with each other. The five Blues patterns provide a way to organize all of the possible notes in a given key within five manageable segments of the fretboard and in a vertical way.

A Blues Scales

Don't restrict yourself to playing inside one pattern when soloing. Your personal exploration of the fretboard should include learning how to move from one Blues pattern to the next – one higher and the next one lower – to take full advantage of the range of the guitar when soloing. Because the Blues scale is a minor scale, you can work with any of the backing tracks that are in a minor key. Have fun with this.

Arpeggios

In this Module you will learn five suspended 4th (sus4) arpeggios. With your theory knowledge of sus4 chords combined with your knowledge of triads, you can probably figure them out yourself. When building a sus4 chord, the 3rd is replaced with a perfect 4th. The interval formula is 1, perfect 4th, and perfect 5th. Take each of the five major triad arpeggios and replace the major 3rd with a perfect 4th.

Here is the Pattern I sus4 triad arpeggio. Notice that the 4th has replaced the 3rd in this shape.

Pattern I sus4 Triad Arpeggio

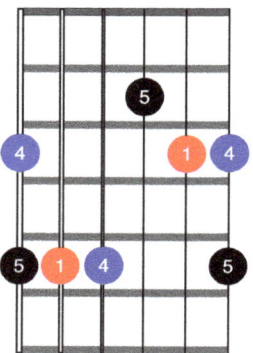

Here is the Pattern II sus4 arpeggio. The 4th has replaced the 3rd in this shape.

Pattern II sus4 Triad Arpeggio

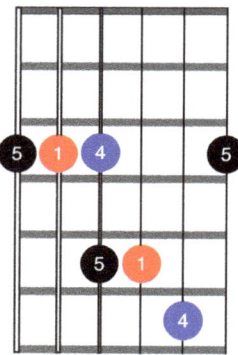

Here is the Pattern III sus4 arpeggio. The 4th has replaced the 3rd.

Pattern III sus4 Triad Arpeggio

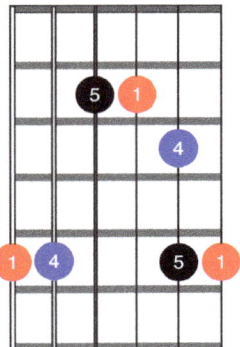

Here is the Pattern IV sus4 arpeggio. The 4th has replaced the 3rd.

Pattern IV sus4 Triad Arpeggio

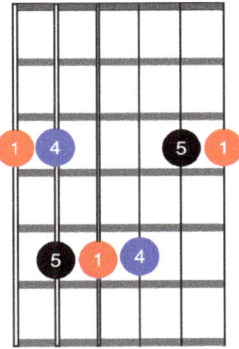

Here is the Pattern V sus4 arpeggio. The 4th has replaced the 3rd.

Pattern V sus4 Triad Arpeggio

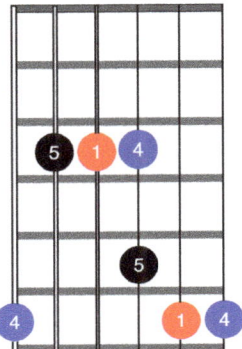

Chords

The last Module focused on the practical major triad chord voicing found inside each of the five Octave Shapes. This Module focuses on the practical minor triad chord voicing found inside each of the five Octave Shapes. The same easy steps can be used to find the practical minor triad chord voicings in each octave shape.

Octave Shape I Minor Triad Chord Voicings

Start with Octave Shape I for E:

Step 1: See the Octave Shape.

Step 2: See the entire minor scale built within the Octave Shape.

Step 3: You know both the minor scale and a minor triad have a minor 3rd and perfect 5th above the tonic of the scale, which is the root of the triad. Highlight all of the roots, 3rds, and 5ths to show every note available to play a triad. Again, notice that these are the same notes of the Pattern I arpeggio.

Step 4: Identify the 3-string voicings, 4-string voicings, or maybe even 5-string voicings that are the most practical to play.

Octave Shape I Minor Triad Chord Voicings

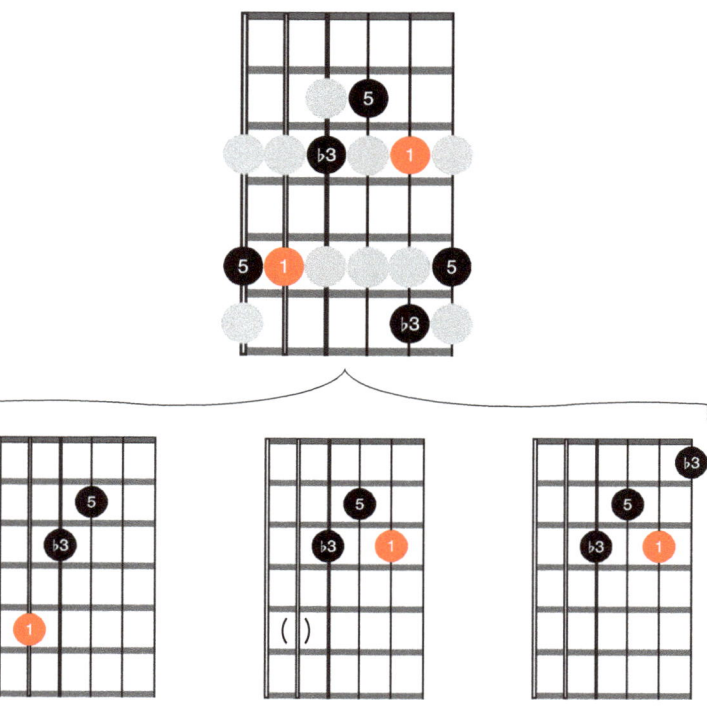

Octave Shape II Minor Triad Chord Voicings

Now let's look at octave shape II for D:

Step 1: See the Octave Shape.

Step 2: See the entire minor scale built within the Octave Shape.

Step 3: You know both the minor scale and a minor triad have minor 3rd and perfect 5th above the tonic for scale. Highlight those three notes in every octave to show every note available for a minor triad. Notice that these are the same notes at the Pattern II minor triad arpeggio.

Step 4: Identify the 3-string voicings, 4-string voicings, or maybe even 5-string voicings that are the most practical to play.

Octave Shape II Minor Triad Chord Voicings

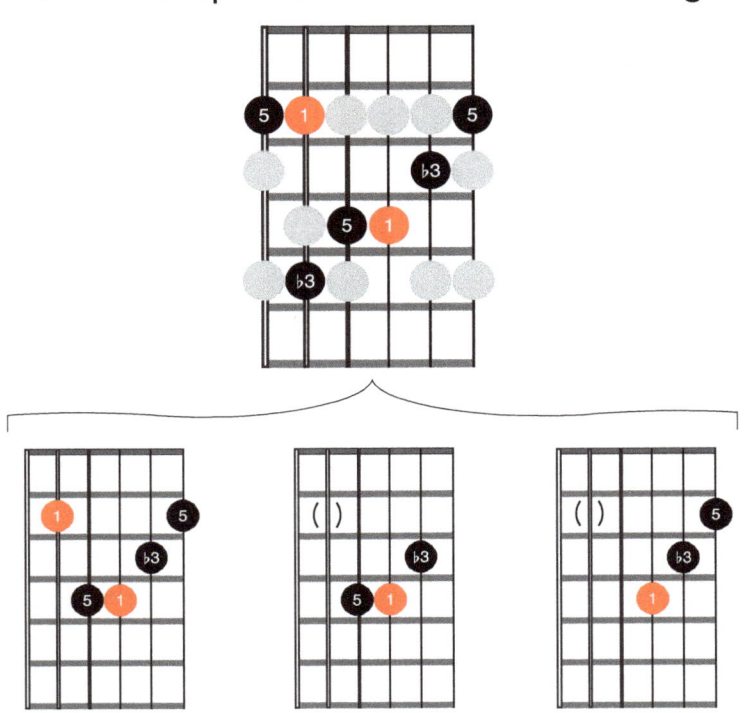

Octave Shape III Minor Triad Chord Voicings

Look at Octave Shape III next and use the Octave Shape for C:

Step 1: See the Octave Shape.

Step 2: See the entire minor scale built within the Octave Shape.

Step 3: You know both the minor scale and a minor triad have a minor 3rd and perfect 5th above the tonic of the scale. Highlight those three notes in every octave to show every note available for a minor triad. Notice that these are the same notes as the Pattern III minor triad arpeggio.

Step 4: Identify the 3-string voicings, 4-strings voicings, or maybe even the 5-string voicings that are the most practical to play.

Octave Shape III Minor Triad Chord Voicings

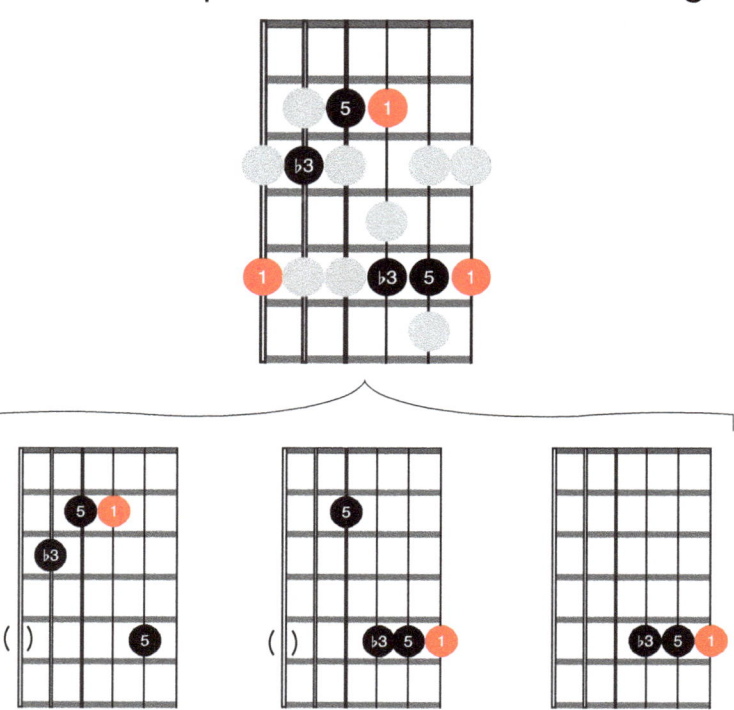

Octave Shape IV Minor Triad Chord Voicings

Look at Octave Shape IV and use the Octave Shape for A.

Step 1: See the Octave Shape.

Step 2: See the entire minor scale built within the Octave Shape.

Step 3: You know both the minor scale and a minor triad have minor 3rd and perfect 5th above the tonic for scale. Highlight those three notes in every octave to show every note available for a minor triad. Notice that these are the same notes at the Pattern IV minor triad arpeggio.

Step 4: Identify the 3-string voicings, 4-string voicings, or maybe even the 5-string voicing that are the most practical to play.

Octave Shape IV Minor Triad Chord Voicings

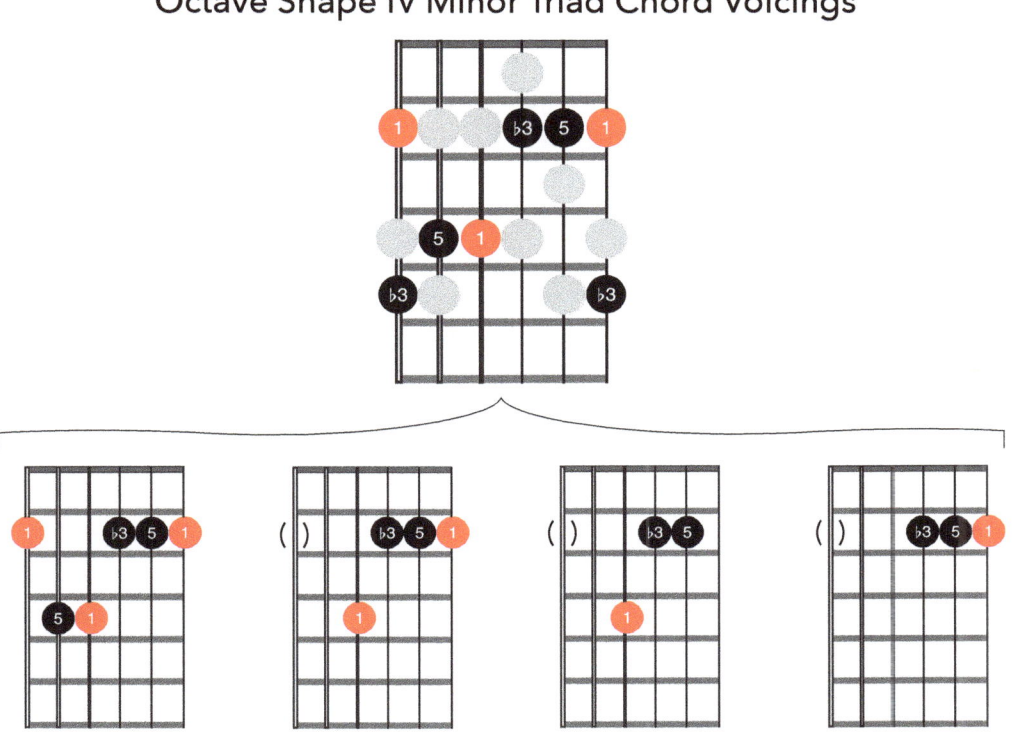

Octave Shape V Minor Triad Chord Voicings

In this example, let's look at Octave Shape V and we will use the Octave Shape for A:

Step 1: See the Octave Shape.

Step 2: See the entire minor scale built within the Octave Shape.

Step 3: You know both the minor scale and a minor triad have minor 3rd and perfect 5th above the tonic of the scale. Highlight those three notes in every octave to show every note available for a minor triad. Notice that these are the same notes at the Pattern V minor triad arpeggio.

Step 4: Identify the 3-string voicings, 4-string voicings, or maybe even the 5-string voicings that are the most practical to play.

Octave Shape V Minor Triad Chord Voicings

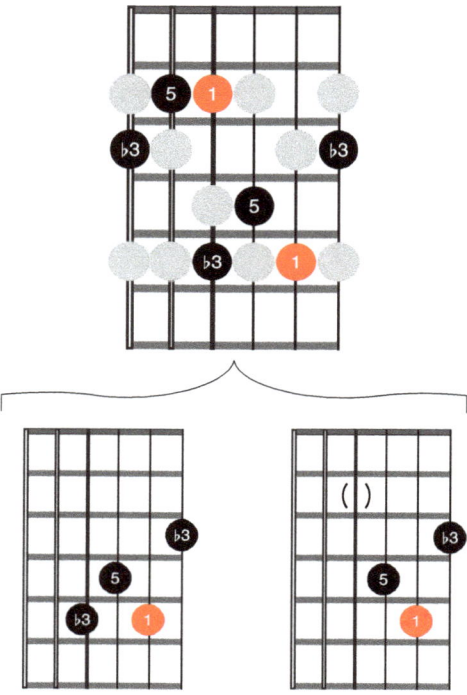

Interval Shapes on the Fretboard

In this Unit you will learn the interval shapes for octaves.

- Play A at the 5th fret of the 6th string and locate the octave two frets higher on the 4th string.
- Play D at the 5th fret of the 5th string and locate the octave two frets higher on the 3rd string.
- Play G at the 5th fret of the 4th string and locate the octave three frets higher on the 2nd string.
- Play C at the 5th fret of the 3rd string and locate the octave three frets higher on the 1st string.

Perfect 8th Interval (octave)

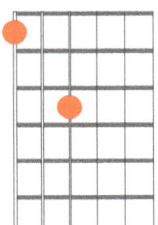 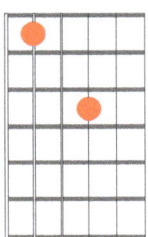 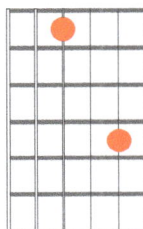 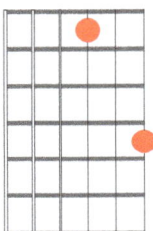

You've got it now. You have learned all of the simple interval shapes on the guitar. Keep refreshing your knowledge of these.

TECHNIQUE

You have learned alternate picking for the most common subdivisions. Alternate picking is important for maintaining steady time regardless of whether you are playing lines or rhythm guitar.

When reading music on the page or learning by ear, make sure your picking hand is following the alternate-picking rules you have learned. Practice with a mirror and watch your hand closely. It is easy to do it wrong without noticing.

It can also be helpful to tap your foot on the beats and make sure you are moving your pick in the right direction in sync with your taps. Don't be too proud to actually write in the pick direction on music you are working on. The picking symbols are easy to write and it is helpful to write them through an entire measure above the notes, rests, or sustained notes with parenthesis around those where the pick does not strike the string. It helps keep your picking hand follow the rules.

Pay close attention to your pick direction while practicing but not so much while performing. If you are using good technique while you practice, it will appear in your performance.

RHYTHM NOTATION

This is the last Module about Rhythm Notation. Your guiding phrase should be:

"Written music should look the way it sounds."

Most musicians have been to a rehearsal where the session is poorly organized, the other musicians are not prepared, and very little gets accomplished. Often, money has been spent renting a practice facility.

Rehearsals go well when these two things happen:

- There is clear communication about what the goals of the rehearsal are.
- The musicians come prepared.

If musicians can read even a simple chord chart, a lot more can be accomplished. Contrast this with the scenario where each musician shows up just having learned the music by ear. With a chord chart, the leader can refer to locations in the song quickly and the whole group will be "on the same page"—literally.

But when a simple chord chart is written, clarity is the key. Clarity starts with proper spacing and grouping of rhythms. Don't forget to slow down; take the time to write neatly. It pays off at the rehearsal and actually saves time.

When performing, a musician's mind can only do so much. If too much brain power is spent deciphering what is written on the page, less brain power is going to playing musically. Take the time to notate clearly so the higher percentage of brain power goes to playing musically and not so much to deciphering a sloppy chart. Always strive to be clear with notation.

RHYTHM GUITAR

The last Module focused on triads and some classic Rolling Stones-like chord moves that live inside the Pattern III Octave Shape. This ties in with the super shape chord system recently learned in the Fretboard Logic Modules. This Module uses the super shapes again and hones in on the three-string triad voicings on string set 2-3-4 and puts them to work for Rock rhythm guitar.

The three major and minor triad shapes found on string set 2-3-4 are the workhorses of so many rhythm guitar parts. A big reason for this is the register. These voicings are in a middle register, which makes them perfect for the full "inner chord sound" of a rhythm section. They are also physically easy to play and it is efficient to move from one to another.

Start by looking at this major key progression.

Rock Progression in A Major

A	D	E	D	A
Ima	IVma	Vma	IVma	Ima

This progression moves from Ima(A) to IVma(D) to Vma(E)—a very common chord progression. You will learn three ways to play this common I-IV-V progression and play each of these with the track.

In the Theory Modules you recently learned how to harmonize major scales and do harmonic analysis so you know that in every major key the I chord is major, the IV chord is major, and so is the V. Those chords are used together so often that it makes sense to map out some common places they can be played together on the fretboard. There are three places using three-string triad shapes on string set 2-3-4 where we can play the common I, IV, and V progression conveniently.

The examples are in the key of A: Ima is A, IVma is D, and Vma is E.

Position 1

Start in the lowest place you can play it:

Ima (A) voiced 5, 1, 3

IVma (D) voiced 3, 5, 1

Vma (E), just use the same 3, 5, 1 voicing and slide it up a whole step.

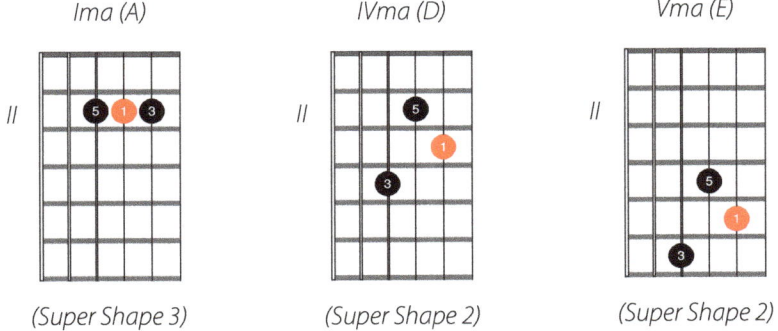

Ima (A)   *IVma (D)*   *Vma (E)*

(Super Shape 3)   *(Super Shape 2)*   *(Super Shape 2)*

Rock Progression in A Major - Position 1

This convenient three-shape combination can be moved to any key as sort of a unit because the relationships are the same in all keys.

Position 2

Do this again, back in the key of A, at the next place higher on the fretboard:

Ima (A) voiced 1, 3, 5

IVma (D) voiced 5, 1, 3

Vma (E), just use the same 5, 1, 3 voicing and slide it up a whole step.

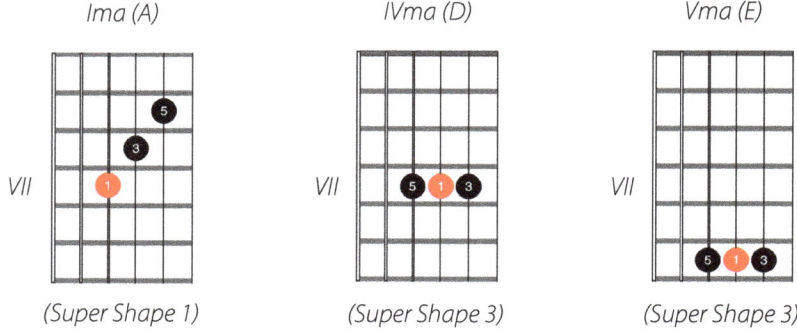

Ima (A)   *IVma (D)*   *Vma (E)*

(Super Shape 1)   (Super Shape 3)   (Super Shape 3)

Rock Progression in A Major - Position 2

And this convenient three-shape package can be moved to any key, too, as sort of a unit.

Position 3

Try this again, back in the key of A, at the next place higher on the fretboard:

Ima (A) voiced 3, 5, 1

IVma (D) voiced 1, 3, 5

Vma (E) just use the same 1, 3, 5 voicing and slide it up a whole step.

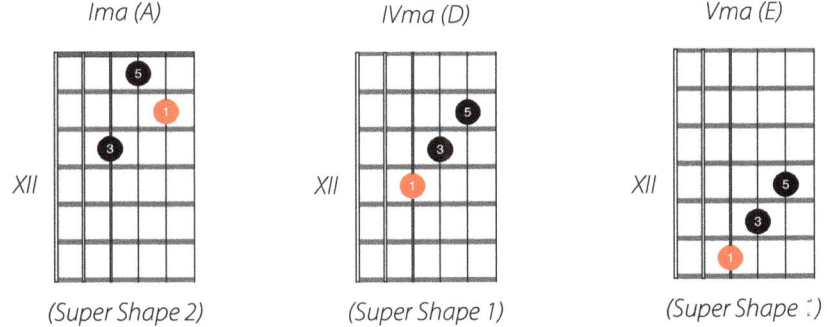

Ima (A)   *IVma (D)*   *Vma (E)*

(Super Shape 2)   (Super Shape 1)   (Super Shape 1)

Rock Progression in A Major - Position 3

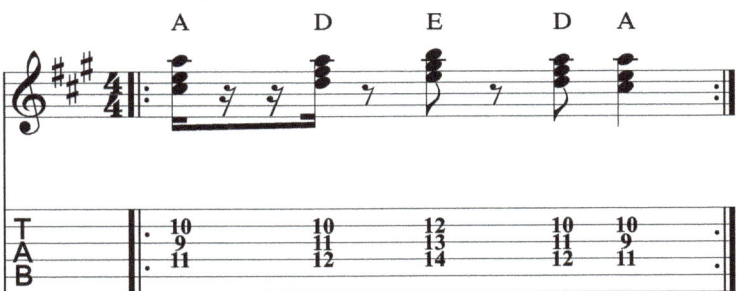

And this convenient three-shape package can be moved to any key, too, as sort of a unit.

Rock Progression in G Minor

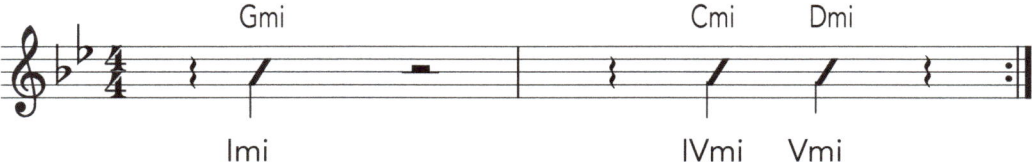

Next, explore minor keys and look at some ways to do the same kind of thing. In the Theory Modules you recently learned how to harmonize minor scales and do harmonic analysis. In every minor key the I chord is minor, the IV chord is minor, and so is the V. This progression moves from Imi (Gmi) to IVmi (Cmi) to Vmi (Dmi).

Like in major keys, those chords are used together so often that it makes sense to map out some convenient and efficient ways to move between them. There are three places using three-string triad shapes on string set 2, 3, and 4 where you can play the common I, IV, and V progression.

The examples are in the key of G minor: I is Gmi, IV is Cmi and V is Dmi.

Position 1

Start in the lowest place you can play it:

Imi (Gmi) voiced 1, ♭3, 5

IVmi (Cmi) voiced 5, 1, ♭3

Vmi (Dmi), just use the same 5, 1, ♭3 voicing and slide it up a whole step.

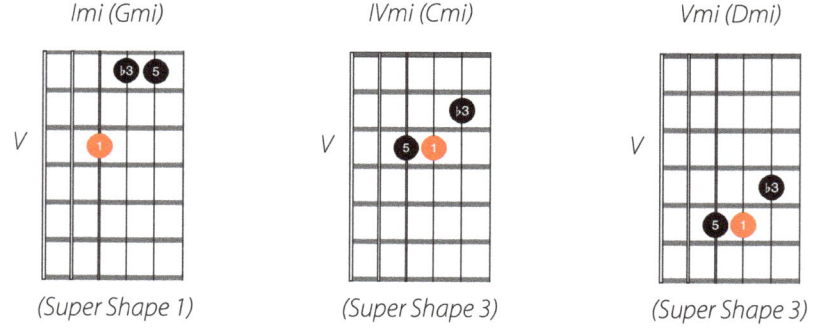

Rock Progression in G Minor - Position 1

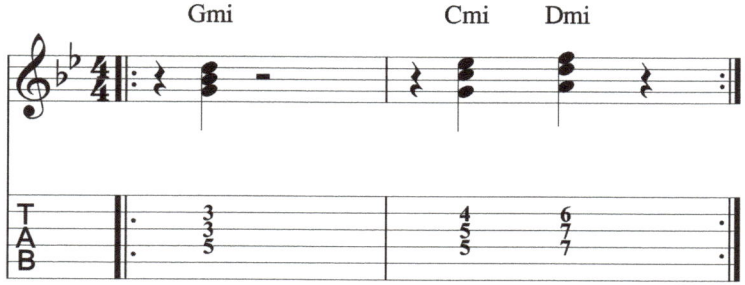

Position 2

Try this again, back in the key of G minor, at the next place higher on the fretboard:

Imi (Gmi) voiced ♭3, 5, 1

IVmi (Cmi) voiced 1, ♭3, 5

Vmi (Dmi), use the same 1, ♭3, 5 voicing and slide it up a whole step.

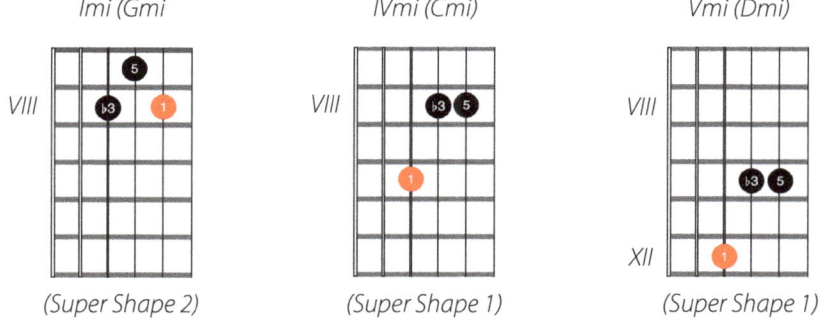

Rock Progression in G Minor - Position 2

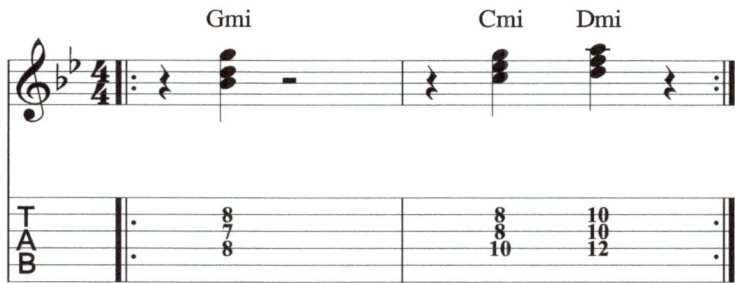

Like all the others, this three-shape combination can be moved to any key as sort of a unit because the relationships are the same in all keys.

Position 3

Try this again, back in the key of G minor, at the next place higher on the fretboard.

Imi (Gmi) voiced 5, 1, ♭3

IVmi (Cmi) voiced ♭3, 5, 1

Vmi (Dmi), use the same ♭3, 5, 1 voicing and slide it up a whole step.

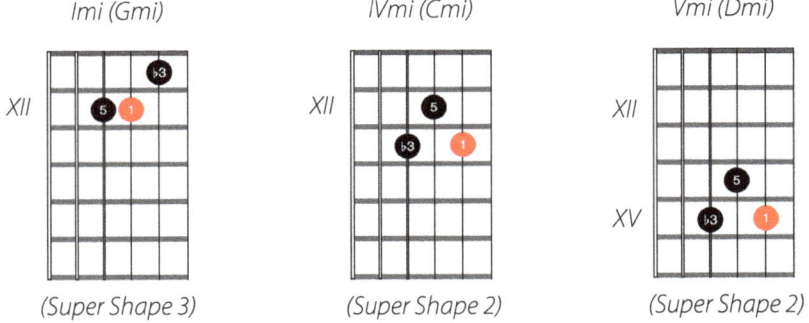

Rock Progression in G Minor - Position 3

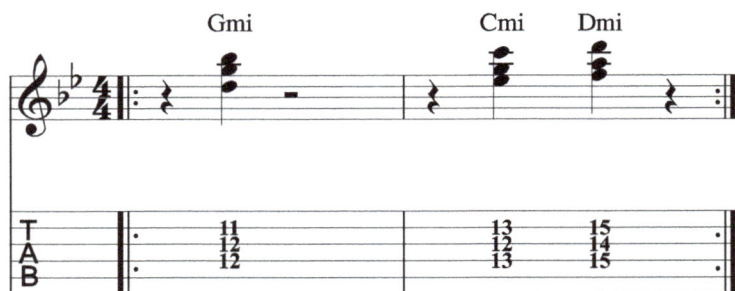

This three-shape combination can be moved to any key as sort of a unit because the relationships are the same in all keys.

Here is a practice example in C that uses all three major shapes and all three minor shapes.

There is a big difference in the sound of the band when this part is absent. These "middle-register voicings" fill out the middle of sound in a rock band. Be sure to spend time with them.

This is the last of our Rock Rhythm Guitar Modules and there is much more to learn. The intent is not to teach you everything about Rock rhythm guitar but rather to teach you how to understand what you are doing technically, musically, and from a theory standpoint. The information provided is intended to give you a solid foundation from which you can build many other parts.

IMPROVISATION

The last Unit opened a whole new phase of learning about soloing and improvising. The study of chord tones is an important step in becoming a mature soloist. The concept is quite simple. Your note choices should, to some degree, reflect the chords the band is playing under your solo. It is easy to understand the idea, but doing it is a whole different matter, so this subject will be presented in a methodical way so it is manageable for you.

When musicians talk about the chords to a song, they often refer to them as "the chord changes" or even just "the changes". Another phrase that comes from that is this: If you are soloing and your lines reflect the chords, you are "playing the changes". Sometimes people will say you are "making the changes".

In this Unit we continue learning about chord-tone soloing.

The progression in this Module is in a major key; C major. It moves from the I chord , C major to the IV chord, F major. The source of notes for a solo could be the C major pentatonic scale or the C major scale. This will sound acceptable but perhaps a little vague and not like the solo is crafted to "fit" the chords.

C Major Progression

If you use chord tones, over the C major chord you have C (the root), E (the 3rd), and G (the 5th) as choices. Over the F major chord, you might focus on or include F (the root), A (the 3rd), and C (the 5th). In other words, the melodic line of the solo can outline the chords.

Remember, too, that you have been learning about arpeggios. The reason for that should be clear: The arpeggio is the musical device used to integrate chord tones into solos. Chord tones are the notes of the chord. Therefore, arpeggios are chord tones. All this to say, you will use arpeggios to play chord tones.

To hear the difference between key-center soloing and chord-tone soling, try this two different ways:

- First, improvise using the Pattern III C major and/or C major pentatonic scale over both chords. This is acceptable but, as I said at the beginning, probably less than satisfying.

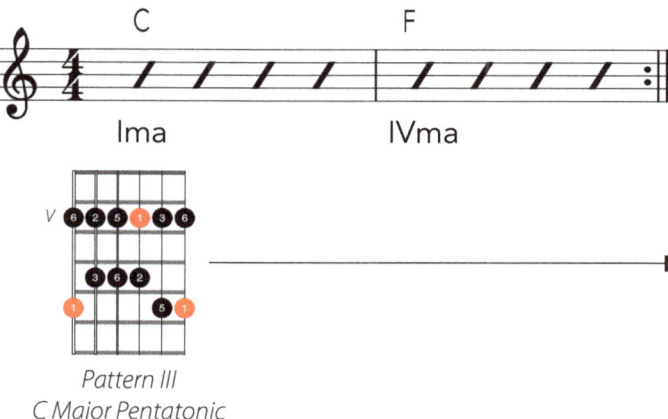

Pattern III
C Major Pentatonic

- Next, take the two arpeggios (Patterns III and I major triad arpeggios) and focus on playing the Pattern III C major triad arpeggio over the C and the Pattern I F major triad arpeggio over the F major, both in 5th position.

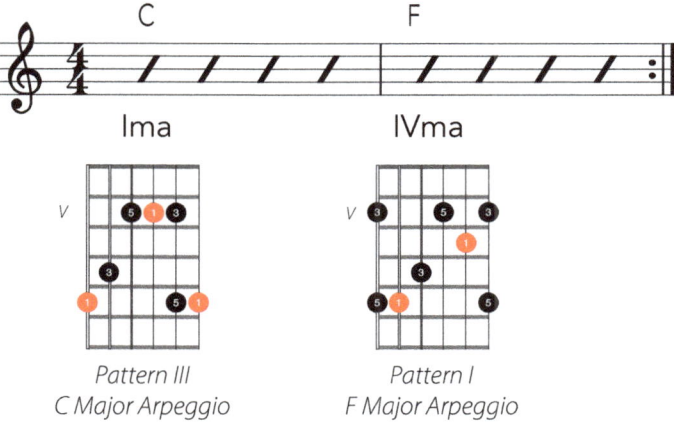

Pattern III
C Major Arpeggio

Pattern I
F Major Arpeggio

All the notes of the C chord (C, E, and G) and all the notes of the F chord (F, A, and C) are part of the C major scale. The goal of the exercise is to be specific and target these specific notes that belong to the chords.

As advised in the last Unit, if you are finding chord-tone soloing difficult, play a chord tone on the first beat of each chord. This will get you started "playing the changes". As you become more confident in your knowledge of the shapes, you can incorporate more chord tones.

You have now reached another important milestone in the Improvisation track of Fretboard Biology. In Level 1 you established a foundation in key-center soloing and storytelling using motif development and the five elements of contrast. In Level 2 you have learned how to play different feels through an understanding of subdivisions and in these last two Units, you have been introduced the important concept of chord-tone soloing.

Keep working hard. You are getting somewhere now. The study of arpeggios and using them to integrate chord tones into solos is just starting.

Level 2 Unit 10 • Example Solo

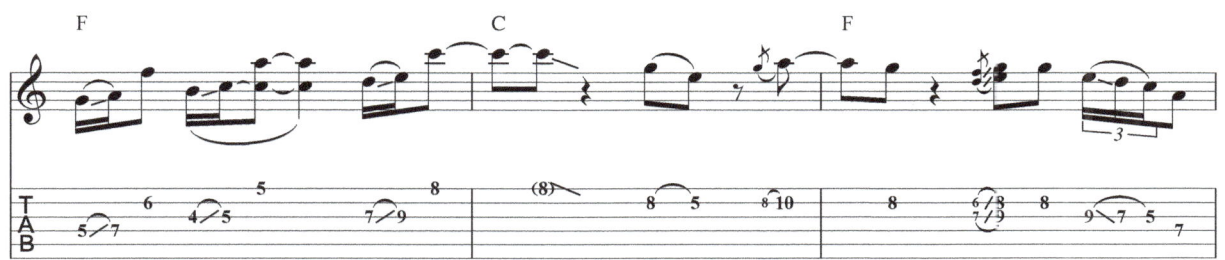

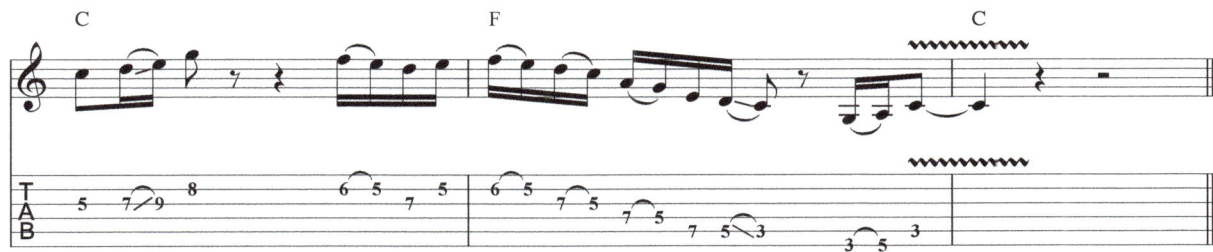

PRACTICE

Theory

- ❑ Go to the tabs below the Theory video on the website and complete the quiz.

Fretboard Logic

- ❑ Learn the Pattern I, Pattern III, and Pattern V Blues scales.
- ❑ Learn the five Patterns of sus4 triad arpeggios.
- ❑ Learn the practical minor triad chord shapes within each Octave Shape.
- ❑ Memorize the octave interval shapes on non-adjacent strings. Use the exercise in the tabs below the video to practice your recognition of intervals on the fretboard.
- ❑ Look at how the new information from this Unit relates to the everything else in the Octave Shape Family Tree.

Technique

- ❑ Practice notating pick direction.

Rhythm Notation

- ❑ Practice clarity in rhythm notation.

Rhythm Guitar

- ❑ Learn Classic Rock moves using Pattern III triad shapes on string set 2-3-4.

Improvisation

- ❑ Practice soloing with chord tones.

Appendix 1: Glossary of Terms

Arpeggio - The notes of a chord played melodically: that is, one note after another rather than simultaneously.

Articulation - Articulation is used to describe the way in which a note is sounded on the guitar. There are numerous articulation techniques including picking, hammer-ons, pull-offs, bends, slides, harmonics, and others.

Barlines - Barlines divide the music into measures, which breaks up the musical paragraph into smaller groups of notes.

Bends - The bend is an articulation device where a string is stretched up or down to change the pitch of a note.

Blend - The merging of sounds in song to create the texture.

Chord - A chord is when three or more notes are played simultaneously.

Chord Tone - A note that is part of a chord.

Clef Sign - A clef sign determines which lines and spaces correlate to letters in the musical alphabet.

Comp - Comp is an abbreviation for "accompany" and refers to any instrument playing the harmony behind a lead part or parts.

Compound Interval - An interval larger than an octave.

Diatonic Harmony - All the chords and melody notes belong to the scale of the key.

Dynamics - Dynamics refers to how loud or soft the music is.

Elements of Contrast - This refers to the specific dimensions a soloist can exploit to create variety in their performance. There are five: Pitch (low vs. high register), speed (slow vs. fast), complexity (simple ideas vs. complex ideas), density (sparse use of notes vs. densely-concentrated notes), and dynamics (soft vs. loud).

Enharmonic Equivalent - An enharmonic is a note that has two names. For example, B and C♭, C and B#, E and F♭, F and E#, G# and A♭.

Feel - Describes the combination of rhythms, placement of attacks, and use of touch to create an emotional effect.

Flat Sign - A flat sign (♭) placed in front of a note head lowers the pitch by a half step or the equivalent of one fret on the guitar.

Genre - Genre refers to a category of music. Genre is often used to describe style or cultural origin. Each genre has a specific musical characteristic that defines its sound.

Groove - Refers to the rhythmic matrix that makes a song feel the way it does but can also refer to the feel.

Hammer-On - A hammer-on is a guitar articulation technique where a noted is fretted and picked, then followed by fretting a note higher on the same string without picking it, causing the second note to sound.

Harmonic Interval - A harmonic interval is two notes played at the same time.

Harmonized Scale - The group of chords that result from building chords on each degree of a scale using only notes from the scale.

Interval - An Interval is the difference in pitch between two notes. If notes are played simultaneously, the interval is a harmonic interval. If the notes are played sequentially, the interval is a melodic interval.

Interval Quality - Quality indicates the exact measurement of an interval based on the number of half steps in the interval. Terms like major, minor, perfect, diminished, and augmented refer to the quality of an interval.

Interval Quantity - Quantity is a term used to describe the general distance between two notes based on the number of letters used in the musical alphabet. Quantity is determined by counting lines and spaces on the staff.

Inverted Chord - An inverted chord has a chord tone other than the root as its lowest note.

Key-Center Approach - This is an approach to soloing that creates musical phrases by using the notes of the scale.

Key Signature - A key signature shows the sharps or flats needed to fulfill the interval formula for a scale built on a given tonic. It is placed on the staff immediately to the right of the clef sign.

Measures - Measures group beats into patterns and help organize the writing and reading of music. The number of beats that are to be contained within a measure is defined by the Time Signature.

Modulation - Modulation is when a song changes from one key to another; there's been a shift in the Tonal Center.

Naturally-Occurring Half Steps - Naturally-occurring half steps are between B and C and between E and F.

Pull-Off - A pull-off is an articulation technique where a note is played and the fretting finger "pulls off" of the string in a kind of plucking motion, making the note below and on the same string to ring without picking it.

Octave Shape - Octave Shapes are physical and visual patterns or shapes based on the location of octave relationships on the neck. There are five and they are numbered I through V using Roman numerals. These are also referred to as Octave Patterns or Patterns.

Melodic Interval - A melodic interval is two notes played one after another (ascending or descending).

Meter - A specific pattern of strong and weak beats is called "meter". Common popular music most often divides pulses into groups of four and sometimes into groups of three. Other combinations are less common.

Natural Sign - A natural sign (♮) next to a specific note returns a sharp or flat note to a "natural" position.

Parallel Keys - Two keys that share the same tonic. For example, C major and C minor are Parallel Keys.

Pattern - Also referred to as Octave Patterns. See Octave Shape.

Pentatonic Scale - A pentatonic scale is a five-note scale. There are both major and minor pentatonic scales.

Pocket - Pocket describes when the feel of the song is just right. The exact point where attacks are placed within the time will affect the pocket. Attacks can be placed in the middle or slightly in front or behind the beat.

Pulse - An important aspect of rhythm is "pulse" which is normally felt as a pattern combining strong and weak beats.

Register - Register refers to how high or low pitches are in a song. High notes are said to be in a high register. Low notes are said to be in a low register.

Relative Keys - Relative keys are two keys that share the same key signature. For example, C major and A minor are relative keys.

Root - A root is the fundamental not of a chord. Scales and keys have tonics; chords and arpeggios have roots.

Scale - A scale is a group of notes assembled above or below a tonic in a stepwise fashion. Scales are named by the note where they start (the tonic).

Sharp Sign - A sharp sign (♯) placed in front of a note head raises the pitch by a half step or the equivalent of one fret on the guitar.

Simple Interval - A simple interval is an interval an octave or smaller.

Slide - A slide is an articulation technique where a note is fretted and the fretting finger either slides up or down to another fret while mainlining pressure against the fretboard so that the note in the target position rings without having to be picked.

Staff - The Staff is a five-line grid on which music is notated. The staff tells you how high or low a note is according to its vertical placement on the staff. The horizontal organization of the staff defines how music happens over time.

Texture - Texture is related to tone and sound but also applies to the nature of the part. For example, dense chord voicings or sparse chord voicings, arpeggiated chords or block chords, etc.

Time - Time describes the steady continuum of music.

Time Signature - A time signature defines how the music is to be counted. It is written at the beginning of the staff and placed just after the clef sign and key signature. Time signatures consist of two numbers written like a fraction. The top number tells you how many beats are contained in each measure. The bottom number tells you what note value is considered a beat: quarter note, 8th note, or 16th note.

Tonal Center - Another name for the tonic. It is the note around which all of the notes of a song revolve.

Tone - Tone refers to the character and quality of sound.

Tonic - The tonic is the fundamental note of a key. It is the key the song is in. For example, if the song is in the key of C, the tonic is C. It is the single pitch around which all the other pitches and chords of a song revolve.

Touch - Touch describes the control of intensity through the use of pressure, dynamics, length of notes, and the various articulation devices.

Triad - A triad is a three-note chord consisting of a root, 3rd, and 5th.

Voice Leading - Voice leading is how the individual components (or voices) of each chord connect linearly when moving from chord to chord.

Appendix 2: Family Trees

The Octave Shape Family Trees

Beginning in Level 2, we will be building the Octave Shape Family Trees that we introduced in Unit 1. With each Level, we will be adding more scales, arpeggios and chords. Although the complete Family Trees look quite daunting, once you understand the logic behind them, you will be able to create these from scratch. I simply cannot over-emphasize what a asset this will be to you as a guitar player.

Each of the five octave shapes are presented over the next 10 pages with the major scales, chords, and arpeggios on the left, and the minor chords, scales and arpeggios on the right. There is also a collection of chords and arpeggios that don't fit neatly into either a major tonality or a minor tonality, such as the various suspended chords and arpeggios, altered scales, and many slash chords. These are presented in the gray box at the bottom of the pages for each octave shape.

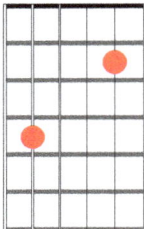

Pattern I

MAJOR

| Pentatonic Scale | | Triad Arpeggio | Augmented Arpeggio | Triad Chord | Augmented Triad |

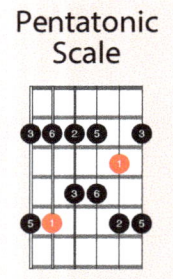 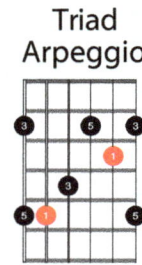  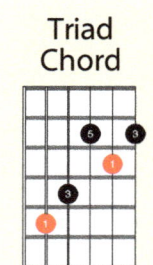 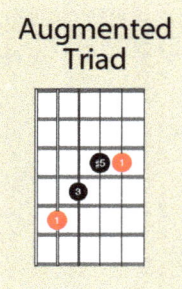

Ionian (Major) Scale

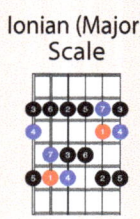

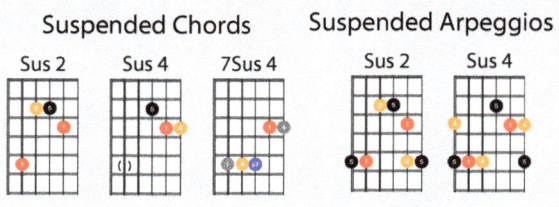

Suspended Chords — Sus 2, Sus 4, 7Sus 4
Suspended Arpeggios — Sus 2, Sus 4

Fretboard Biology — Appendix 2: Family Trees

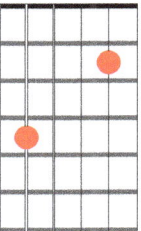

Pattern I

MINOR

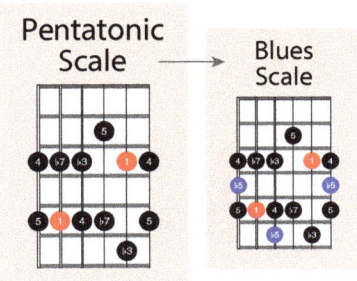 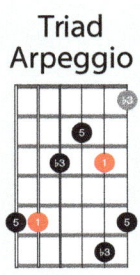  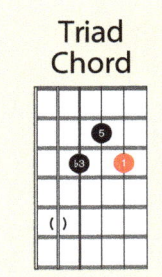 

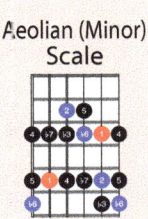

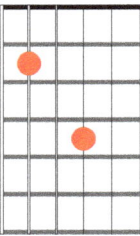

Pattern II

MAJOR

Pentatonic Scale	Triad Arpeggio	Augmented Arpeggio	Triad Chord	Augmented Triad

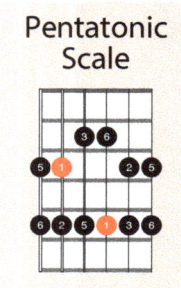 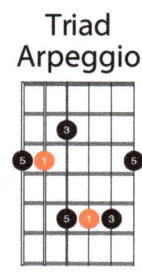 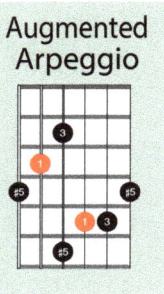  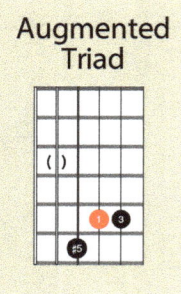

Ionian (Major) Scale

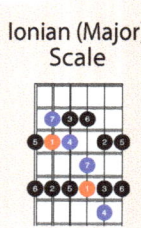

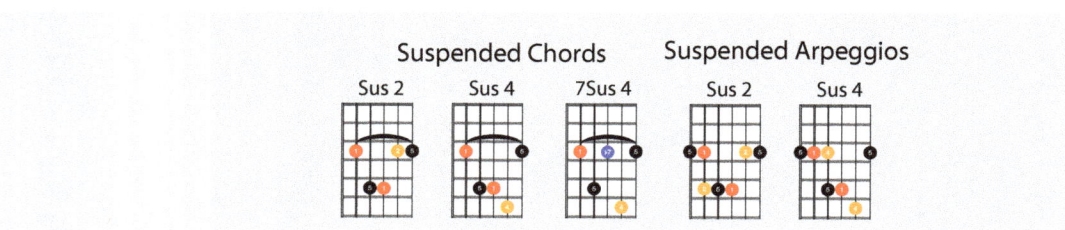

Suspended Chords — Sus 2, Sus 4, 7Sus 4
Suspended Arpeggios — Sus 2, Sus 4

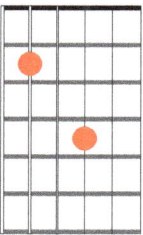

Pattern II

MINOR

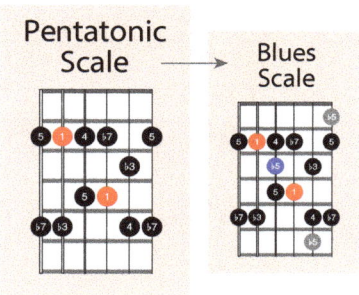 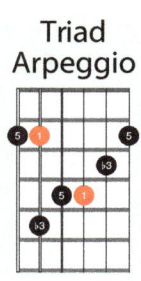  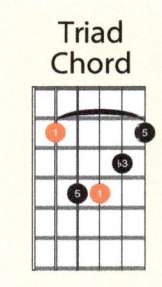 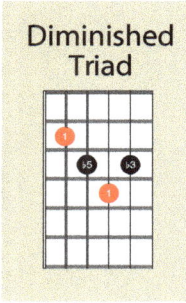

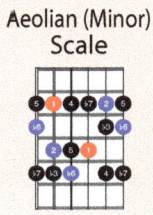

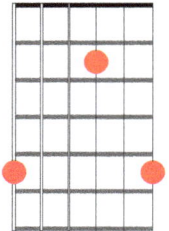

Pattern III

MAJOR

Pentatonic Scale
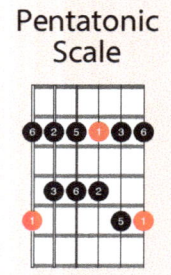

Triad Arpeggio
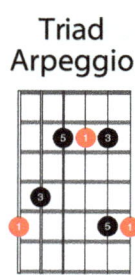

Augmented Arpeggio

Triad Chord
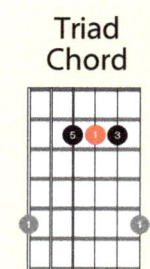

Augmented Triad
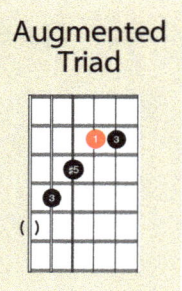

Ionian (Major) Scale
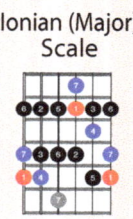

Suspended Chords — Sus2, Sus4, Sus6/4, Sus2/4, 7Sus4 Suspended Arpeggios — Sus2, Sus4
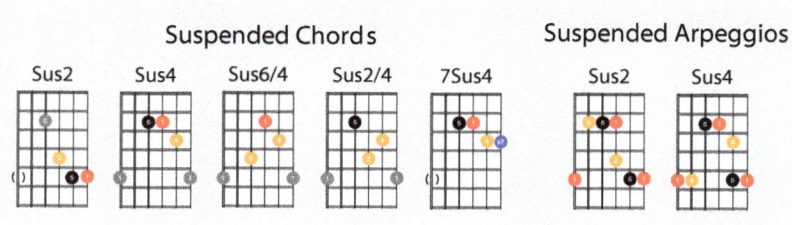

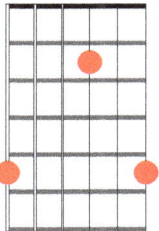

Pattern III

MINOR

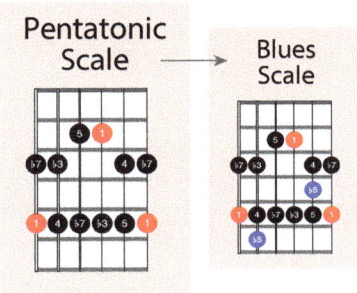

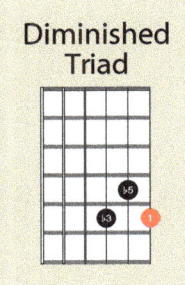

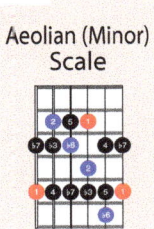

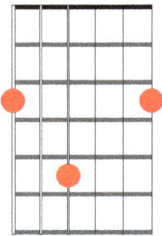

Pattern IV

MAJOR

Pentatonic Scale
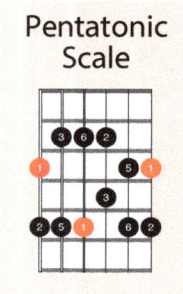

Triad Arpeggio
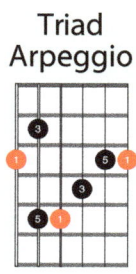

Augmented Arpeggio
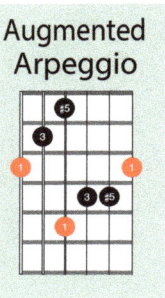

Triad Chord
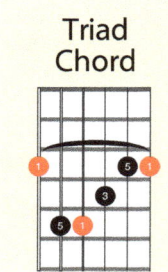

Augmented Triad

Ionian (Major) Scale
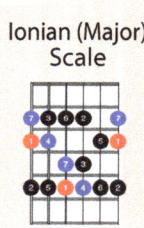

Suspended Chords   **Suspended Arpeggios**

Sus4   Sus6/4   Sus2/4   Sus2/4   Sus4

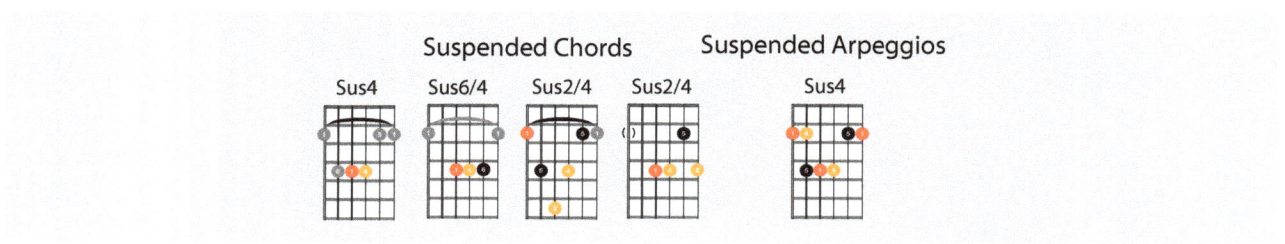

Fretboard Biology — Appendix 2: Family Trees

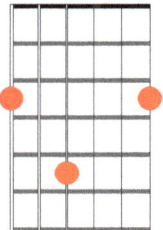

Pattern IV

MINOR

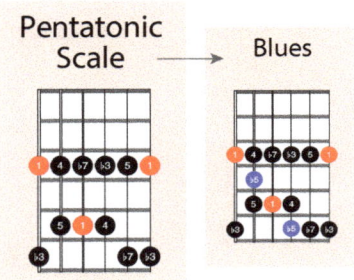 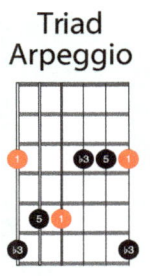  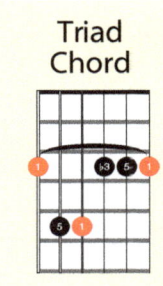 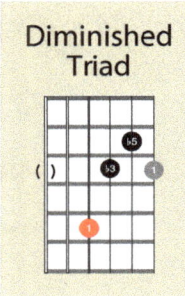

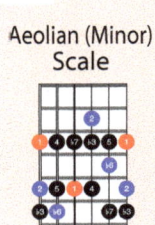

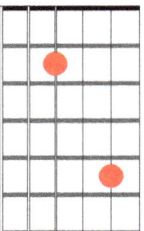

Pattern V

MAJOR

| Pentatonic Scale | Triad Arpeggio | Augmented Arpeggio | Triad Chord | Augmented Triad |

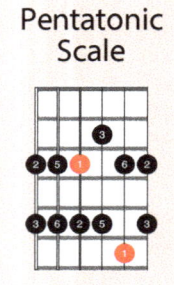 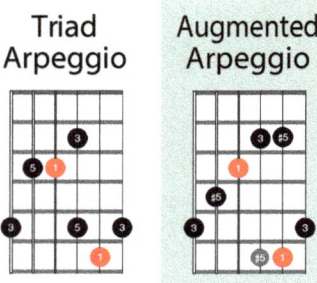 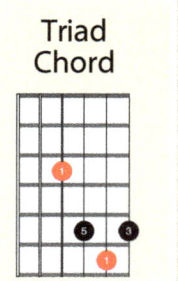 

Ionian (Major) Scale

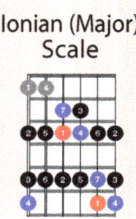

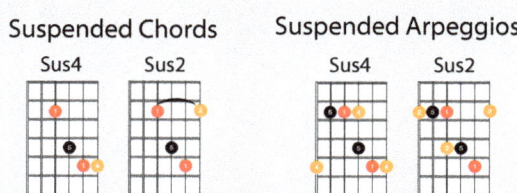

Fretboard Biology   Appendix 2: Family Trees

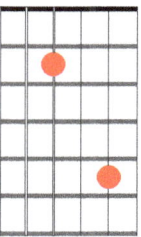

Pattern V

MINOR

Pentatonic Scale	Blues Scale	Triad Arpeggio	Diminished Arpeggio	Triad Chord	Diminished Triad

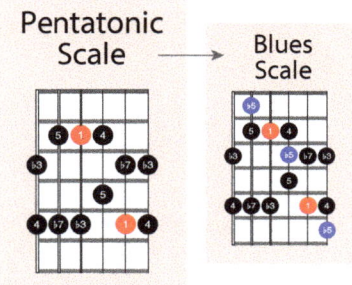 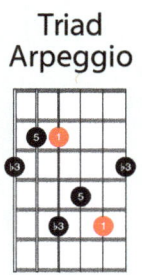  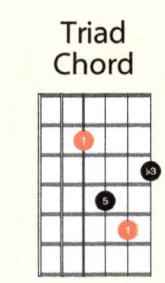 

Aeolian (Minor) Scale

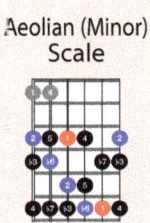

Other Chords

Pattern II and IV Barre Chords

Pattern II Major · Pattern II Minor 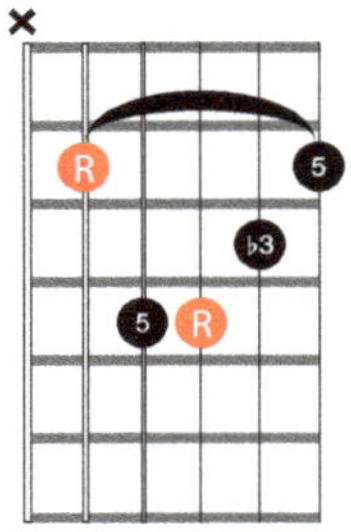 · Pattern IV Major 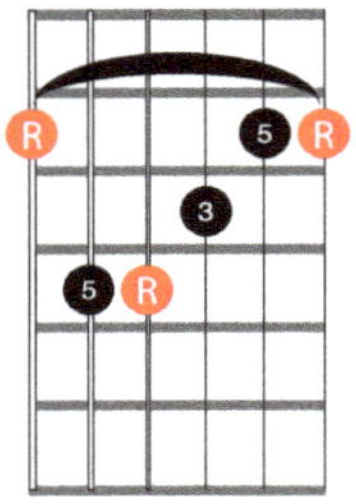 · Pattern IV Minor

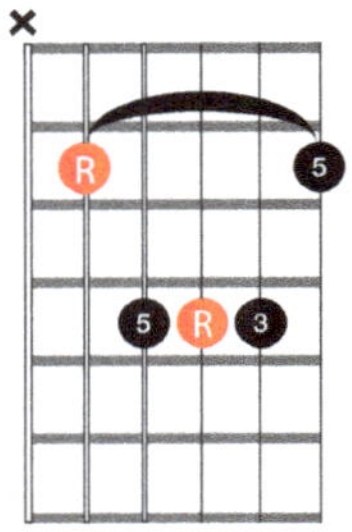

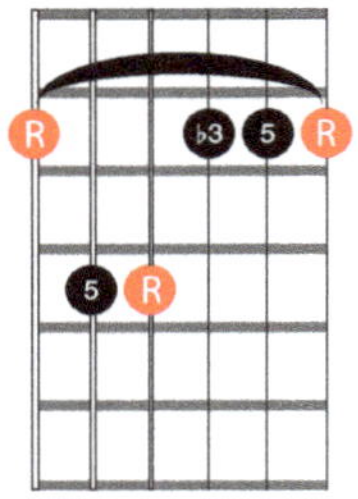

Open Chords

C · A 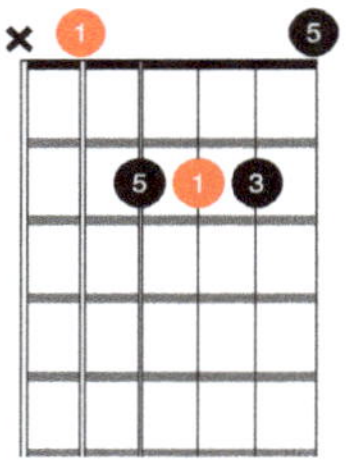 · G  · E 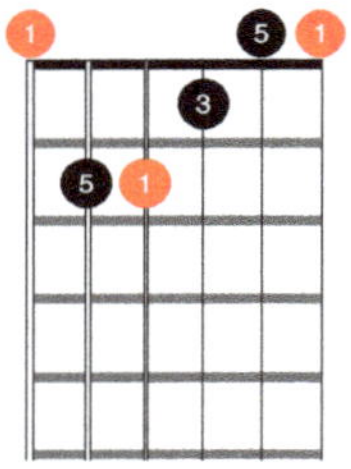 · D 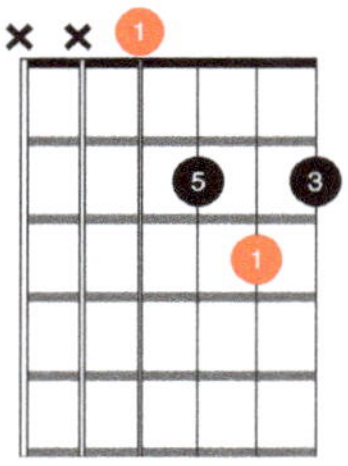 · F

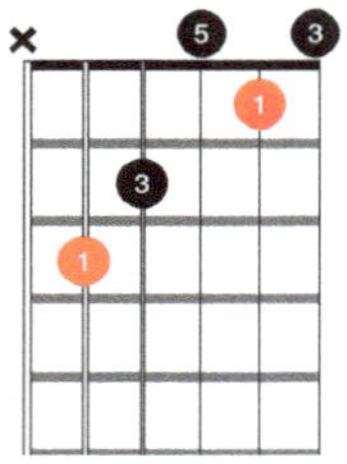

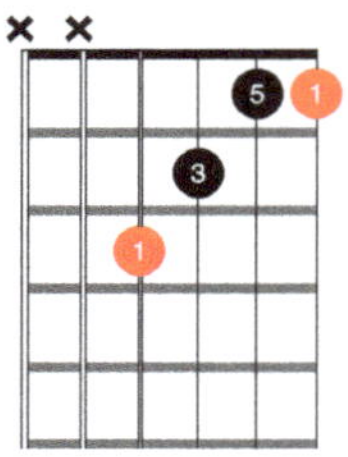

E mi 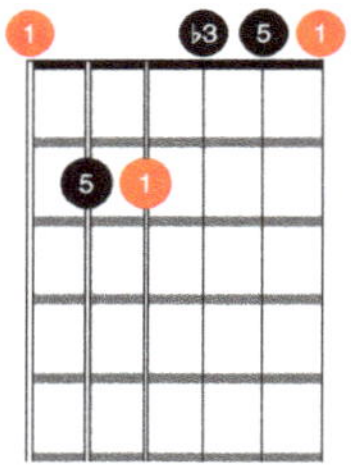 · A mi 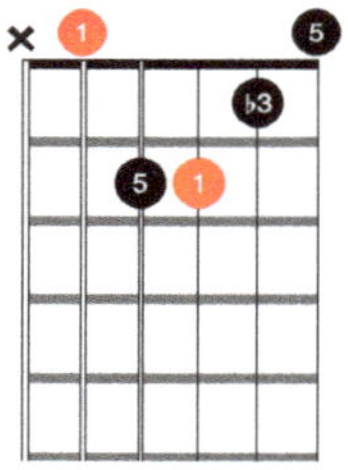 · D mi

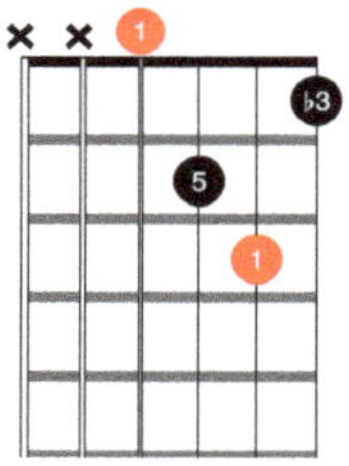

Suspended Open Chords

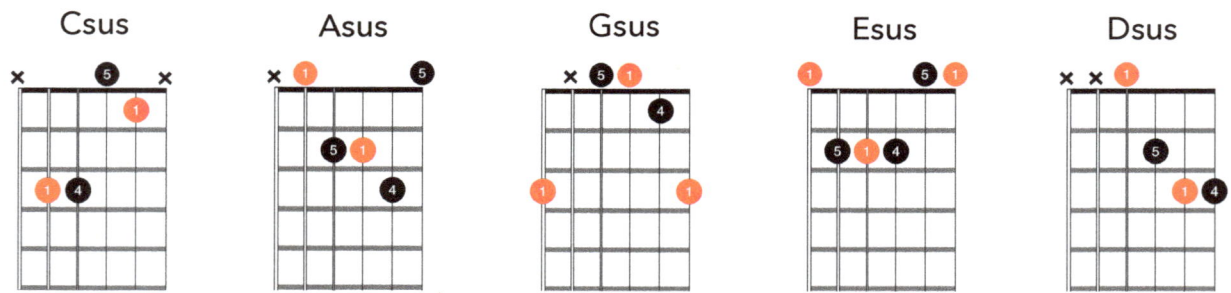

Csus · Asus · Gsus · Esus · Dsus

Unit ___ Practice Routine

Date:	Routine #	1	2	3	4	5	6	7	8	9	10
Exercise	Time/Reps										

Unit ___ Practice Routine

Date:	Routine #	DAY									
Exercise	Time/Reps	1	2	3	4	5	6	7	8	9	10

FRETBOARDBIOLOGY
COMPREHENSIVE GUITAR PROGRAM

About Joe Elliott

Joe Elliott is an American guitarist, author, composer, and music educator.

Joe's professional experience as an educator includes 23 years of teaching at Musicians Institute (MI) in Hollywood, California, at the Guitar Institute of Technology (GIT). Joe has taught numerous clinics throughout the U.S. While at MI, Joe wrote and edited courses for GIT and MI's Baccalaureate programs. He spent three years as GIT Department Head and nine years as Vice President and Director of Education at Musicians Institute. He spent seven years as the Guitar Department Head and Director of Academic Administration at McNally Smith College of Music in St. Paul, Minnesota. He is currently the co-founder, CEO, and Director of Education of the guitar education website FretboardBiology.com and Music Biology, Inc.

Joe has authored several instructional books for guitar, including *An Introduction to Jazz Guitar Soloing* and *The Fretboard Biology* series of books, and has co-authored *Ear Training* with Carl Schroeder and Keith Wyatt.

Joe has released two solo guitar albums, *Joe's Place* and *Truth Serum*, as well as an instrumental country album, *Country Grit*, is currently a composer for APM Music in Los Angeles, and has composed numerous scores for television and film.